Chris Morgan

FUTURE MAN

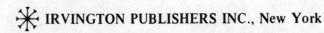 IRVINGTON PUBLISHERS INC., New York

Library of Congress Cataloging in Publication Data

Morgan, Chris.
   Future man.

   Bibliography: p.
   Includes index.
   1. Twenty-first century—Forecasts.   2. Evolution.
I. Title.
CB161.M668   909.83   79-26886
ISBN 0-8290-0144-1

Contents

Preface   6

Introduction: On Prediction   7

1 The Story So Far   12

2 Evolution—Theories and After   29

3 The Changing Shape of Man   38

4 Future Mind   64

5 The Twenty-First-Century
   Schizoid Man   87

6 The Limits of Extrapolation   115

7 Man in Space   139

8 When Man Becomes Not-Man   165

Notes   193

Bibliography   202

Index   205

To Pauline,
with love

FUTURE: That period of time in which our affairs prosper, our friends are true and our happiness is assured.

MAN: An animal so lost in rapturous contemplation of what he thinks he is as to overlook what he indubitably ought to be. His chief occupation is extermination of other animals and his own species, which, however, multiplies with such insistent rapidity as to infect the whole habitable world and Canada.

Ambrose Bierce *The Devil's Dictionary*

Preface

1   The terms 'future man' and 'mankind' and the use of the pronoun 'he' in connection with them should not lead anyone to suppose that the world of the future will be populated exclusively by the male members of *Homo sapiens*. These terms must be understood to refer equally to men and women, and are employed for reasons of brevity and style rather than sexism.

2   Whenever the word 'billion' is used it refers to the American billion (a thousand million) rather than the British one (a million million).

3   The abbreviation LDCs refers to Less Developed Countries.

Introduction: On Prediction

The more you go ahead, the more you seem to get entangled with the burning questions of your own times. You may cast your tale a century or so ahead, and even then something may happen next week which might knock your most plausible reasoning crooked.' H. G. Wells, 'Fiction of the Future'

Prediction is largely guesswork, whether one is looking only into next year or much further ahead. The crystal ball and the fall of the tarot cards have been superseded by the intelligent extrapolation of statistical trends but, *plus ça change, plus c'est la même chose*, there is no greater certainty of accuracy.

Statistics of any kind are, by definition, historical data. Thus, using statistical trends to plan for the future is analogous to driving a car while able to see out only through the rear window; it is a dangerous practice. One is safe only as long as the invisible road ahead remains straight. As soon as a bend (a change of trend) is noticed it may already be too late to stay on the road (the path of optimum progress) and a waste of resources occurs. Such waste—it may be of life, not just of crops or facilities—is a regular feature of the economies of most countries today due to faulty economic forecasting. Mostly this is due to bad planning, political changes, strikes and over-optimism. Also to blame are 'unique' events such as war, freak weather or scientific innovation; although these occur fairly frequently they are irregular and unpredictable as to time and place. In the longer term (say ten or twenty-five years) a certain number of such events can be expected and planned for, even though their individual effects cannot be.

In one respect the car analogy, above, is misleading. There is not just a single future ahead of us but many, any of which can be steered for by taking particular decisions now. The many potential futures are approaching us at such a rate that we can choose the most desirable type of future for mankind as a whole, aim for it and see whether or not it is achieved—all within a person's lifetime. Selecting a particular future as a goal presupposes recognition of the existence of multiple futures and the ability to apply sophisticated planning techniques consistently over decades to ensure that the most favourable future is arrived at, or at least that the less favourable options are avoided. Because this planning, to be fully effective, needs to encompass all aspects of industry, commerce, science, education and public services, in most countries of the world, on a permanent basis, its success is bound to be limited for some time to come.

Even selecting the most desirable future to aim for is fraught with difficulty. Different nations or political parties have different long-term goals, and organisations interpret statistical trends in the way which suits them best. Additionally, many desirable futures are unreachable because of constraints. For example, it might seem highly laudable to aim for a future in which every family owns a substantial house with all modern conveniences and domestic appliances, plus two cars. If applied solely to Britain or the USA this is possible; if applied to the whole world it is not. Not only would the countries in which most potential recipients live be unable to pay for these goods (wealth constraint), but also the families concerned would mostly be unable to operate the appliances and cars (educational constraint), which in any case could not be properly sited or connected up (infrastructural constraint). Even if such an enormous number of extra vehicles (perhaps a billion) could be produced at all (it would require an exponential increase in productive capacity, including skilled labour) there would certainly be insufficient fuel reserves for the length of the cars' lives. An infinitely better goal would be the development of an alternative to petroleum (its world reserves will probably be exhausted during the twenty-first century, even without an increase in demand) and of an alternative to the motor car, which is an extremely wasteful form of transport.

Although the world's mineral reserves (including petroleum) are finite, all predictions of the respective amounts and the numbers of years before they are exhausted have had to be revised regularly over the last half century because of new discoveries.[1] As the more easily obtained supplies are used up so deeper or more awkwardly sited reserves will be tapped. The closer we appear to be to the exhaustion of reserves in any particular case, the more effort and capital will be put into finding new reserves and improving the methods of scrap recovery.[2] But there will come a time, probably during the twenty-first century, when some metals can no longer be mined on Earth (or only with the greatest difficulty, so that it is a very inefficient process), so capital should be invested now in finding alternatives—glass fibre and aluminium, for which the raw materials exist in huge quantities—or new sources, elsewhere in our Solar System.

One factor which critically affects all our predictions of the future is knowledge—especially the lack of it. Whenever we interfere with nature by mining or damming a river or polluting the sea or cutting down a forest we are making largely irreversible changes to our planetary ecology. In most cases we do not yet know the full effects of our actions, even though we realise that we are making life more difficult for the people of the future, or at least limiting their options. This trade-off between present and future is inevitable. One cannot have one's cake and eat it too. A barrel of oil which we use today might be of enormous value to our descendants in 2080 (because their use of it might be far more efficient than ours) or it might be worthless—a curiosity in a world where the internal combustion engine is found only in museums and transport is based on different concepts. More worrying is the fact that a species of insect or bacteria which we deliberately exterminate (or fail to protect) will turn out to have been a vital link in a food chain. Our imperfect knowledge of the systems which keep our ecology in balance could lead us to make decisions which will damage the future beyond repair.

Practitioners in the business of predicting the future have always been divided—though the division has never been particularly clear cut—between 'serious' prophets and science fiction writers. Many of the former have, since Old Testament times, claimed divine inspiration even though their methods of divination have rather tended to resemble magic. It is in order to escape the crystal ball image that futurists in the second half of the twentieth century have increasingly attempted to make their predictions appear more rigorous and worthwhile by the use of advanced statistical techniques and computer-fed econometric models. In most cases these futurists lack imagination; they exclude such factors as wars and revolutionary scientific achievements as being unquantifiable;

too often they do not consider, for example, after-the-bomb or intensely polluted futures. (See FIGURE) On the other hand, science fiction writers (few of whom claim divine inspiration) are only just managing to escape from their juvenile-oriented, aliens-and-spaceships image created during the 1920s and 1930s by Hugo Gernsback's pulp 'scientification' magazines.[3] Although science fiction set in the future is written for many different reasons and only some of it is intended as prediction, this segment is at its best highly imaginative, providing warnings of unpleasant futures and allowing us to carry out no-risk tests of certain areas of advance (behavioural and scientific).[4] Dedicated readers of science fiction may well be the best equipped members of society for life in the future.

So how do all these introductory remarks on prediction (and mainly concerning economic or ecological prediction, at that) tie in with the future evolution of the human race? Well, in the near future, long before evolution will have had the opportunity to alter *Homo sapiens sapiens* into some new species, human society, human bodies and human minds will

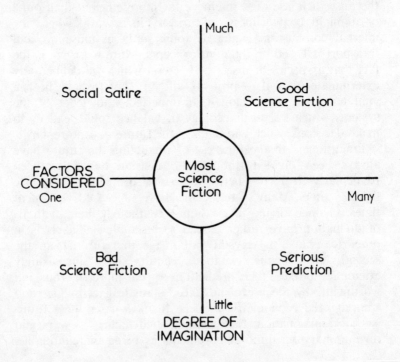

all have been changed because of the actions of our descendants and their reactions to the changed world around them. Even in fifty or a hundred years' time life will be nothing like it is today. Our descendants will be alien to us in their beliefs and assumptions, they will alter their bodies with prosthetics, with organ transplants and by genetic manipulation, they will develop the powers of the mind; their society will be incomprehensible to us.

We cannot remember the future, like the White Queen in *Through the Looking Glass*, so, barring the sudden invention of time travel, prediction is our only means of knowing what forms this alienness will take.

1 The Story So Far

'Evolution ever climbing after some ideal good.'

Tennyson

Creation

About 4,700 million years ago the Sun was a vast, diffuse nebula, thousands of millions of miles across, which was being broken up by gravitational forces. Outer rings of this nebula, which had become detached, fell together in orbit around the shrinking Sun, colliding and coalescing to form spherical clouds which condensed to become protoplanets. Though mostly composed of hydrogen and helium, they contained many dust particles swept up by the Sun in its passage through space, which settled to the centres by gravitational attraction. Solid, spherical cores formed, still enveloped by huge gas clouds. One of these protoplanets was the Earth. Never at any time during this period of accumulation was it in a molten state, though increasing internal pressure liquefied part of its centre.

This process occurred in darkness. The Sun's gas clouds had not yet condensed sufficiently to create fusion and emit any light or heat, but it was shrinking, becoming more dense. At a certain point its temperature soared by thousands of degrees. It began to pour out intensive radiation into the area of space around it, lighting and heating its family of planets. The nearby planets, including the Earth, had their veils of hydrogen and helium stripped off. Earth was left with its solid, rocky core and only small amounts of the original gases.[1]

Then, after sweeping it clean, the solar radiation began to provide the Earth with another gaseous covering, this time of oxygen and nitrogen which was liberated from the crust to form an atmosphere. Below the surface several different processes distributed the elements. Although there was a tendency for heavier materials to gravitate towards the centre,[2] the crust contains some deposits of even the heaviest elements due to the effects of metamorphosis, the transport of material dissolved in heated or superheated water, and volcanic action. The atmosphere produced by liberated gases consisted of water vapour (mainly originating as volcanic steam), hydrogen, ammonia, methane and hydrogen sulphide. The oxygen released was, initially, totally consumed in the oxidation of ammonia to nitrogen and water, and of methane to carbon dioxide and water. It is thought that the very first organic molecules appeared during this period, within a few hundred million years of the Earth's solidification. The oldest known fossil traces of living matter are 2·5 to 3 billion years old and include bacteria and blue-green algae.

Some 700 to 800 million years ago a very important process began: free oxygen started to accumulate. At this stage it probably came from the chemical dissociation of water vapour. Its importance was paramount, because until there was at least a small amount of free oxygen land-based plant life could not develop.

The origin of life has been ascribed to five major causes. Three of these need not detain us long. The more fanatic adherents to certain faiths (including Christianity) believe in a supernatural creation, and no amount of scientific evidence is going to affect their belief. A second theory, not necessarily inconsistent with supernatural creation, is that life can originate spontaneously from non-living substances in very short periods of time; it was a view held by mankind for thousands of years and only disproved by science in the seventeenth century. At the end of the nineteenth century it was fashionable to believe in life as having existed as long as matter— as long as the Earth itself—and thus having no beginning. It was more of a sidestep than an explanation.

The most widely held view of the origin of life is that it resulted from a series of chemical reactions amongst non-living substances. Put forward at about the middle of the nineteenth century as the true scientific explanation, its early proponents included T. H. Huxley, though he was very vague as to the details.[3] The creation of simple organic molecules in the laboratory was first achieved in 1953, when an electric spark (representing lightning) was discharged through a mixture of methane, ammonia and hydrogen in a water solution. Amino and hydroxy acids were produced. The fifth and final theory is that life began elsewhere than on the Earth and was brought here in meteorites. Although this smacks of science fiction rather than of science fact it has recently received some scientific approval because of the work of Professors Fred Hoyle and N. C. Wickramasinghe who have suggested that microbes could be stored deep-frozen in the middle of comets or similar pieces of interstellar debris for thousands or millions of years, eventually reaching Earth in meteorite fragments and becoming active again.[4] It seems a remote chance but cannot be ruled out as impossible.

All these theories as to the origin of life on Earth are just theories. No firm evidence exists or is expected to be found. In fact the early period of Earth's development, that 4,000 million year stretch called the Precambrian, which lasted until about 570 million years ago, is still a time of mystery. Despite the widespread existence of Precambrian rock strata and the large number of varied and fully formed species of plant and animal fossils found which date from the following era (the Cambrian), Precambrian fossils are very rare. One of the exceptions is a clam-like brachiopod some 720 million years old from Canada.

Life before man

Each geological period since the Precambrian has left behind it a profusion of fossils to show the gradual development of higher forms of life from lower. Until 400 million years ago the only animals were invertebrates, such as molluscs, crustaceans and sea-urchins. During the Devonian period, 350 to 400 million years ago, the first vertebrates appeared—primitive bony fishes similar to the coelacanth. Also at this time the first land plants developed, initially rising up out of the water. The next period was the Carboniferous, during which the first animals left the seas and became land-living. These included land snails, arthropods (spiders, scorpions, millipedes and early insects) and, most significant, many amphibians, some of which (*Cotylosauria*) were developing into reptiles. Over about 100 million years the early reptiles became the dinosaurs, which existed in a variety of forms—many of them gigantic and well known—for about 120 million years, although for most of that time they coexisted with the first of the mammals.

The early mammals remained small and insignificant throughout the Mesozoic era—for a period in excess of 100 million years. They evolved from the therapsid reptiles about 175 million years ago but did not achieve a position of importance until the last seventy million years. The very earliest of them were probably similar to opossums in behaviour and appearance. Gradually they acquired the mammalian characteristics of hair, milk glands and so on, but these refer to soft parts of the animal and almost nothing is known of them, since normally only bones and teeth have survived in a fossilised state.

After the dinosaurs disappeared at the end of the Cretaceous period, about seventy million years ago, the first placental mammals evolved. A great variety of forms of mammals developed, some of a considerable size to fill the carnivorous niche abandoned by some dinosaurs. But among the small mammals there were some types, not unlike the present-day lemurs, but only the size of shrews, which have been identified as basal primates.[5] Other primate families appeared during the two succeeding epochs; they can be linked by skull shape and dental features with later simian types. During the next epoch, the Oligocene, came *Oligopithecus* (that was about forty million years ago) which has dentition that connects it both with earlier mammals and with the anthropoids (the suborder which contains the monkeys, apes and man) which came later. Similar but slightly later fossil types are *Propliopithecus* (thirty-five million years old) and *Aegyptopithecus* (thirty million years old) which also arose during the Oligocene. These were small animals (an *Aegyptopithecus* skull is much the same size as that of a present-day domestic cat), and probably tree-dwelling. They were, in essence, small primitive monkeys, though with ape-like teeth. The evolutionary implication is that these types gave rise to modern apes and to man.

From the Miocene epoch, which came next (from twenty-two to seven million years ago) there is fossil evidence of several species of *Dryopithecus*, which seems to have been an ancestor of our present-day great apes—the gibbons and gorillas. Probably it was not an early hominid, judging from the dental evidence, though it must have existed at the time when the evolutionary links leading to man and ape diverged. A degree of uncertainty exists here, in the relationship between

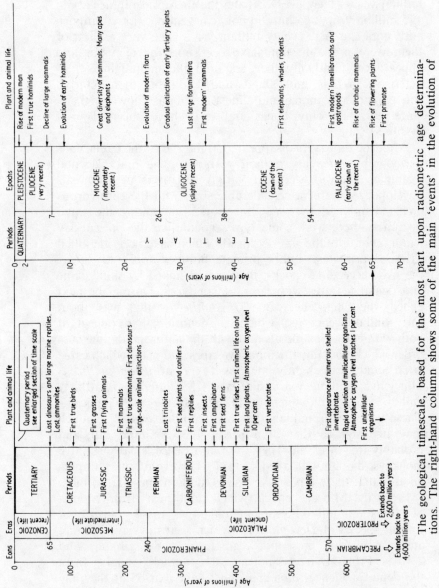

The geological timescale, based for the most part upon radiometric age determinations. The right-hand column shows some of the main 'events' in the evolution of plants and animals.

the early forms (to each other and to ourselves), and in their geographical distribution. Some were intermediate forms and some were evolutionary deadends. Different chains of development occurred on the different landmasses. In time more fossil evidence will come to light and the relationships will become clearer.

The Early Hominids

Nor is our knowledge adequate of the early hominids. (The hominids, family *Hominidae*, include all fossil and living evidence of man, not just of the genus *Homo* but also of primitive types.) Although the early hominids are clearly closer to modern man in skull shape and, particularly, dental features, than to the apes, there are timegaps between the different types and it is unclear which is the chain of development that led to us. Confusion is multiplied (especially for the layman) by the proliferation of different names for the same form, just because specimens were found at different times and in various localities.

To clarify the position, there were only three types of pre-*Homo* hominids (so far known) which existed between one and fifteen million years ago. These are *Ramapithecus*, *Australopithecus* (which came in two forms), and *Gigantopithecus*. All other names, such as *Sivapithecus*, *Zinjanthropus*, *Kenyapithecus*, *Paranthropus* and *Pleisanthropus*, refer to one of the three.

One of them, *Gigantopithecus*, is probably not an ancestor of modern man, but instead 'the latest survivor of an Asiatic stock which more or less parallels the human line'.[6] Some authorities disagree with this, claiming *Gigantopithecus* as a hominid which later became reduced in size when tools came to be used, while others class *Gigantopithecus* with the apes. In fact the evidence is awfully meagre, resting on a few examples of exceptionally large hominid-type teeth and jaw fragments.

Ramapithecus ('Rama's ape'—named after Rama, an incarnation of the Hindu deity Vishnu, although the teeth are distinctly different from those of the apes) was first identified and named from jaw bones found in the Siwalik Hills of Northern India in 1934. Since then many other teeth and bones (skulls, jaws, and recently some limb bones) have been discovered in India and Pakistan, in Turkey, Greece and Hungary, and at Fort Ternan in Kenya. The timespan covered is about fifteen to nine million years ago, and the wide geographical range suggests that *Ramapithecus* might have lived in (or at least roamed across) most parts of the world. But was there separate evolution in Africa and Asia or, as seems more likely, a single evolutionary advance followed by migration? Although it is difficult to be sure of appearance or behaviour from such slender evidence it seems likely that *Ramapithecus* was, at least initially, a tree-dweller (most of its habitats were forested at the time) but that it descended to live on the ground after the forested lands were reduced by climatic changes during the Miocene epoch. Dr Bjorn Kurten has speculated as to what *Ramapithecus* looked like:

> Our tree-living ancestors perhaps 15 million years ago were creatures about the size of a five-year-old child. They were furred (a naked skin bruises too easily in the trees); we would probably have called them apes, yet they lacked the projecting snouts and big eye-teeth seen in many apes. Their faces were probably more expressive than those of apes and may have had an 'ape-baby' quality. The eyes looked straight forwards, with stereoscopic vision; the ears were like those in man. The lips were thin and the mouth large: the nostrils, over a short upper lip, faced somewhat downwards rather than forwards.[7]

They were certainly omnivorous and probably had relatively long arms suitable for tree-living, but they must have been capable walkers, too, judging from their wide geographical distribution and from the open savannah regions where they lived in late-Miocene times. Dr Kurten suggests that their reason for leaving the trees was not the reduction of the forests, because this might well have led to extinction rather than adaptation; it was because ground-living offered a more favourable way of life, a new habitat which suited them better than the old.

Between *Ramapithecus* and the next hominid development, *Australopithecus*, is a gap of some four million years without any fossils to show what happened. In all probability the African examples of *Ramapithecus* eventually evolved into *Australopithecus*, but this cannot be proven. However *Austral-*

opithecus specimens have been discovered only in Africa, at sites in South Africa, Tanzania, Kenya and Ethiopia. Except for one site in Kenya where fossils have been dated as about 5·5 million years old, all Australopithecine remains are from four to one million years old. Hundreds of fossils have been found at these sites, mainly skulls but including most other bones. A complicating factor is that there were two distinct forms of *Australopithecus*, which coexisted during the same period and in some cases at the same sites. These are commonly called the 'gracile' and 'robust' forms.

As the names suggest, the robust form is more heavily built than the gracile. Both are at first sight fairly ape-like, with protruding jaws and heavy eyebrow ridges (more pronounced in the robust form), though their teeth are smaller than those of *Ramapithecus*. Their cranial capacity was about 480cm^3 for the gracile, similar to that of present-day gorillas but only just over a third of our own. The robust form had a slightly larger cranial capacity. (Some studies give lower figures, such as 450cm^3 for the robust form.) It seems that the robust *Australopithecus* made use of stone implements, for some of these have been found in the same strata, but the evidence for the graciles using tools is inconclusive. It has been suggested that one difference between the forms was dietary, the graciles being omnivorous and the robusts herbivorous; this alone could account for the slightly larger tooth size and heavier jaws of the robusts.[8] The same author has deduced that the graciles were better built for running, as omnivorous hunter-gatherers would need to be. Other writers have maintained that the two forms were in fact the same, since two competitive species would not occupy the same ecological niche.[9] There is even some support for the suggestion that the graciles should be reclassified within the genus *Homo*, because they seem to be direct ancestors. Further evidence will be needed before this could be done, but further evidence could clear up a lot of problems pertaining to the early hominids.

Genus 'Homo'

To classify any early forms of man as being a member of our own genus, *Homo*, is to proclaim a close relationship with us, though the exact degree of relationship necessary for inclusion has never been universally accepted. No particular feature, such as a minimum cranial capacity, or achievement, such as tool manufacture, seems to be appropriate. While it might be both useful and acceptable to employ a classification which would apply to all types of man since the most recent branching point, to apply this would be particularly difficult due to conflicting evidence and is generally not an easy procedure in any case because the type differences close to a branching point tend to be more blurred than normal. In fact, the classification as *Homo* has tended to become looser over time, with more primitive types being admitted. At present three species are recognised, *Homo habilis, Homo erectus* and *Homo sapiens*, with the Neanderthals as a sub-species of *Homo sapiens*. (Other named species are merely the result of duplicated names referring to specimens found at particular sites.)

One of the greatest difficulties in making categorical statements about the evolutionary progress of man within the genus *Homo* is the extent of overlapping in time between the different species. Also there is some disparity between specimens which have been attributed to the same species—which is perhaps only to be expected in a developing line, but makes identification difficult and sometimes arbitrary.

Homo habilis, which was recognised as a species only in 1964, is a case in point. More or less a half-way stage between the robust *Australopithecus* and *Homo erectus*, it seems to have coexisted with the former for at least two million years (ie for the vast majority of the time during which each existed) and with the latter for about half a million years. *Habilis* seems to have an average cranial capacity of about 640cm³, at least twenty-five per cent greater that the robust Australopithecines, and it has smaller teeth. Not enough fossil evidence exists for a height figure to be suggested, though hand bones found suggest a manipulative ability. They lived at many of the same African sites as *Australopithecus*, and no specimens from other parts of the world are known. The bulk of fossils identified as *Homo habilis* have been dated as between 3·3 and 1·3 million years old. Older material discovered with them has led to suggestions that these sites were permanently occupied, that there was some cooperation between individuals (the carcass of a hippopotamus was found at one site in Kenya; this could only have been transported to the living area by joint effort), and that stones were brought to the sites and shaped as tools.

A couple of distinctly different fossil finds have been made. One of these, known as 1470, is an incomplete cranium found by Richard Leakey in Kenya in 1972. This appears to have a cranial capacity of 775cm^3 (twenty per cent more than *habilis*) but a mixture of Australopithecine and *Homo* features. It has been dated at 2·6 million years old and represents a considerable puzzle. Antedating most specimens of both *Australopithecus* and *Homo habilis* it suggests that neither of them is a direct ancestor of ours. On the other hand, 1470 is a solitary, incomplete example: it may be a freak. It has been classified as *Homo* without a species being mentioned. The other puzzling case is of fragments discovered in Tanzania which have been dated at 3·7 million years old yet appear to be from a *Homo* type which is not *habilis*. These could be from a more highly developed gracile Australopithecine.

The implications of all this data are, as B. A. Wood suggests, that the gracile Australopithecines may be our direct ancestors, that they may be a later branch off the robust Australopithecine branch, or that they may be a later branch off the *Homo* lineage than the robusts.[10]

Homo erectus presents fewer problems. Although its name is fairly meaningless, because all *Homo* species have been capable of an erect stance and because it was by no means the first primitive man to adopt such a stance, it is a species which occurred in Africa, Asia and Europe over the period 1·75 to 0·25 million years ago. But within this timespan are some interesting points. *Erectus* appears to have evolved simultaneously in Asia (Java) and Africa (Kenya) prior to 1·5 million years ago and then to have migrated to temperate regions in Europe, where the earliest fossil evidence is from about 0·5 million years ago.

The cranial capacity of *Homo erectus* averages about 950cm^3, although this average masks the contrast between earlier specimens (about 800cm^3) and later ones of over 1,000cm^3. This quite speedy increase in brain size is reflected in the changing skull shape—a flat forehead at first, and a more domed one later. It is a rate of growth of about 4·6 per cent per 100,000 years,[11] and one author, Oscar Kiss Maerth, has suggested that the reason was cannibalism—men gaining intelligence by eating the brains of other men.[12] While the practice of cannibalism among early man (particularly *Homo erectus*) was possibly widespread and is attested by the finding of battered craniums obviously used as drinking bowls, the idea that intelligence can be enhanced by this means has received a singular lack of support from authorities on the subject of prehistoric man. The mysteries of evolution are not to be so glibly solved.

Homo erectus was about five feet tall, bigger than the Australopithecines or *Homo habilis*, though the bony eyebrow ridges and protruding jaws were still present but reduced in size. He was an accomplished hunter, particularly of deer, who chipped flints into a range of tools and made regular use of fire in his caves (presumably for warmth and for cooking food) and outside (perhaps for driving game). Not all authorities accept that *Homo habilis* was our direct ancestor, but certainly he was a widespread and developing species. Many synonyms exist for *Homo erectus*, based on different site names, including *Atlanthropus* (Ternifine man), *Cyphanthropus* (Broken Hill man), Solo man, Djetis man and Peking man. Just as some samples of *Homo habilis* show advances on the norm, so there are some *erectus* populations which show evidence of change towards the *Homo sapiens* shape.

But there is one more morphological group of early man, a fairly distinct and problematical group, Neanderthal man. Current thinking is for its classification as a sub-species of modern man, as *Homo sapiens neanderthalis*. The neanderthals existed from about 130,000 years ago to 25,000 years ago, which makes them contemporaries of other *Homo sapiens* forms more like present-day man. Hence their status presents difficulties. They might have been a stage in man's ancestral line, though this seems unlikely, or they might have been a variation away from the direct line which appeared, spread and eventually disappeared—perhaps through interbreeding with the main line of *Homo sapiens*. The placing of the neanderthals in the same species as ourselves is an acceptance that such interbreeding would have been possible, even though there is no direct evidence for it.

Neanderthal man had a fairly distinctive stature and skull

RAMAPITHECUS

ROBUST DARTIANS

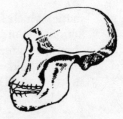

GRACILE DARTIANS

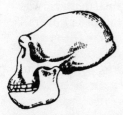

HOMO ERECTUS

NEANDERTHAL MAN

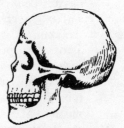

HOMO SAPIENS
(including modern man)

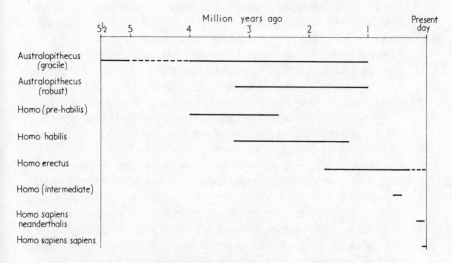

Chart showing the periods during which the various species of *homo* lived and, in some cases, overlapped.

shape, which has become well known to most laymen through fictional sources. The neanderthals were short and stocky— about five feet tall. They were extremely powerfully built, broad-shouldered and heavy-boned, with great physical strength. As Dr Kurten puts it they were 'probably excellently suited for bursting forth through the dense scrub forest'.[13] For many years it was accepted that they could not stand up straight and moved with a stooped, shambling gait, but this was due to the skeleton of an aged and arthritic specimen having been studied. It is now known that the neanderthals walked much as we do. Their most exceptional feature was the skull. It was particularly large—as high and broad overall as of most modern men, but longer. Even allowing for greater thickness of bone, the cranial capacity of the Neanderthals appears to have averaged 1,450 or 1,500cm^3, as compared to the modern average of 1,350cm^3. This does not necessarily mean that their level of intelligence was greater than ours; the extra capacity was at the rear of the brain whereas most of the important determinants of intelligence are connected with the forebrain. Their faces still possessed bony ridges over the eyes but with a slightly domed forehead (less so than modern man, but not *much* less so), properly developed nasal cavities and more indication of a chin than in any previous hominid. If suitably attired for 1980, one of them could walk down a busy city street today without attracting attention.

As a culture they appear to have been similar to *Homo erectus* but perhaps rather more advanced. They made great use of flaked flint tools in hunting and in the preparation of food and hides. Besides meat they ate vegetable matter. Commonly, their teeth are defaced by innumerable scratches, which can only be explained by the habit of stuffing food into the mouth and using a flint knife to chop off whatever hung out, thus scratching the enamel regularly. It can be presumed that the neanderthals possessed a language of sounds and signs.

As for the origins of the neanderthals there is something of a mystery. They seem to have occurred only in Europe and the Middle East, while contemporary populations in Asia and Africa show none of the distinctive neanderthal traits. Three possible ancestors of the neanderthals have been found, as skull fragments at Verteszollos in Hungary, as Steinheim man in Germany and Swanscombe man in England. The dates of all three are in the region of 0·5 to 0·4 million years ago. The Verteszollos skull has been classified as an advanced form of *Homo erectus*; its cranial capacity is possibly as large as 1,400cm^3. The Steinheim skull is smaller, perhaps 1,150cm^3, which would be an acceptable size for *Homo erectus* although on the large side, but the skull shape is wrong for *erectus* (the forehead is slightly domed and many details resemble modern man far more than either *erectus* or the neanderthal type). The Swanscombe skull is far from complete but suggests a cranial capacity of 1,300cm^3. It bears some similarities to the Steinheim skull, but there are also differences. From such uncertain evidence it is possible to suggest, though only tentatively, that there may have been at least two branches of hominids after *Homo erectus*, one leading to the neanderthals and one to modern *Homo sapiens*.

Examples of *Homo sapiens sapiens*—that is, men who are anatomically undifferentiable from those of today—are known to have existed for the last 30,000 years, though some Asian remains may be 10,000 years older than that. In Europe there seems to be no firm evidence of *Homo sapiens*—other than neanderthals—from before 30,000 years ago, which suggests a migration, presumably from Africa or Asia. A few scattered fragments of bone which might be from modern man have been discovered at African sites. These suggest the existence of *Homo sapiens* as early as 130,000 years ago, though no earlier than 35,000 years ago for *Homo sapiens sapiens*. It does seem that *Homo sapiens sapiens* appeared relatively suddenly at around that time, spreading across Europe, Asia and Africa to replace the existing neanderthals and other early *Homo sapiens* populations. Or there might have been simultaneous evolution among relatively isolated populations. The latter seems more likely in the cases of America and Australia, where migration appears to have taken place ahead of the emergence of modern man. Some North American fossil evidence of *Homo sapiens* is up to 48,000 years old. It is accepted that there was a migration of early *Homo sapiens* across the Bering Straits perhaps 50,000 years ago, when sea levels were lower than they are today. Australian evidence is inconclusive but indicates the possibility of a fairly primitive type of man (*Homo erectus* or early *Homo sapiens*) existing there until maybe 10,000 years ago. The linking together of both the migratory and separate development theories can be achieved by suggesting the interbreeding of' the neanderthals with migrating *Homo sapiens sapiens*, as W. W. Howells does.[14]

Looking at modern man over the last 50,000 years it is convenient to use Alvin Toffler's concept of the 800th lifetime.[15] This period may be divided into eight hundred lifetimes of man (assuming about sixty-two years per lifetime) of which at least six hundred and fifty were spent living in caves. For some seven hundred and thirty of these lifetimes it was not possible to communicate effectively over periods of time (such as from one lifetime to the one-after-next) because there was no writing; anything memorable was handed down by word of mouth if at all.

> Only during the last six lifetimes did masses ever see a printed word. Only during the last four has it been possible to measure time with any precision. Only in the last two has anyone anywhere used an electric motor. And the overwhelming majority of all the material goods we use in daily life today have been developed within the present, the 800th, lifetime.

That is the story so far—the evolution of man from Sun-birth to atomic technology over a period of about 4,700 million years. The Sun will probably continue to pour out life-giving radiation at about its present level for another 6,000 million years, despite occasional doubts as to its stability.[16] This enormous period gives man plenty of time to develop in directions and by amounts which we are not able even to imagine (though in chapter eight a valiant attempt will be made).

The Evidence for Evolution

This book most definitely is not intended as a textbook of evolutionary theory. Nevertheless, a brief outline of evolution on Earth has been given and something needs to be said about the evidence supporting it. The fossil record has been referred to frequently. This consists of sedimentary rocks of various datable ages which contain fossilised remains of the hard parts (bones, shells, scales, woody stems, etc) of early forms of plant and animal life. Although the record is far from complete the age distribution of different species, together with certain in-between forms, gives an indication of the course of evolution. A second aspect is comparative anatomy. All vertebrates (including extinct types known only from fossils) have certain skeletal similarities, particularly the vertebral column itself, and all living vertebrates are built on roughly the same lines with regard to internal organs. As Darwin put it, 'Man still carries in his bodily frame the indelible stamp of his lowly origin.' The most likely explanation for this is evolution from a common ancestor. The geographical distribution of particular species of animals is a third piece of evidence. While Europe, Asia and, to a certain extent, North America have a fairly uniform fauna, the more isolated continents of Africa, South America and Australia each have many species which do not occur elsewhere. This tendency is further exaggerated on some islands, notably Madagascar, New Zealand and the Galapagos group. The inference is that ancestral stocks of

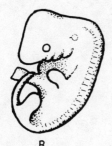

B

A

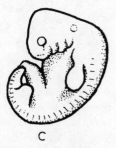

C

The embryos of: A a bird; B a dog; C a man. (Not drawn to scale.)

animals migrated from Eurasia at a time when land bridges existed, then developed separately when continental drift isolated them. Comparative embryology is a fourth strand. The adult forms of fish and mammals, for example, are not very much alike despite some basic similarities, but in their embryonic stages there is a much greater degree of similarity, with the mammalian embryo possessing gill slits. There are many examples of common embryonic features between widely separate groups of animals, which provides good evidence of one type having developed from the other (see FIGURE p 27). This evolutionary path is reflected in taxonomy—the classification of organisms. Although taxonomy is primarily done for convenience and is a result of evolution rather than evidence for it, classification does show up the small differences between orders and families, and the relationships between groups of animals, because this is the basis of taxonomy.

2 Evolution – Theories and After

LUBIN: *I am sound on the garden of Eden. I have heard of Darwin.*
SAVVY: *But Darwin is all rot.*

G. B. Shaw, *Back to Methuselah*

'Even if we are descended from worms they were glorious worms.'
J. M. Tyler

Before Darwin

There is a tendency for the average person to believe (in all complacency) that theories of evolution began and ended with Charles Darwin, that nobody knew anything about the subject before him and that nobody has added anything since. Although this is comprehensively wrong in both respects it is a belief which highlights the great extent to which 'evolution' and 'Darwinism' are held to be related—indeed, synonymous —in the minds of the public. A score or more of researchers can be said to have had as great an influence upon the theories of evolution and genetics as Darwin, yet none of their ideas has achieved a tenth—perhaps not even a hundredth—of the impact of Darwin's *Origin of Species*, on its first publication in 1859.

Until the seventeenth century there was no concept of evolution, or even of the relationships between species of animals or plants. Human beings were thought always to have been human beings since the time of the creation, while a variety of small creatures—insects, spiders, mice, etc—were imagined to be generated spontaneously from non-living substances. During the Middle Ages it was common for magic to posture as science (in order to escape the persecution of the church), and supposedly scientific treatises gave instructions for the creation of small creatures from inanimate matter.

During the seventeenth century it was demonstrated that

meat which is going bad does not spontaneously generate maggots, and John Ray devised systems of plant and animal classification which were, during the eighteenth century, adopted and completed by Carolus Linnaeus. But Linnaeus was primarily a classifier, content to accept that all species had been created as such, though later in his life he speculated that the genera might have been created and that the species might have developed separately. Other eighteenth-century naturalists began to suggest that a process of descent and transformation was at work. Buffon, a French count, was one of these; Erasmus Darwin (grandfather of Charles) was another. Best known of these eighteenth-century figures was another Frenchman, Jean Baptiste Lamarck, whose theories included one of evolution which, though unsupported by firm empirical evidence, sounds convincing and persists among non-scientists even today. It is not very different from Darwin's theory.

The essence of Lamarckism is that the driving force in the process of evolution is the organism's need for a particular evolutionary advance, based on the idea that those parts of the body which are used greatly will become larger while those which are unused will atrophy. According to Lamarck, the mechanism by which this happened was the transmission of acquired characteristics. The usual example given is of the giraffe, which needed to be able to reach the branches of trees. Its fossil ancestors had shorter necks but, by the Lamarckian theory, the continual stretching tended to increase the length of the neck, a characteristic which was passed on to the next generation. This is an appealing argument until one realises that, if it were true, it follows that the children of weight-lifters should be born with particularly strong arm muscles and that the children of famous musicians should be born with great musical talent and at least a basic grasp of harmony and counterpoint.

Darwin and After

By contrast, Charles Darwin's theory of evolution suggests that there is a continuous variation within most species but that some variations will make the organism better suited to its environment than its fellows (whether it is a plant, a fish or a man). In the struggle for existence in an overcrowded ecological niche the organism possessing the favourable variation (or mutation) will prosper and go on to raise young, while others will not. This survival of the fittest[1] is the mechanism by which Darwin said that new species originate.

So Darwin was not the first to put forward a theory of continuous evolution leading to man. All he did was to suggest a mechanism by which this could happen. He was not even the only one to think along the lines of the survival of the fittest: Alfred Russell Wallace independently worked out an identical theory at the same time, and a joint paper by Darwin and Wallace was read out to the Linnaean Society in 1858 and published in its journal. Yet it was the publication of Darwin's book *On the Origin of Species by Means of Natural Selection, or the Preservation of Favoured Races in the Struggle for Life* which was noticed by the public because it was a clear exposition of the way in which evolution worked, written in a way which was intelligible to the layman. The book sold out on its day of publication. It became a sensation, a *cause célèbre*. 'Darwin's theory of evolution made an impact on the imagination of the layman far greater than any other set of ideas in 19th century science. It challenged all man's cherished beliefs and called into question his self-image.'[2]

It was not so much that the idea of evolution of one species from another was new; breeders of horses, dogs and pigeons were quite aware that breeds could be created. It was that, in particular, Darwin's theory brought it firmly to the Victorian attention that *man* had not been created whole, perfect and intelligent, but had evolved from the lowest of beasts, fighting with tooth and claw all the way. It claimed that man had a close family connection with the apes which, with their dark faces, thick fur, lack of cleanliness and jungle habits, epitomised everything that the Victorians tried so hard not to be. Furthermore, it attempted to prove that the world had been in existence for millions of years rather than having been created by God at 9·00 am on 23 October 4004 BC, as calculated by the Reverend Dr Lightfoot of Cambridge in the seventeenth century.[3] The *Origin of Species* was denying what was clearly laid down in the Bible about Adam and Eve in the Garden of Eden. Also, by suggesting that natural selection was responsible for improving species, Darwin was saying that God's creation had not been perfect to begin with. It was blasphemy!

Most churchmen reviled Darwin, but many important figures in science and literature supported him. There was a celebrated confrontation between T. H. Huxley (the biologist, and later to be the teacher and inspirer of the young H. G. Wells) and Dr Samuel Wilberforce, the Bishop of Oxford, on the occasion of a British Association meeting at Oxford in 1860. Huxley was one of Darwin's greatest supporters. (But not all scientists followed his example; Lord Kelvin, the physicist, said: 'We find something at every turn to show the utter futility of Darwin's philosophy.')

The affair rocked the nation. There were debates in Parliament. Disraeli described the issue as one of 'whether man is an ape or an angel'. Darwin, who had been in poor health almost ever since his voyages of discovery on HMS *Beagle* during the 1830s, was a semi-recluse. He was unwilling to defend his theories in public debate for this reason. He was pilloried by the cartoonists of the day.

But Darwin's *Origin of Species* was not the last word on evolution. It contained some misconceptions and some vagueness. It was conceived and written at a time when nothing was known of heredity or genetics. Even those who accepted Darwin's theories did so—in some cases—as a means of perpetuating their own fiercely held bigotry.

> A vast body of research 'proved'—to no-one's great surprise— that if the ethnic groups were ordered in terms of their distance up the ladder of evolution, white Anglo-Saxon Protestants would be in the lead, followed by Northern Europeans, Slavs, Jews, Italians, and so on, with Negroes trailing in the far rear. By the 1860s natural scientists could pinpoint woman's place on the evolutionary ladder with some precision—she was at the level of the Negro.[4]

After Darwin came Abbot Gregor Mendel, an Austrian monk, who researched heredity exhaustively, providing the basis of current theories, but whose work was almost unknown for thirty years, until 1900. William Bateson, a British biologist who has been called the founder of the science of genetics, extended Mendel's work, and the American T. H. Morgan carried this work even further, making experiments with the fruit fly *Drosophila melanogaster* to establish the existence of genes and describe their role in heredity (and evolution). The research goes on still, with genetic engineering pointing the way ahead while new fossil evidence and improved methods of dating fill in gaps of the past.

The Influence of Darwinism

The impact of Darwin's *Origin of Species* can hardly be overemphasised. It disrupted the stability of life by its insistence that there *is* no stability, that life itself is a dynamic process. Its effect on science was less great than its effect upon society and, in particular, upon literature. The idea of continuous evolution—of an enormously long past, and presumably an equally lengthy future, stimulated much thought (and no small number of books) on the subject of change. This was not simply a continuation of the early Victorian ideal of progress, which was optimistic, confident, taking advancement for granted. Rather it was an examination of change, laced with doubts and reservations. This is best exemplified by the works of Thomas Hardy, who had been excited by the appearance of *Origin of Species* (he was nineteen at the time) and allowed it to influence him in many of his books and in his attitude to life. There was something of science about this, on occasion, as when he lectures the reader on the primitive sea-life of the Silurian period (in *A Pair of Blue Eyes*), but more importantly it took the philosophical form of man (insignificant to all but himself) caught up by destiny. It culminated in a spiritual evolution, described in *The Dynasts*.[5] The idea that change was not necessarily for the better was hammered home by Robert Louis Stevenson in *Dr Jekyll and Mr Hyde* (1886) which can be interpreted as an allegory about the grim and brutal origins of all mankind which may still be locked up inside us.

Darwinism greatly influenced the way in which the contemporary novel investigated past and future. Jules Verne took the popular 'hollow Earth' theme, added a mixture of prehistoric life left over from different periods and wrote *Journey to the Centre of the Earth* (1864) which at one level is a tour of past eras of the Earth's development. Enclaves of the past, well stocked with dinosaurs, early races of man, or both(!), hidden away in a remote corner of the world, became regular backgrounds for adventure fiction. Conan Doyle's *The Lost World* (1912) is one of the more memorable of these. But Darwinism also gave rise to a new sub-genre of stories about primitive man, demonstrating the existence of 'missing links' and showing how many early technological advances might have occurred (the invention of fire, the first log boat, and so on). The earliest of these was written by the Frenchman J. H. Rosny *aîné* in 1892 (*Vamireh*), but the first to be published in English was Austin Bierbower's *From Monkey to Man* (1894), which tells of the struggle for supremacy between two early types of 'ape', the Lali and the Ammi, of which one will survive to evolve into mankind. A similar book, published three years later, *The Story of Ab* by Stanley Waterloo, was admittedly written to put the theory of evolution in such a simple form that anybody could understand it. Among the many others are H. G. Wells' novella 'A Story of the Stone Age' (1897) and Jack London's *Before Adam* (1906); both of them show primitive man making important discoveries.

It is in the sphere of novels set in the future that Darwinism had the greatest effect upon literature, and this is one of the aspects of Darwinism most relevant to the present book. Prior to 1859 a few stories were set in the future.[6] Even if one ignores the political satires, these tend to be somewhat staid in their predictions, envisioning new gadgets and sometimes new social orders, but avoiding fundamental changes. After 1859 there is both an increase in tales of the future and a gradual use of evolutionary ideas.

One of the first such is E. G. Bulwer-Lytton's *The Coming Race* (1871). Although not set in the future it shows an advanced race of man living below ground. They are clearly the product of further evolution and have achieved greater size as well as enormously increased mental powers. But, as J. O. Bailey points out, Bulwer-Lytton makes the mistake of describing a 'static perfection . . . He fails to realize one implication of the theory of evolution, that life is dynamic, so that whatever stage of perfection man may reach is only a stage.'[7] The next year (1872) Samuel Butler, who was opposed to Darwin's theories, wrote *Erewhon* which (at one point) satirises evolution by applying it to machines. The Erewhonians have, in fact, rid themselves of all machinery because of the danger of it developing a consciousness of its own and replacing man.

Evolution is not always synonymous with continuous improvement. Richard Jefferies, in *After London* (1885), shows late Victorian civilisation toppled and London slowly reverting to a natural state, with weeds and animals encroaching further each year. (He offers no explanation; probably he wrote what he felt *should* happen, for he far preferred countryside to city.) This is followed by a kind of medieval romance indicating the rise of humanity from a second period of barbarism. W. H. Hudson writes of another 'after-the-catastrophe' future in *A Crystal Age* (1887), an important novel of future evolution which is fully described in chapter eight.

During the 1880s and 1890s an increasingly large number of authors of speculative works began to draw upon the ideas of *Origin of Species*—or just assumed them in passing. All conceptions of future societies tended to show evidence of evolution. In Edward Bellamy's *Looking Backward 2000–1887* (1888) and in William Morris's rebuttal of it, *News From Nowhere* (1890), this was social and organisational evolution, though there is also some indication that Bellamy envisaged a spiritual evolution which would bring together men and God: 'The long and weary winter of the race is ended. Its summer has begun. Humanity has burst the chrysalis.' (Chapter XXVI.) *The British Barbarians* (1895) by Grant Allen varied the pattern by having a twenty-fifth-century social anthropologist come back in time to investigate the primitive customs and taboos of late Victorian England. He is mystified by the many irrationalities and concludes that they are caused by our descent from monkey-like animals. Camille Flammarion predicted Earth's future evolutionary pattern in *La Fin du Monde* (1893). Percy Greg even did the same for the planet Mars in his interplanetary adventure novel *Across the Zodiac* (1880).

H. G. Wells whole-heartedly embraced Darwin's theories. He learnt them from T. H. Huxley's lectures when he was a student of biology at the Normal School of Science in London in 1886. Throughout his writing—fiction and non-fiction—one can see the Darwinian message, though sometimes compounded with the ideas of Marx or Nietzsche. The far future of *The Time Machine* (1895) is an obvious example, with its two separate races of future man and 'wonderful flowers countless years of culture had created'. (This novel is considered at greater length in chapter eight.) There is also *The Island of Dr Moreau* (1896), where Wells shows that 'there is no essential difference between man and animal, nothing which cannot be affected by surgical manipulation'.[8] This was an essential part of Darwinism; it had offended the Victorian mind in 1859, and Wells' repetition of it offended the more traditional readers in 1896, accounting for the novel's hostile reception in some quarters. *The War of the Worlds* (1898) is a Darwinian struggle for survival between the men of Earth and the invading Martians. The latter, by their inability to withstand Earth's microbes, show themselves less fitted to live here than man. At one point the narrator considers the evolution of the Martians:

> To me it is quite credible that the Martians may be descended from beings not unlike ourselves, by a gradual development of brain and hands (the latter giving rise to the two bunches of delicate tentacles at last) at the expense of the rest of the body. Without the body the brain would of course become a more selfish intelligence, without any of the emotional substratum of the human being.[9]

The insect-like Selenites in *The First Men in the Moon* (1901) are the specialised end results of controlled evolution, and the land of Utopia in *Men Like Gods* (1923) is a Utopia precisely because men have learned to control evolution, creating 'a nobler humanity', 'different in kind'.

Among Wells' short stories are many which deal with some aspect of evolution—past, present or future. In 'Aepyornis Island' (1895) a man stranded on a desert island has to eat the priceless egg of an 'extinct' bird to avoid starvation. 'In the Abyss' (1896) shows a bathyscaphe discovering a city of humanoids living at a great depth beneath the sea. Wells justifies this by having his narrator say:

> They [eminent scientists] tell me they see no reason why intelligent, water-breathing, vertebrated creatures, inured to a low temperature and enormous pressure, and of such a heavy structure that neither alive nor dead would they float, might not live upon the bottom of the deep sea, and quite unsuspected by us, descendents like ourselves of the great Theriomorpha of the New Red Sandstone age.

In 'The Empire of the Ants' (1905) it is a species of South American ant which is evolving, gaining intelligence and threatening to displace man as ruler of the world. There are several of Wells' articles which speak of evolution, notably 'The Man of the Year Million' (1893) and 'The Limits of Individual Plasticity' (1895), and his major premise in *Anticipations* (1899), a book of serious prophecy, is of an evolving human society during the twentieth century.

As the decades passed, as the Victorian age ended, and as more people came to believe in evolution (having been taught it at school or college), no author writing about the future could afford not to consider how evolution might affect man. It came to be taken for granted that man would evolve further. *The Hampdenshire Wonder* (1911) by J. D. Beresford is about the childhood of a 'future man'—a super-intelligent being born to apparently normal parents presumably because of spontaneous genetic mutation. The child has a large, bald head but is otherwise physically normal. Yet he forgets nothing and at the age of four is already capable of reading and comprehending anything in a very large private library to which he is given access. 'He is too many thousands of years ahead of us,' says one character.

George Bernard Shaw, who was always willing to express a strong opinion upon any subject, wrote two plays which deal markedly with evolution, *Man and Superman* (1901–3) and *Back to Methuselah* (1921), adding to each a preface on the subject almost as long as the play. But Shaw, as one might perhaps guess from the quotation heading this chapter, was not a Darwinist; he was a convinced Lamarckian. He dismissed the Darwinian theory of natural selection as 'a chapter of accidents' and argued vehemently that although acquired characteristics are plainly not transmitted *in toto*, each generation passes on just a trifle more in this respect than the last. He was a great believer in man being able to alter himself if he wanted to do so badly enough, and this is his chief premise for the acquisition of increased longevity presented in *Back to Methuselah*. At a purely mechanical level—via improved technology—Shaw was, of course, correct. Mankind wants to change itself and is doing so in many ways without waiting for that 'chapter of accidents', as the next two chapters of this book will demonstrate.

3 The Changing Shape of Man

'The body is just something to carry the brain around in.'
Thomas Alva Eddison

Slowly, all of us are changing shape. Not just individually, with advancing age, but all together: the human bodily norm is evolving—mutating, if you like—though with a tremendously ponderous slowness. The interaction between man and his environment is resulting in the languid erosion of our genetic material. Millennia are too brief for this change to become manifest. We cannot even be sure which parts of our bodies will alter first. The human body possesses many dozens of vestigial features which could disappear without disadvantage. Some of the functionless muscles of the ear, or the fold of epithelium at the corner of the eye could go without being noticed. As for larger changes, the loss of our outermost toes, or wisdom teeth, or remaining body hair (though not in the pubic and armpit regions, where it retains a sexual role), or a change in skull shape are all possible, even likely. In tens of thousands of years our descendants will know—perhaps.

Caution is necessary because over that same period mankind—always the most impatient of animal species—will have changed its shape by artificial means many, many times. Such changes will be brought about by a combination of organic means (including transplant surgery and genetic engineering) and by the addition of mechanical parts (either as necessary replacements or deliberate enhancements) to the human body, tending to upset and blur the effects of natural evolution. Although small changes in both these categories—organic and mechanical—have already become commonplace, the pace of research in these fields is fast and accelerating: today's science fiction is becoming tomorrow's established fact. The possibility of human clones and largely mechanical cyborgs existing before the end of the present century is widely accepted. That state of affairs will raise a number of taxing social and moral problems. What constitutes a person's identity? At what stage of the substitution of mechanical for organic parts does a man cease to be a man? What right do we have to radically alter human genetic material? Can those not 'born of woman' claim the same social status as those who are? These and similar questions will be analysed in the last part of the current chapter.

Increased Longevity

Dreams of immortality have been around for as long as man himself. Elixirs of life, potions of eternal youth—these have been sought eagerly by generation after generation of the rich and powerful. But all such seekers have been disappointed. Magical cures for old age exist only in fiction, and there they abound. All mythologies confer immortality upon their deities and many works of utopia refer to it as having been achieved in their perfect country.[1] Nor has lack of success led to any diminution in the numbers of magicians (or, since the Middle Ages, scientists) hunting for a solution. As a sphere of research it has always been as popular as the search for a means of turning base metal into gold. Many eminent scientists, particularly during the nineteenth century, have forecast that the increasing powers of medicine would lead to the doubling of lifespans at the very least.

Only fairly recently has it come to be generally realised that medicine, as such, has done nothing to increase the natural lifespan of the human race. What medical advances have done is to allow a much greater proportion of people to attain their natural lifespan of three score years and ten. This has been due to the vast reduction of mortality levels from certain 'killer' diseases such as smallpox, diphtheria and pneumonia; enzyme abnormalities and diet deficiences which would have reduced life expectancy have become curable; cancer and heart disease can in many instances be combatted and controlled, affording the sufferer a decade or two of active life. Thus it can be said that 'people are living longer', because average life-expectancy has increased dramatically over the last century or so (see FIGURE), but man's natural lifespan seems not to have increased at all since biblical times. Some individuals survive to over one hundred, but the numbers of these, taken as a proportion of people reaching the age of seventy, are not increasing. Even if mankind were not counterbalancing the good work of preventive medicine by the detrimental effects of cigarette smoking, over-eating and air pollution, it is doubtful whether average life expectancy could be pushed past seventy-five or eighty without a revolutionary breakthrough.

Increases in life expectancy during the past century

ENGLAND & WALES (figures in years)

Period	Male	Female
1838–54	39.9	41.9
1901–10	48.5	52.4
1910–12	51.5	55.3
1920–22	55.6	59.6
1930–32	58.7	62.9
1937	60.2	64.4
1948–60	68.3	74.1

UNITED STATES (figures in years)

Period	Male	Female
1850	38.3	40.5
1900–02	47.9	50.7
1909–11	49.9	53.2
1919–21	55.5	57.4
1929–31	57.7	61.0
1939–41	61.6	65.9
1948–60	66.5	73.0

There is, however, one part of the human body which does survive death: the gene. It has been suggested by molecular biologists that some of our genes are identical copies of those possessed by our remote ancestors, perhaps tens of thousands of years ago. Some may in fact antedate the emergence of *Homo sapiens* more than a hundred thousand years ago. This is one of the factors which makes Richard Dawkins, in his book *The Selfish Gene*, assert that the human body's major function is to ensure the survival of the gene. It may indeed be pleasant to reflect that a minute part of us will still be around in an identical form in thousands of years' time (assuming that we have children and that they have children . . .) but this is only of very limited comfort to somebody dying of old age at seventy-five who wishes for a few more decades of life.

Today many hundreds of scientific teams, all over the world but particularly in the USA, are, by different approaches, trying to achieve a breakthrough in the prolonging of life. It has been proven, by experimentation with rats, that a restricted diet (to sixty per cent of normal) increases life expectancy, sometimes considerably, though this involves the prolonging of immaturity and so is of limited use. (Even if this were possible in the case of humans, who would want to spend a hundred years stuck at the age of ten?)

Relatively little is known of the ageing process, especially in man. The three major hypotheses are 'that ageing is timed by the irreplaceable cells and structures, that it results from faulty copying in cells which divide clonally, and that it is a mechano-physical process involving the "setting" of low-turnover colloids and other macromolecules'—a succinct resumé by Dr Alex Comfort.[2] Dr Comfort is the leading British specialist in the field. He predicts that 'we shall know by 1990 of at least one way of extending vigorous life by about twenty per cent'.

Current research is concentrating on the 'faulty copying' hypothesis, as it has been proven from cultured cells that mistakes can be made during the replication of DNA—and the older the chromosomes the more faults there are that occur. There is a gradual multiplication of these errors until cell function becomes impaired. Possibilities of repairing DNA are being investigated—it is a trick which some long-lived plants and animals seem to manage.

The most important thing about any period of extended life is that it must be vigorous. Living to the age of, say, two hundred is of no benefit if one is still going to become increasingly frail physically and vague mentally from the age of seventy onwards. To be of any practical use, these years of extra life—whether they number ten or a hundred—must be accompanied by an apparent physical age of thirty or forty. Apart from anything else, society could not survive if the periods of old age (or pre-pubescence) were to be extended dramatically. In any case, the age of retirement would need to be adjusted so that it still came only five or ten years before death could be expected.

Among fictional accounts of increased longevity the secret is often a drug of some kind, usually with side effects. In

Aldous Huxley's novel *After Many a Summer* (1939) it is suggested that the intestinal flora of that notoriously long-lived fish the carp account for its longevity by preventing an accumulation of cholesterol. Discovering this at the end of the eighteenth century, the Fifth Earl of Gonister keeps himself from growing old by the consumption of carp viscera. He lives to an age in excess of two hundred years but regresses evolutionarily, growing coarse red hair all over his face and body, and a sharp bony ridge just above his eyesockets. In a more modern novel, *One Million Tomorrows* by Bob Shaw, an immortality drug is widely available. It is administered by a single injection and people can choose for themselves when to take it—choose at what age to remain for the next thousand years or so. The side effect there is sterility.

But perhaps an elixir of life is unnecessary. George Bernard Shaw, in his play *Back to Methuselah*, suggests that men might live to the age of three hundred if they wish it strongly enough (though this desire might well be subconscious), and that such an age would enable them to achieve great mental maturity. ('Can't you see that three-score-and-ten, though it may be long enough for a very crude sort of village life, isn't long enough for a complicated civilization like ours?') On the other hand, Lazarus Long, in *Time Enough For Love* by Robert A. Heinlein, has a lifespan of thousands of years as a result of a careful eugenics programme, the interbreeding of families with proven longevity, which is, in our present state of knowledge, the only sure way to increase natural lifespan—and then only for a small group.

The main problem of increasing longevity is that it can result in a rapid increase in population. (If everybody marries, with each couple producing two children and everybody dying at the age of seventy, the population will remain steady, neither increasing nor decreasing. But if longevity is increased to two hundred years, *with birth rate remaining unchanged*, the population will grow to about two and a third times its former size before stabilising itself, because seven generations will be alive at any one time, rather than three.) Even the increase in life expectancy which has occurred during the twentieth century has resulted in an ageing population in developed countries, where an ever-rising proportion of GNP has been devoted to the welfare of the elderly.

A totally different approach to longevity must be considered. This is the practice of freezing the bodies of those recently dead (normally using liquid nitrogen, at a temperature of −196° Centigrade) in the hope that at some time in the future they can be unfrozen and cured of the cancer, heart disease or whatever else it was that led to death. It seems reasonable to assume that, eventually, medical science will be able to reverse death however it was caused (so long as most of the body is present), but this is not the same as suggesting that cadavers frozen in 1980 will be unfrozen and returned to full, active life by the super-scientific techniques of 2080. Many of the drawbacks to this were examined by Robert C. W. Ettinger in *The Prospect of Immortality*. The act of freezing can cause far more damage to the body than the disease which led to death, because of the expansion of the water contained in the body as it turns to ice. A fast rate of freezing produces very small crystals of ice but many of these will be inside cell membranes and may damage the nuclei. A slower rate of freezing induces the ice to form between cells, though in larger crystals; the concentrated salts remaining in the cells may cause damage. In any case there will be some considerable degree of shock sustained by the body, and many cells will die. If the body is stored for a very considerable time (multiples of centuries) there is likely to be damage due to natural radiation, because the body will be unable to repair itself and the normal minimal damage will accumulate. The result of all this is that if a body is skilfully thawed in 2080 it will require an enormous amount of effort to make it function normally again—probably extensive transplant surgery. Even then, there is a strong chance that the brain will have been irreparably damaged at some point. The cancer or heart condition will have been curable but the patient will be the oldest living cabbage in the world—with storage and surgical bills amounting to hundreds of thousands of pounds (at today's values).

For these reasons the practice of freezing the recently dead must at present be regarded as a complete waste of time and money. But once a high level of reliability has been achieved one can forsee a great many of the rich—either those suffering from a terminal disease or those who are simply curious—taking a one-way trip into the future by this means. Then there will arise a whole new set of problems—ethical, moral and legal. Should a dying spouse be frozen, even if it means considerable monetary sacrifice on the part of the surviving partner? If a dying person adamantly refuses to be frozen, is this a form of suicide? If the surviving partner refuses to pay out for his spouse to be frozen, is he guilty of a form of murder? Indeed, is it possible to commit murder if the 'victim' is able to be frozen and later revived? But if one deliberately allows a frozen body to warm up (and thus rot), what crime has been committed—surely not murder? And if a man is convicted of murder and executed, would it be possible to freeze his body, too? If freezing, particularly of the still-living, becomes popular, new laws will need to be drafted covering their rights. If a person 'dies' and is frozen, should any life insurance he carries be paid out? Should his spouse be free to remarry? Should his money and possessions be dispersed to next of kin or held in trust in case he is returned to life in twenty, fifty or a hundred years' time? If a living person is frozen, will he still be classed as a living person, even though there is no heart beat, respiration or brain activity? This will require new definitions of death to be established. Since the frozen person will be expected to pay taxes on any income from his investments, will he be entitled to vote in elections (by proxy)?

One of the biggest problems connected with freezing is money. What happens to a frozen body when the money runs out, leaving not even enough to pay for resuscitation and necessary organ replacements? What happens if the freezer company goes bankrupt with frozen customers in its charge? Even when freezing is safe and relatively common, it is never likely to be cheap, though this will be no problem for the very rich. It might even become fashionable someday, among the rich, to be frozen and unfrozen regularly, spending only a day or two awake in every year or every decade. By such means a man's life could span several millennia, even if the total time spent unfrozen did not exceed seventy years. This has been used as the basis for a story by Roger Zelazny, 'The Graveyard Heart'.

Organ Transplants

The heart transplant operations performed by Dr Christian Barnard in South Africa since December 1967, and by teams of surgeons in the USA, Britain, France, and so on, have continued to make headline news and to cause no small amount of controversy. Generally speaking these operations have been performed upon ageing patients (almost all male) whose hearts had failed completely and who were being kept alive by machinery. The donors have tended to be young people, quite often the victims of road accidents, though in a few cases the heart has come from a baboon.

These facts raise a number of important points. In the first place, the relatively small number of heart transplants (little more than a hundred in eleven years) and the large percentage of failures mean that this remains an experimental operation —a last-ditch attempt to give the patient a few months of normal life—which receives far more public attention than it deserves. The less glamorous transplants of skin, corneas and kidneys are an everyday occurrence with much lower failure rates. The major cause of failure in any type of transplant is the defence mechanism by which the body rejects all strange tissue (a function of the body's human lymphocyte antigens, which recognise HLAs from a different body and react against them). This means that all tissues must be matched in the same way as blood for transfusion (though the task is much simpler with blood). Any drugs given to the patient to diminish rejection will also lower resistance to infection. What is needed here is a technique which will eliminate the rejection of a transplant without affecting the rest of the body's de-fences. In the case of skin grafts this seems to be achieveable by the use of enzymes, which are employed to dissolve away the proteins that identify the skin as 'foreign'. The system is still being tested.

A second problem in transplant surgery is the lack of sufficient donors. Although skin and corneas, like blood, can be stored for considerable periods at low temperatures with no deterioration, the technique has not yet been perfected for organs, which must be transplanted as soon as possible after the death of the donor, and normally within four to six hours.

(In exceptional cases organs have been frozen and kept for up to forty-eight hours without deterioration.)

The problem of a lack of donors can be solved in several ways. Now that the death criterion of zero brain activity has become widely accepted by doctors, it may be possible to keep 'vegetable' patients alive by means of heart-lung machines until operations requiring several of their organs have been set up, and then to perform all the operations within a very short space of time at the same hospital. Alternatively, a much larger proportion of the population could be persuaded to carry donor cards, giving permission for their organs to be used should they meet with a fatal accident. Or perhaps blanket permission could be given by law for accident victims' organs to be used in this way. It is probable that within twenty years the freezing and storing of organs will be a routine procedure, with vast organ banks in existence; all undiseased youthful corpses may be sent to the organ banks for dismemberment and storage, with burial or cremation reserved only for the bodies of the very old, which are unsuitable for transplant purposes.

A different approach would be the breeding in large numbers of some particular animal—presumably a species of baboon—specifically for transplant purposes. This is being strongly advocated at present by some doctors who feel that research into artificial organs is a waste of time and money. The main disadvantage of utilising non-human material in this manner is that only internal organs could be transplanted from them, whereas if a human organ bank were to be set up it could include limbs too. Considerable protest could be expected from anti-vivisectionists at the idea of animals being bred as transplant 'donors'. But these protests, however loud, will be nothing when compared to the outburst of condemnation that is to be expected if another solution is ever put into practice—the use of human foetus parts. These have been taken from three and four month aborted foetuses and kept alive in tissue cultures, the results suggesting that a normal, but accelerated, development can be expected in such circumstances.

Two other techniques which should become possible for the provision of replacement organs or limbs must be mentioned here, though they are genetic rather than solely surgical.

It may soon be possible to grow new organs from a single cell, in the same way as the cloning of a whole animal or person. (See below for cloning.) If only the correct signals could be given to cause activation of the particular genes, normal healthy organs could be grown in a nutrient solution—and because the initial cell would be taken from the patient there would be no rejection problem. The second technique is the regeneration of an organ which has been surgically removed because of disease, or of a limb which has been lost in an accident. This *in situ* cloning may be a fairly easy procedure, but once again it depends on the correct signals being given to the patient's genes. Experiments are in progress with frogs and chicks which suggest that success with humans is likely within twenty-five years.

Whatever the techniques used it is probable that all difficulties will be overcome by the end of this century, so that transplant surgery will increase greatly, both in total numbers and in variety. It will be possible to replace any part of a human body with an organic substitute. (In animal experiments the head of a monkey has been transplanted from one body to another with some degree of success—the recipient monkey lived for a few days with a limited amount of motor control.) The main problem in transplant surgery, as in many other developing fields which will lead to the changing of mankind, is not technical but monetary. Even where there are plenty of funds for research, the costs of operations are almost prohibitive, limiting many transplants to the rich.

Previous applications of transplant techniques will all have been for sound medical reasons, but once this level of sophistication has been reached it should not be long before a new category of transplants appears. This will be the grafting on of grotesque additions (presumably grown in culture) such as head crests, tails, claws or wings, all for cosmetic purposes. This frivolous misuse of the advance of science has been prophesied by Samuel R. Delany in his novel *Babel-17*. The author suggests analogies with tattooing. The grafts, often combined with the attachment of precious stones or other items of jewellery, or even offensive weapons, are in fashion amongst certain sub-cultures—particularly the crews of spaceships. A similar misapplication of transplant surgery occurs in 'The Pugilist', a story by Poul Anderson, where a man's penis is replaced with a miniaturised fission gun so that he becomes a political assassination weapon. (The penis is later re-grafted.)

Genetic Engineering

This is perhaps an overdramatic term rather loosely applied to a great variety of experimental techniques, all of which somehow tamper with evolution, sometimes by the manipulation of cell contents (nuclei, plasmids, etc) and sometimes by less fine means. It was thought that such research posed a threat to the health and safety not just of those directly involved but also of the community at large. This was because of the widespread work with recombinant DNA material, particularly the DNA of the intestinal bacterium *Escherichia coli* which, it was feared, would mutate to cause a new disease.[3] Recognition of this possibility by Professor Paul Berg and ten other US researchers led to the 'Berg letter', published in 1974, alleging the dangers of genetic manipulation. Following this, the US National Institutes of Health introduced stringent safety procedures.

These precautions have largely been shown to be excessive, and conditions have since been relaxed. In other countries the degree of governmental control varies. In Britain the Genetic Manipulation Advisory Group is a toothless committee set up in the autumn of 1976. Its brief, defined by GMAG itself, was to watch over 'the formation of new combinations of heritable material by the insertion of nucleic acid molecules produced, by whatever means, outside the cell, into any virus, bacterial plasmid or other vector system so as to allow their incorporation into a host organism in which they do not normally occur'. Obviously, some such body is necessary to watch over genetic experimentation.

Much genetic engineering has been carried out using strains of *E. coli* because it is far easier to manipulate the DNA of bacteria than of higher organisms. Some research is aimed at creating new strains of bacteria which will be more efficient in the production of enzymes in various chemical processes, such as sewage disposal, the preparation of pharmaceutical drugs, and fermentation for the brewing industry. One application still being worked on is the development of plastic-eating bacteria, to ease the problem of breaking down plastic containers when they become refuse—though this has been used in fiction, in *Mutant 59: the Plastic Eaters* by Kit Pedler and Gerry Davis.

Using similar techniques the nuclei of animal and plant cells have been fused to produce hybrids. These are not monstrous walking plants like John Wyndham's triffids, but fairly normal plants with certain animal qualities. The intention is to cause some food plants to incorporate animal proteins for additional nutritional value, as well as the taste of meat to increase palatability. Development work is still at an early stage, but, this could be a major world food source by the middle of the twenty-first century.

Other projects are aimed at identifying the genes which perform certain functions, such as isolating the active DNA ingredients of oncogenic (cancer-causing) viruses, or learning what chemical signals switch particular sets of genes on and off (this work is being done with genes of *Drosophila*, the fruit fly). Work with human genes includes various projects (at hospitals in London and Los Angeles) into the connections between the specific cell surface markers (antigens) and a type of inflamatory arthritis. It is hoped that this approach will lead eventually to the eradiction of gene-controlled susceptibility to this and other diseases, if the genes responsible can be switched off permanently or persuaded to change their roles.

All these projects with human and non-human genetic material are providing valuable experience; they are leading towards the achievement of something that has been a theme of science fiction for half a century—the improvement of the human race by genetic engineering. This, in centuries to come, will be the main means by which man changes his shape. Because all physical and mental details of an individual are held as coded information in his genes, any particular inheritable factor is capable of being altered: height, build, colouration, hair and skin types, susceptibility to disease, many bodily characteristics and (to a limited extent) intelligence. Eventually people will be able to choose their own physiques, and those of their children—unless there is government intervention. Aldous Huxley's *Brave New World* (written in 1931) shows a world six hundred years hence in which the ruling powers use genetic engineering to perpetuate a society stratified by intelligence and physique, of which the small, semi-moronic workers of the Epsilon caste form the lowest level. Robert Silverberg's *Up the Line*, set in the mid-twenty-first century, shows genetic engineering in private hands, with a 'helix parlor' almost on every corner. Probably neither of these situations will come to be, but one thing is certain: genetic engineering *is* going to be used to improve the human body and mind. Individual governments may attempt to control or suppress these techniques but in other countries they will be instrumental in producing olympic gold medal winners and a lot of strong, healthy citizens. Genetic engineering is going to bring about profound changes in the future of man; the possibilities are endless.

Cloning

Cloning is the taking of a single cell from an animal or plant and causing it to develop into an identical animal or plant. Until the spring of 1978 it was just another genetic engineering technique, factually possible with frogs, rabbits and some plants and popular with writers of science fiction as a means of duplicating human beings. Then the book *In His Image: the Cloning of a Man* by David Rorvik was published. This purports to tell the true story of an ageing American millionaire who, in 1973, secretly had a clone made of himself. No names or locales are given. The loud mass-media ballyhoo which attended the book's appearance was exceeded only by the concerted shouts of indignation on the part of biologists and geneticists. Seemingly without exception they have condemned Rorvik's book as a hoax. In a hearing before a congressional sub-committee (June 1978) it was agreed by a group of leading US genetics researchers that the cloning of animals had not yet been shown to be a practical possibility with adult frogs, let alone with adult humans.

But in theory it may be possible. Seventeen years ago Drs Robert Briggs and Thomas King successfully cloned frog tadpoles, and in 1975 Dr Derek Bromhall managed to clone rabbits (more difficult due to the smaller size of the rabbit egg). The procedure for cloning a tadpole is as follows. An unfertilised egg is removed from an adult female frog, and the nucleus of that egg is destroyed. Cells are taken from a tadpole and the nucleus of one of them is inserted into the egg. This effectively 'fertilises' the egg, which will develop into a tadpole identical to the cell donor. This will become an adult frog in the normal way. It is possible because every cell nucleus carries a complete set of genes, giving full details of the individual, as with human beings. But it is widely accepted that the nucleus of an adult cell is not sufficiently 'plastic' to allow its genetic package to develop into an identical individual, into a clone. The early stages of embryonic development are still not perfectly understood, in particular the relative importance of different influences (egg cytoplasm, female genetic package, etc). Another point is that a human clone, if produced, would probably not be an identical twin of its 'parent' due to the thousand-and-one divergent influences of having a different mother (even if only a host-mother) and a separate upbringing.

Despite these difficulties, science fiction writers continue to deal with clones as if all the problems are capable of solution within the next couple of decades, and clones are portrayed as being exactly identical to their parent (*The Ophiuchi Hotline* by John Varley) or, when produced in small groups, shown as having secret, extrasensory methods of communication (*Where Late the Sweet Birds Sang* by Kate Wilhelm). Perhaps David Rorvik's intention in suggesting that cloning had already been achieved was to stimulate interest in the subject among scientists and members of the public, making it easier for success to be achieved.

In the world of plants, though, cloning is already a commercial process. Non-seed propagation, using only a few cells from callous or meristem, has been shown to be a speedy method of producing new plants. The technique also makes the creation of new varieties easier.[4]

Androids

Definitions and pseudo-scientific explanations vary, but the term android can generally be taken to mean an artificially produced human creature made out of organic materials. Frankenstein's monster, built from pieces of grave-robbed corpses, does not qualify. It seems to be important that the parts should have been artificially synthesised from the basic elements (oxygen, hydrogen, carbon, nitrogen, etc) and the end product either grown in a glass vat or else fitted together as if being made with an organic Meccano set. The android is normally very similar to a human being, or even identical (except for the lettering which some have around their navels, saying 'Made in USA'). It may or may not be capable of breeding with its own kind or with humans. Its role is typically one of subservience to its human masters, and android revolutions have become a hackneyed plot element. Less often is the android sub-culture described in detail, the most important treatment of this occurring in Robert Silverberg's *Tower of Glass*.

Of course, androids belong wholly to fiction. The completely artificial organic man is a long way from being a scientific possibility, so far so that scientific prophesy declines to treat it as a serious topic. And with a burgeoning world population already, who would want to create artificial men of any kind? Yet some of the scientific prerequisites for android building are already being achieved. Within a hundred or a hundred and fifty years the construction of an android from the basic elements may be feasible, and by then the world situation may have changed sufficiently to warrant their existence. Just the possibility of creating an almost identical type of mankind which is dubbed 'inferior' raises important ethical questions; these will be dealt with later in this chapter.

Cyborgisation

So far, this chapter has outlined possible organic changes which mankind may make in himself. Parallel developments can be expected in the non-organic sphere—the production of plastic and metal devices to replace or enhance parts of the human body. Once again, the initial stimulus for research has been medical need, but future applications may well be for less high-minded purposes. Historically, the process of cyborgisation began with wooden legs—so popular with eighteenth-century pirate captains, but in fact two thousand years older than that. These were little more than crutches, desperately uncomfortable for their wearers. It was not until this century, when large-scale modern warfare combined with improved medical facilities to leave more combatants and civilians maimed than ever before, that the techniques of prosthesis began to improve. During World War II, English air ace Douglas Bader was able to continue to pilot aircraft despite wearing two artificial legs.

Since 1945 the development of artificial parts—for both external and internal use—has proceeded at a tremendous pace, and the variety now in common use is astonishing. Artificial limbs have been very greatly refined. Fitting them to the stump is now an exacting process, while limited mechanical control of the limb is obtained by amplifying the tiny electrical impulses given off by the muscles (not the nerves, though this is being worked on) of the stump, via electrodes fastened to the skin.

In Sweden, Dr Rolf Sorbye and his team are currently making good progress in the design and fitting of complex artificial hands for children with congenital below-elbow amputations. The hands can be opened, closed and swivelled through almost 360° by the wearer, via stump muscle signals. Due to first fitting a prosthetic hand when the child is very young—before the age of four and preferably before the age of two—the stump muscles have not had time to atrophy, so myoelectric control is good. Children make better subjects for this kind of prosthesis than do adults. They are more adaptable, far less likely to suffer bodily rejection, and gain finer control. Some of the children Dr Sorbye's team have treated are able to handle delicate objects blindfold, and obviously possess some form of limited tactile sense, which is not yet fully accounted for.[5] In the USA similar teams are developing working artificial arms, but no artificial limbs are yet as strong or capable as the real thing. At the Boston Children's Hospital researchers are attempting to plug directly into nerve signals in order that future artificial limbs will operate in this way, being controlled directly by brain messages in the same way that natural limbs are.[6]

Artificial joints—used in cases of arthritis or accident—have been around for more than a quarter of a century. Hips came first, then knees about twelve years ago, and now there are artificial elbows, ankles and shoulders available too. They may be made of metal (usually a stainless alloy steel) or plastic, or a combination of the two, or of ceramics. Millions have been implanted, particularly hip and knee joints. Metallic pins and screws to strengthen broken bones are even more common, in repairing the neck of the femur, for instance, which is frequently fractured by elderly people. Such joints and pins can allow many years of painless use of the leg involved. Generally the surfaces of all implanted parts are either so slick that no organic material will adhere to them, or else they have a surface of polymer flock to which cells can adhere well, building up an organic layer. Surfaces of in-between slickness, such as glass, cause an accumulation of blood platelets, leading to internal blood clots, which are dangerous. It is most important that the materials used for cyborgisation should be unaffected—even over a period of thirty or forty years—by the amazingly corrosive properties of the human body, which does, after all, consist largely of warm salty water.

Electronic pacemakers for hearts were first developed about twenty years ago. To begin with, thin silver wires or electrodes were painstakingly sewn to the wall of the patient's heart during lengthy operations. If the patients survived this ordeal the wires were connected up to an external power supply. Nowadays the electrode can be more easily sited by passing a fine wire along a vein and into the heart, while tiny batteries and control units are shallowly implanted in 'easy access' areas, such as the armpit or beneath a breast. New technology has meant that the control units are able to speed up or slow down the heart beat according to the varying requirements of the body. Similar pacer units, attached to the phrenic nerves, can control respiration, thus freeing patients from iron lungs. Most pacers are now powered by radio-isotopes, which only need be replaced every ten years.

Among other artificial parts currently being implanted are plastic corneas and woven polyester arteries. Artificial hearts, lungs, livers, kidneys and pancreases have all been developed, but so far these are all for external use; most are large, cumbersome machines, connected to the body by wires and tubes. The idea, of course, is to be able to make these machines sufficiently compact and reliable for self-contained implantation within the body, so that the patient can live a normal life. But it is not until one attempts to duplicate the function of a heart, say, in metal and plastic, that one realises what a miracle of compact efficiency it is. Despite a good deal of experimentation, no artificial organs have yet been successfully implanted. (As long ago as 1969 there was an attempt to implant an artificial heart. The patient died, as have all other recipients—during the operation or soon after.) The greatest degree of success seems to have been achieved by the University of Utah Artificial Organs Division. They have replaced calves' hearts by artificial ones, and calves have survived for up to seven months. These hearts are powered by compressed air, with an external power source, though for humans the hearts might be nuclear or electrically powered. A complicating factor is that the two ventricles of the heart pump blood at different pressures.

The concept of replacing more and more of the body's natural parts with machines has given rise to the term 'cyborg' (a contraction of 'cybernetic organism'), in other words a creature part man and part machine. The term 'bionic' is also used, with the same meaning. Although none of these replacement parts are an improvement upon nature, progress is so rapid in this field that within a few decades artificial organs and limbs may be so good that it will be an advantage to have them. What will happen then? Will cyborgs with superhuman strength and speed be constructed deliberately? Martin Caidin's novel *Cyborg*, which led to the TV series *The Six Million Dollar Man* and *The Bionic Woman*, suggests that the answer is yes. Unfortunately, not only would it cost six billion dollars, rather than six million, to turn a crash victim into a cyborg superman but, as he pounded along at forty miles an hour in pursuit of criminals, he would need to be accompanied by a truck-load of control and power equipment for his mechanical innards, presumably attached by rather long cables. And every time the bionic woman uses her enormously strong prosthetic arm to lift a car it should by rights cause her unstrengthened shoulder to crumble, but it never does.[7]

Almost three decades ago, in 1952, Bernard Wolfe envisioned a future society where it had become fashionable to undergo voluntary amputations of arms and legs, because the prosthetic replacements were so much better. That was in his novel *Limbo 90*. If the idea seems repulsive, this is only because it is an unfamiliar one. To a professional sportsman the chance of exchanging his breakable bones for a set made of alloy steel would be a godsend. Also, it must be remembered that artificial parts, should they ever wear out, can always be replaced by new ones; the cyborg will almost certainly have an improved life expectancy.

Is there any limit to the proportion of the human body which can be successfully replaced by cybernetic parts? In the foreseeable future it seems that only the brain is unlikely to be capable of replacement, at least by a unit of comparable size and complexity.[8] The idea of removing a man's brain and keeping it alive without an organic body has long fascinated science fiction writers. Recent experiments in the USA with the disembodied brains of monkeys have shown limited success (the brains have been kept alive for a while). There are ethical problems, though, which are likely to prove equally troublesome, if not more so, than scientific or medical ones. After all, with a protective covering and a constantly renewed blood supply a disembodied brain should stay alive—perhaps for many years. But what of the personality inside the brain? Unless it can be linked with the outside world it will suffer acute sensory deprivation, leading to insanity. Contact should be possible via carefully sited electrodes, so that the brain will regain all its senses and be provided with some control over its environment. Once this has been achieved, what can a disembodied brain do? The answer seems to be: almost anything. It could be fitted into a man-shaped cybernetic body. It could be fitted into a cybernetic body of any size or shape—a wheeled vehicle, or a war machine, or a space vehicle.

It would have three major advantages over a normal man: compactness, range of control and adaptability. Even allowing for its blood recycling system, which would require supplies of oxygen, glucose and trace elements, the brain and its life-support system would be much smaller than the space needed by a human being still in his body. (Think of food storage and preparation areas, washing facilities, space for exercise, etc.) Range of control refers to the close contact between the brain and the machine or system which it is controlling; it is anticipated that the faint electrochemical signals of the brain itself could be harnessed to a large number of complex controls simultaneously, with greater efficiency than if a human hand were employed. Adaptability means that such a brain could operate a spaceship, or a factory, or a city transport system, simply by being unplugged from one and (allowing for training) plugged into another. Some of these jobs might be very boring, but perhaps the brain might agree to them from economic necessity, or might be sentenced to this as a punishment.[9]

Children of the Atom and Other Sudden Changes

It is a familiar occurrence for science fiction stories to be set a few years or a few decades after a nuclear war. The survivors have, by dint of much hard work, succeeded in dragging themselves back up to the level of frontier settlers in the American colonies or, if the author is British, the level of the English peasant farmer of one or two centuries ago. But the fruits of all this effort are not what they might be. The crop yield, the births of animals and children—these are all reduced by the curse of radiation. Invisible except for its effects, it produces some sterility and causes the appearance of hideous mutations. For centuries after the initial catastrophe the struggle continues, with isolated handfuls of homesteaders battling against what has effectively become an alien environment. Their numbers barely increase over the years. They beat some of their ploughshares into guns with which to defend themselves against giant animal predators (for some reason—presumably entertainment value—the mutated animals of fiction always seem to be gigantic) and roving bands of semi-human 'muties'. Then they visit one of the nearby ruined cities to look for spare metal which can be beaten into new ploughshares and they are decimated by acute radiation sickness. And then, after many years of killing all their newborn children who deviate in any way from the human archetype, they discover that many, if not all, of the children possess telepathic abilities and are in touch with the muties by this means. Finally, human and mutant come together, forgetting their differences, to found a new and better society where physical and mental deviations are accepted without question. The chief homesteader's beautiful daughter marries a mutant with two handsome heads on his shoulders, and they all live happily ever after.

So much for a typical fictional scenario. In fact the situation would probably be very different—better in some ways and worse in others. Because of the warhead detonation pattern (see chapter six for more on this) any nuclear war would probably leave the greater parts of most countries unscathed except for some wind-borne radiation. Thus there would not be just 'isolated bands of survivors', but there would be some decreased fertility due to radiation. The appearance of beneficial mutations would be very slight, so the mutants of fiction —the two-headed people, the telepaths and the rest—must be dismissed as overdramatisation. So *The Chrysalids* by John Wyndham, in which a small group of children living in post-disaster England develop telepathy but conceal it because their parents destroy mutants for religious reasons, is scientifically suspect. So is *Children of the Atom* by Wilmar H. Shiras, where the children of parents caught by an atomic weapons development plant accident all turn out to be mental giants. But any small group of people caught in a highly radioactive area would be more likely to die from chronic radiation sickness than to found a lasting community. And while it is not impossible that the higher ambient radiation levels following a nuclear war might help to produce a progression from *Homo sapiens* to something better in a shorter time period than otherwise, the odds against it happening are very long and the time period involved would still need to be measured in centuries, probably millennia. But a book title like *Great, Great, Great . . . Grandchildren of the Atom* would be lacking in impact.

Leaving aside the effects of atomic radiation, science fiction makes liberal use of the unheralded appearances of exceptional children due to genetic mutation in their parents. Of these, J. D. Beresford's *The Hampdenshire Wonder* was mentioned in chapter two. Olaf Stapledon's *Odd John* (1935) is better known. It tells of the extended childhood and adolescence of a superman who is sufficiently advanced on *Homo sapiens* to be a member of a different species. Physically he is odd but more-or-less human, being long-limbed with a big head, very large eyes and short, wiry hair, negroid but for its extreme fairness. He possesses extremely high intelligence and develops mental powers including telepathy. His body is always immature, for he is slow-growing, but he achieves superhuman strength even so. He finds a score of others like himself around the world and together they found an island colony. The implication is that they are all the result of a peculiar genetic combination of excessively rare recessive genes (or the spontaneous mutation of ordinary genes on rare occasions). In the case of a condition such as albinism (caused by rare recessive genes) its rate of occurrence is about one in 20,000 people, though the gene itself is more common. In *Odd John* Stapledon suggests that the supermen are as rare as about one in twenty or forty million people. The older ones have been driven mad by human society; only the youngsters are able to adapt and be superhuman—and then only if allowed to develop naturally without being forced into the human mould.

Whether Stapledon intended Odd John and the other children to represent a self-sustaining evolutionary jump is not clear. It was the philosophy of the superman about which he wrote rather than the scientific implications. But Arthur C. Clarke, in his novel *Childhood's End,* does describe just such an evolutionary jump. This is a mental advance rather than a physical one. It is not genetic in the normal sense of the word, but time-based, possible only when *Homo sapiens* has reached the requisite level of maturity:

> Like an epidemic spreading swiftly from land to land, the metamorphosis infected the entire human race. It touched practically no-one above the age of ten, and practically no-one below that age escaped.

But the sudden change need not be so dramatic as this— ending the human race as we know it. An evolutionary change of a different kind is described in L. Sprague de Camp's admittedly farcical story 'Hyperpilosity'. In this the human race grows a coat of hair all over their bodies. (The cause is given as an accidental change in a protein molecule—effectively DNA, though the story was written in 1938, before DNA was christened—which is self-replicating and infects the whole world population, male and female.) The results are, at first, a great effort to clip or shave it off. People are so disgusted with their appearance that the marriage rate drops off. Even in winter they find themselves overheated; dress fashions change and near-nudity becomes the norm. Eventually everyone grows used to the hair and when a 'cure' is found which will alter the protein molecule in question nobody is interested.

To a certain extent the idea of sudden change (from one generation to the next) is scientifically accepted. Genetic mutations are always occurring. Most are tiny or recessive, so they go unnoticed or are not passed on, but occasionally something more major happens. There seems to have been a spontaneous mutation in the genes of Queen Victoria of England which made her a carrier of haemophilia (see FIGURE). Certainly there was no record of it in her ancestry, yet one of her sons suffered from the disease and two of her daughters were carriers, passing it on to some of their children. There is always the possibility that other genetic mutations have happened and will happen, producing quite startling changes.

Social Problems

It is very likely that within two centuries several—if not many—varieties of man will exist. This refers not to skin colour or ethnic origin but to physical shape, constituents and genetic origin. Although some lines of research will prove more fruitful than others it is possible that advances in genetics and cybernetics will lead to competition between them in the market to provide bodily enhancement and increased longevity. Some humans will not appear so, due to exotic extras grafted on to their bodies; these may be pointed ears, horns on the head, a prehensile tail or whatever else fashion or their own whim has conceived. Others will possess one or more prosthetic limbs—possibly with transparent coverings so that everybody will know they are artificial and realise that their owner is a person of wealth—or even totally prosthetic bodies. But there may also be robots in existence which are barely distinguishable from either rich men in prosthetic bodies or from normal humans. Some of the most exotic shapes around may be worn by men who have been bred for survival upon an alien planet and have come to Earth for some reason. Then, again, the so-called 'normal humans' may have, inside them, prosthetic parts, transplanted organs from an organ bank or regenerated organs. Some bodies may be inhabited by brains which have been surgically transferred into them. Some 'normal humans' may be clones, others may be androids. How will they all react towards each other?

In response it must be asked, how will each know what the

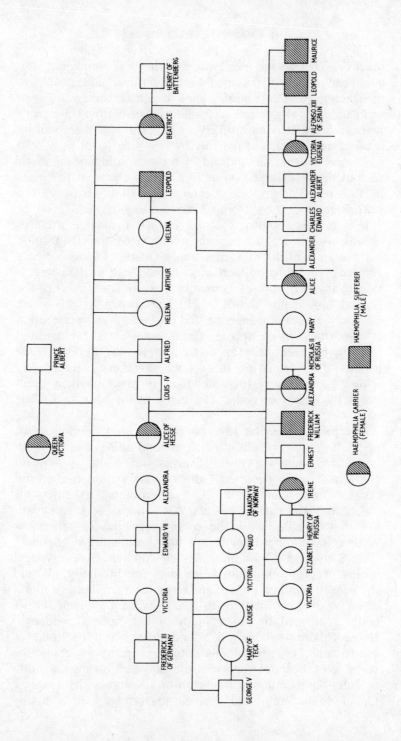

other is? There is the possibility that they will simply not *care* about each other's make-up and origin but will judge people by their actions and capabilities, though human beings *en masse* seem unlikely to achieve such maturity of outlook in a mere two centuries. It is more likely that certain categories will be marked as non-human, possibly by law—the robot by a bold serial number and the android by a clear distinguishing mark such as an 'A' stamped on its forehead, perhaps, or red irises in its eyes. Perhaps these categories will be barred from possessing property or from taking certain jobs.

If it becomes known that a certain individual is a clone, or was brought to term in a glass container rather than inside his mother, will this stigmatise him? Or might there not be a *volte-face* in public opinion which would lead to the deprecation of anybody born of woman in what we consider to be the normal fashion (as shown in Huxley's *Brave New World*)? Certainly one cannot imagine that all bigotry and persecution of minorities will disappear. Because not even true age and sex will be necessarily apparent, people may develop acute instincts for identifying the origins of others. Alternatively it may be necessary for individuals to proclaim their exact status by means of coded badges or as an adjunct to their names.

There will be terrible legal problems to be decided upon. If, say, John Smith, who is growing old and infirm, has his brain transferred into the twenty-five-year-old body of William Jones, a recently deceased brain tumour victim, can he still claim to be John Smith? Can he continue to enjoy his possessions and run his business? It is not difficult to answer yes to these. But could he continue to draw a retirement pension (assuming John Smith had been entitled to one)? Would his wife, Mrs Smith, or their children, have any legal means of preventing him from changing his body? Would the wife or children of William Jones have any legal or moral claim on the body of William Jones? What if William Jones's body, controlled by John Smith's mind, fathers children— whose children will they be? And if John Smith refused, or was unable, to pay for the transfer operation, could the surgeon or hospital repossess the body, throwing the brain of John Smith into a debtor's prison of sensory deprivation? Or, if John Smith had decided to transfer into a totally prosthetic body or to be directly linked electronically with his business, could he still claim to be human? Could he still carry out his duties as a husband and a father?

The permutations are endless; the potential situations grow more complex the more one looks at them. But the future is never going to be less complex than the present. Each time man changes or varies his shape an extra layer of complexity is added.

4 Future Mind

*'On Earth there is nothing great but man;
in man there is nothing great but mind.'*

The human mind is still very much an unknown quantity,
though today its mysteries are being probed simultaneously
from many directions. The future of mankind will be dominated
by the powers of the mind, and by man's powers over the
mind, even though we cannot yet be sure how strong or wide-
ranging any of these powers will be. So far the foremost power
of the mind has been intelligence. Most of man's scientific
progress has been the result of genius-level intelligence, and
despite the constraining effects of present day educational
systems and research methods this trend will probably continue. Obviously it would be highly desirable if intelligence
could be raised, either in special cases by the selective breeding
and rearing of future generations or universally by the administration of a wonder drug. The determinants of intelligence
and the ramifications of increasing it will be examined.

The functions and abilities of the mind are imperfectly
understood because of its complexity. The physiologist Sir
Charles Sherrington referred to the mind as 'an enchanted loom
where millions of flashing shuttles weave a dissolving pattern,
always a meaningful pattern, though never an abiding one',
which helps reinforce the idea of enormous complexity. The
mind (or the brain, if it is referred to in purely physiological
terms) manufactures some complex chemicals, such as enkephalin, which are still being discovered and studied. It manages
to record and store much information in a very small volume
by means which are uncertain. It produces dreams—an
enigmatic phenomenon if ever there was one. It reacts in
peculiar ways to the administration of certain vegetable
derivatives, producing hallucinations and distortions of sensory-
input information. Certainly the mind can be used consciously
to control various parts of the body which have always been

considered as autonomic. And does the mind possess extra-sensory perception? This is a 'grey' area between science and superstition; it is an ability which, if real, is unduly reticent in the presence of scientific investigation.

Hand in hand with exploration of the mind go control and imitation of the mind. As more is learned so will it be easier for unscrupulous governments (or individuals) to control others. Control is not necessarily a bad thing, though; the other side of the coin is control of mental disease or abnormality, and the enhancement of the mind's function by the implantation of electrodes in the brain itself. Thus electronics joins with psychology, endocrinology and parascience to draw forth the enormous potential of the mind.

Intelligence

This is the major factor which sets apart man from all other creatures and has enabled him to obtain control over them. In order to gain more complete mastery over his environment and over his own actions, so that his future development will proceed smoothly, man should seek to improve his intelligence. But having made these undeniable assertions one must ask, as a preliminary step to investigating the possibility of increasing intelligence, whether intelligence can be accurately measured and what its determinants are. Although IQ tests have been employed for many years to 'measure intelligence' for educational, industrial and military purposes, they do not necessarily achieve this. What they do in fact measure are the individual's mental abilities in various areas such as verbal dexterity, numerical dexterity, pattern matching and problem solving. The emphasis placed on one or more of these abilities (all of which are capable of being learned to a greater or lesser extent) will result in a score which determines the tested person's suitability for a particular job or type of training. It is well known that people who are gifted at manipulating numbers are quite often slow and inept with words, and vice versa. Who is to say that one such talent is more important than another, especially when many of these talents have been developed (or allowed to atrophy) by the nature of the person's upbringing and education? It must be mentioned, though, that new, open-ended or 'culture-free' tests are continually being devised to measure aspects of intelligence which are less reliant upon education or environment. Despite the claims of some psychologists such as Professor Hans Eysenck (who has written many books on the subject of IQ testing) intelligence is a slippery concept which manifests itself in many different forms.

As for the determinants of intelligence, these are (according to Professor Eysenck) 70 to 80 per cent hereditary and only 20 per cent or so environmental. Various opponents of this theory (including the National Union of Teachers, in Britain) assert that the major influence is environmental. This argument frequently extends to the inflamatory topic of whether there are significant genetically based differences in intelligence between the different races of mankind, or whether all such apparent differences can be explained away by environmental circumstances. As one is dealing with individual human beings rather than with inanimate objects or laboratory animals it is impossible to carry out foolproof experiments in order to accumulate irrefutable proof to back up either side of the argument.[1]

Whatever the merits of heredity versus environment there is no doubt that improvements in nutrition, medical care and educational facilities (especially in the less developed countries) would enable many millions of children to attain their full potential of intelligence. Many studies have been carried out to determine the optimum way of bringing up a child, and while all authorities may not agree on matters of detail it does seem that continuous stimulation of the child's physical and mental faculties from birth by its parents or teachers is very important in the development of its intelligence—though this is all too often impossible for economic reasons. Hence, while widespread enhancement of intelligence levels is possible it is likely to be a slow process.

The genetic factor in intelligence seems not to be associated with a single gene but to be the cumulative result of characteristics transmitted by a lot of separate genes. This does not make it impossible for genetic engineering to be used to increase intelligence, but it does render the problem more complex and the solution more distant. Eugenics programmes aimed at producing highly intelligent offspring by means of parents carefully chosen for their intelligence would probably succeed, if only because the offspring would receive all necessary care and attention, with presumably no expense spared. The amount by which intelligence could be increased in this manner is uncertain (animal experiments, with monkeys, rats and even fish, are no guide, since animal brains react differently to human brains) and in any case, even if ethical considerations were to be overcome and such a programme begun, it would involve so few people (presumably) as to make no significant difference to the overall intelligence of mankind. Indeed, as described more fully in chapter eight, genetic factors tend towards a reduction of intelligence at present because of differential fertility: the less intelligent, less well educated sections of the world's population are producing a disproportionately large number of children.

Even if intelligence as such cannot be much increased there is hope that certain aspects of it, such as learning ability, specific aptitudes and memory, can be improved by chemical means and improved teaching techniques, not to mention electronic enhancement. Pills to aid the memory have been available in the USA for a few years now, and it has been shown that a period of deep sleep soon after learning will aid retention of the information learnt. Research with human RNA suggests that it may be possible in the near future to combat the loss of memory which almost inevitably accompanies old age. In these ways future man may be able to speed up the process of learning and to preserve the full power of his brain right up to the time of death, so extending the period over which he is able to make use of his level of intelligence. This, coupled with superior teaching techniques to enable potentials to be reached, will raise the effectiveness of intelligence which is, certainly over the medium-term future (the next two hundred years), as good as raising the actual level of intelligence.

Perhaps it is just as well that science is not, at the moment, able to raise all of humanity to a genius level of intelligence. After all, genius is an abnormal state, not all that far removed from madness. Dickens refers to the 'eccentricities of genius', and those people with very high IQs seem to be more difficult to live with and more prone to nervous breakdowns than the rest of us. Stability of personality is as important an attribute as sheer intelligence. Also, if all those with IQs of less than

100 suddenly had them increased to over 100 (by a new miracle pill, perhaps) it would be extremely difficult to persuade them, or anyone else, to perform the menial unskilled jobs which they had previously held without complaint. Society needs a range of IQs among its population in order that there should be leaders and subordinates, administrators and (assuming such jobs will not have been fully mechanised) road sweepers. In Aldous Huxley's *Brave New World* (1932) the technology of the twenty-fifth century enables all foetuses to be given first-class treatment as they grow in their bottles. Everyone could be developed into an Alpha—a physically perfect specimen with very high intelligence—but instead most foetuses and young children are made less intelligent and conditioned to their lower castes, so that Betas, Gammas, Deltas and Epsilons are produced to do all the physical work. While a general increase in intelligence would benefit mankind, clearly the increase must be gradual and of modest proportions, or else it must be delayed for a century or two, until mankind can cope with it.

One of the most stimulating books dealing with future intelligence is Michael Young's long satirical essay *The Rise of the Meritocracy*. This takes the enthusiasm shown for IQ tests during the 1950s and extrapolates it into the twenty-first century. Instead of almost all non-manual occupations being age-graded, as is still largely the case today (with promotion coming automatically by the death or retirement of the boss at the top of the ladder), a 'meritocracy' is postulated. Looking backwards as if from the year 2034 Michael Young says, 'By dint of a long struggle, society has at last been prevailed upon to conform: the mentally superior have been raised to the top and the mentally inferior lowered to the bottom.' In other words social structure, income and the filling of jobs are based entirely on the individual's state-certified IQ, everyone being retested at five-year intervals. All high-IQs are automatically given the very best education possible at school and college. They marry partners of similar IQs, becoming a self-perpetuating élite (despite some degree of regression, whereby the children of high-IQ parents have high IQs but not quite as high as their parents). In fact, a few low-IQ children from élite homes are exchanged (plus dowries) for high-IQ ones from lower class homes. Eventually the élite acquire a privileged position not only for themselves by virtue of their IQs but for their children too, and such inequitable iniquity provokes revolt.

Exploring the Mind

Although it was discovered over a hundred years ago, in 1875, that the brain produces electric currents, it was not for another fifty years that any significant research work was carried out on the human brain (except for the purely mechanical process of weighing the brains of some deceased persons). The reasons for this were twofold: the difficulty of experimenting with living brains without injuring the patient, and the reluctance on the part of physiologists of that time to accept that the brain was a fit subject for study because its functions were too complex and disparate.[2] It was not until almost 1930 that Dr Hans Berger, working in Germany, succeeded in recording the voltage changes in the electrical impulses of the human brain—a difficult feat due to the infinitesimal size of such changes. This was the first electroencephalogram (EEG).

Over the last fifty years the EEG has become a highly sophisticated technique. (The electrical impulses are now picked up by electrodes implanted in the brain itself rather than by pieces of silver foil held against the scalp by rubber bands.) The initial 'wobbly lines' have been divided up into a number of different components, which are these days analysed by computer. Changes as small as a few millionths of a volt can be picked up, and different standard brain rhythms can be isolated by their frequency (such as the alpha rhythm, the most prominent, with a frequency of between eight and thirteen cycles per second).

Among the uses to which the EEG readings have been put are diagnosing and studying various mental illnesses or abnormalities, such as epilepsy, in analysing sleeping and dreaming, in identifying the different ways in which people think so that personality clashes can be predicted and avoided, and even in picking up brain commands. The last of these was the discovery of Dr Grey Walter, who isolated the expectancy wave (or E-wave) from the complex mass of brain wave patterns. The E-wave appears about a second before any and every voluntary action, whether this is a physical movement

of a firm mental decision. The exciting aspect of this is that
it has proved possible to channel the E-wave, together with
the similar intention wave (I-wave), into an electronic switching
device so that the subject, by deciding to operate a switch, can
actually operate it by amplified brain waves alone. Initial
experiments have shown that a person can learn to switch a
TV set on and off by this means. This will give a form of motor
control to those who are totally paralysed. Work is proceeding
to discover whether finer analysis of the E and I-waves will
enable this on–off interface between mind and machine to be
qualitatively extended so that a variety of control devices can
be operated simultaneously. The applications of this would not
be limited to incapacitated hospital patients but could extend
into many areas of life and work.

Dream studies are another aspect of research into the way
the brain works, or even the way the mind works, for dreaming is less tangible, more of mind than brain, than is EEG
analysis. Nonetheless, it was EEG analysis of sleeping subjects which helped to establish most of what is known about
dreaming. All humans, young and old, engage in dreaming for
between three and five periods every night, each period being
of approximately twenty to thirty minutes' duration. In other
words about a quarter of all sleeping time is spent in dreaming.
Although a great deal has been discovered over the last
quarter of a century about dreaming it remains an imperfectly
understood phenomenon. It is known that dreaming is accompanied by relatively shallow sleep, an EEG pattern of relatively
small, frequent waves (similar to the pattern when awake and
in sharp contrast to the slower, higher-voltage waves which
accompany non-dreaming sleep), random eye movements
(REMs) and small body movements. If a person is prevented
from dreaming for more than two or three nights they will
suffer increasingly from hallucinations, personality changes
and, eventually, psychosis—even if they are being allowed to
engage in non-dreaming sleep. This finding has led to the
theory that human beings do not require sleep as such, only an
adequate period of dreaming every twenty-four hours. The
obvious extension of this thought is that if a way can be found
to isolate dreaming sleep from non-dreaming sleep and com-
press it into one two-hour spell, all of mankind will be granted
an extra five or six hours of conscious, active time per day;

to all intents and purposes this would be equivalent to a thirty per cent increase in the length of one's life. Because of the concentration of research it is possible that a breakthrough of this nature will come within the next five years.

The questions of why we dream and what those remnants of our dreams which we remember really mean have exercised some of the world's greatest thinkers for thousands of years. Many primitive tribes have beliefs to the effect that the human soul or spirit wanders from the body during dreaming. Dreams have long been associated with prophecies of the future, and throughout the first half of this century the British philosopher J. W. Dunne attempted to base his theories of the serialism of time upon the many recorded instances of apparently prophetic dreams. Although present-day authorities are highly sceptical of this idea it must be regarded as not proven rather than as totally defunct. Freud saw dreaming as a safety valve which allowed suppressed desires to be satisfied. One possible explanation is that the brain is merely keeping itself active during the night to avoid sensory deprivation. The most popular current hypothesis is that dreaming is a byproduct of the process of assimilating and storing away that day's experiences. (This is backed up by the finding that in most cases the first dream of the night refers to the events of the past day, though later dreams tend to focus on episodes from one's earlier life.) The significance of dream studies for the future are that they should aid understanding of how the brain works and, in particular, how it stores information, so that these methods can possibly be applied to the development of artificial intelligence, as well as the explanation for dreaming being used to help concentrate it into a single block while non-dreaming sleep is abolished.

In 1975 it was discovered that, among all its other functions, the brain produces its own brand of morphine. This, known as enkephalin, is a natural painkiller which is very efficient and non-addictive. It consists of two peptides and is found in a hormone called Beta endorphin which the pituitary gland produces. Although enkephalin is rapidly dispersed and destroyed if it gets into the blood stream it is thought that, providing it can be made synthetically outside the body in large enough quantities, it can be used to treat several mental disorders, including schizophrenia. There are complications involved, but it may be possible to derive substances from enkephalin (or from associated peptides) which can be used for selective mood control.

Mind over Matter

The mind's control over the body is potentially much greater than was ever thought possible. One means of achieving such control is meditation. Although practised by Zen Buddhists in Japan and Hindus in India for some six thousand years this was largely ignored by the western world (except for inane jokes about fakirs and beds of nails) until the mid-1960s when Transcendental Meditation was introduced, first into the USA and then into Europe. Easily learned, the TM trance is not a hypnotic state yet it turns the practiser in on himself, shutting out distraction, bringing relaxation and diminishing anxiety. Oxygen intake is lowered and heart rate reduced, due partly to the position (sitting upright with legs crossed) and partly to the semiconscious state. It has been found that practitioners enjoy significantly less dreaming sleep than other people. Possible explanations are that the TM trance acts as a form of dreaming sleep, or that the amount of dreaming sleep experienced is positively correlated to the level of anxiety in the individual.

More dramatic control is provided by biofeedback training (BFT). Among the bodily processes which one can learn to control in this way are brain state, heart rate, local skin temperature, blood pressure, autonomic muscles and gastric activity. Training is accomplished by attaching the relevant part of the subject's body to a suitable BFT instrument and allowing him to go on trying to influence that part by mental control until he succeeds, success or failure being shown by a dial on the instrument. For example, if the object is to control the temperature of one's left little finger, an extremely sensitive thermometer (clearly indicating changes as small as one hundredth of a degree Centigrade) will be attached to the finger. Eventually one acquires the knack of that particular form of control and can exercise it at will, whether or not the feedback device is attached. The immediate advantages of such training should be obvious. Those suffering from heart trouble can be trained to treat themselves without recourse to regular doses of drugs, which are not only expensive but often produce unwelcome side effects. Also, acid indigestion, migraine, insomnia, epileptic seizures, muscular tics, headaches and various muscle pains can all be relieved. A novel use of BFT occurred in 1972 when a concert was given in New York of music produced by the composer/performer controlling and altering his mental state to give different brain wave patterns and feeding these changes into a Moog electronic synthesiser. But the boundaries of possibility have not yet been reached. It is hoped that BFT can be used to control ovulation, providing a form of mental birth control, and there are many illnesses and injuries which may soon be alleviated in this way. Even serious injuries may be helped by mental control over internal muscles and blood flow, and certainly the effects of shock can be minimised. It is likely that BFT will become much more widespread very rapidly—over the next ten years. The routine checking and analysing of everybody's brain wave patterns can be foreseen, with the object of spotting tendencies towards neurosis or psychosis before they become noticeable from behaviour patterns. Treatment could be by BFT, too, so long as the patient has a standard pattern to aim for. By controlling individual cells and preventing their death it may be possible to delay the process of ageing, though this is just a hope at the moment. There is the further possibility that the widespread use and development of these techniques over a few generations might lead to the appearance of extra-sensory perception—not such a wild science-fictional idea after what has already been achieved.

Extrasensory Perception

ESP or psi, as it is sometimes known, is part of parascience, along with ghosts, UFOs and the hodgepodge of unusual phenomena collected and recorded by Charles Fort. Some former branches of parascience, such as dowsing, Kirlian photography and acupuncture, have become scientifically respectable because their bases have been shown to fit in with accepted scientific theory. ESP, despite having been sought vigorously over a period of about a hundred years by many teams of scientists in several countries, has only appeared fitfully or (debatably) not at all. As one of ESP's longest-serving seekers, Dr J. B. Rhine, says:

> Psi is both uncertain of demonstration and heretical of inter-
> pretation. Uncertainty plus unorthodoxy equal superstition.
> Men are so constituted that before they can accept an orthodox
> claim they want to be particularly certain about the phenomena
> offered in support of it. The degree of uncertainty that attaches
> to the demonstration of ESP and PK have made the way of
> psi research especially rugged.[3]

It must be disappointing to spend one's entire life trying to
find repeatable and irrefutable proof of ESP's existence, as
Dr Rhine has, and never to discover more than a few runs of
coincidence against which the odds are astronomical.

But there are always the apologists who say, as Professor
C. E. M. Hansell does, 'While all the years of research into
ESP have failed to provide a clear demonstration for its existence, this does not necessarily imply that it does not exist.'[4]
Could that really be true? Has the scientific approach been
frightening away any ESP talent it came across by imposing
all kinds of harsh, impersonal test conditions? Before we look
at tests for ESP, and at the successes and failures they have
produced, let us define what is meant by ESP.

As one might expect of a subject so hedged about with
uncertainty, there are various definitions and classifications,
but four major categories can be distinguished. *Telepathy* is
extrasensory communication—the sending or receiving of
thoughts, or both. *Clairvoyance* is a knowledge of persons,
objects or events by ESP powers. Included with this is necromancy, prophesying the future through communication with
the dead.[5] *Psychokinesis* (PK) is the moving of objects by
mind power alone; when the object is oneself the correct term
is levitation or teleportation. *Precognition* is the accurate fore-
telling of the future (as opposed to the combination of inspired
guesswork and divers borrowed prophecies which makes up
this book).

Often there is an overlap between types of ESP, or it is
unclear which type is responsible for a particular phenomenon.
There is the story about a man who owned a dog which he
claimed was telepathic. Each day he sent the dog out to a
local news stand for a newspaper and the dog always returned
with the correct one, even if the man changed his mind when
the dog was already on its way. Demonstrating this to a friend
the man said, 'Isn't that wonderful? Clearly, my dog's tele-

pathic.' 'No he isn't,' said the friend, 'he's only clairvoyant.' In fact, presuming that no trickery is involved, one could argue convincingly for any of the following: that either the dog or both the man and the dog are telepathic, that either the man or the dog is clairvoyant, that either the man or the dog had precognition, or even that the dog waited outside the door for its master to change his mind and then snatched the correct newspaper from the stand by means of psychokinesis.

Various categories other than the main four occur in fiction, but these tend to be specific magical talents for which (one presumes) no scientific institute has ever thought to test its subjects. Imagine an ESP tester saying to one of the subjects, 'I know it's broad daylight and the wrong time of the month for a full moon, but can't you try just a bit harder to turn yourself into a wolf?'

Tests have been devised to locate any trace of each of the four categories separately. Telepathy tests are most often carried out with a set of five symbols on cards. These may be the ESP (Zener) symbols (see FIGURE) or they may be drawings

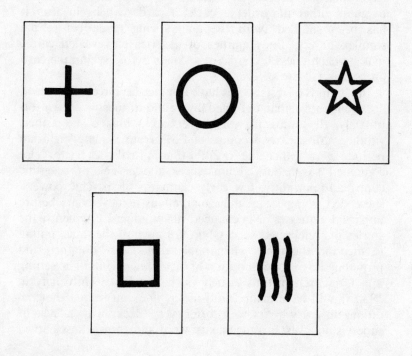

of animals, as used in some UK experiments. Person A (who is sometimes the tester) thinks of one of those symbols while person B, normally in another room, tries to guess which one. Trials consist of a large number of guesses, for example 200 in tests at Duke University, USA, under Dr Rhine. A score of forty correct answers per trial would be expected from guess-work alone. As an alternative, A looks at a particular design or picture while B tries to make a copy of it, the disadvantage of this being that it is an unquantifiable test, the result often being a matter of opinion. Some trials for telepathy have been carried out over distances of hundreds of miles. In the case of tests for clairvoyance only one person is involved and the most common idea is to try and identify cards (either ESP cards or playing cards) from looking at their backs only. It is important that nobody should know the order of the cards until afterwards, so that any hint of telepathy can be excluded.

Subjects being tested for psychokinesis have to try to influence the fall of dice, sometimes many at once. Coins, plastic discs and the ball on a roulette wheel have been used in some experiments. Precognition is tested for by getting the subject to guess either the order a pack of cards will be in after it has been shuffled (with the guess being made before the shuffle), or else the identities of a series of revealed cards, making each guess a couple of seconds before seeing the card guessed.

In all kinds of tests scores have at times been recorded which are well above that expected by random guesswork. Unfortunately all successful tests have had doubts cast on their validity.[6] Most early accounts of ESP, from the late-Victorian period, were either the result of admitted trickery or else contained suspicious circumstances and a lack of scientific control. Importantly, few early claimants of 'psychic powers' succeeded in repeating their marvellous achievements before impartial witnesses or in changed surroundings. Frequently the stories of 'celebrated success' do not give all the facts, failing to mention the times when poor results were obtained and providing no exact description of test arangements. The setting up of research institutes such as that at Duke University in 1930 should have made fraud impossible, but in fact the conditions in early years were often very slack, with a lack of supervision. Test arrangements were sometimes unscientific, choices by testers were non-random, recording was not always accurate and collusion between tester and subject was not unknown. In fact many testers appear to have been singularly unobservant when faced with blatant cheating, as in the case of two Welsh schoolboys tested in 1955–6. Over many sessions these two thirteen-year-olds coughed, stamped and whistled signals to each other without being caught, though eventually they were found out. It was suspected that they had made some use of dog whistles which they could hear but which were inaudible to the middle-aged testers. Even when some partly automated experiments were carried out in the 1930s, to avoid tester error, the equipment tended not to be tested for bias. But when the USAF carried out a series of highly automated tests during the early 1950s, under conditions which allowed no room for trickery, error or collusion, no trace of ESP was found. As recently as 1974 a leading tester at Dr Rhine's own institute of parapsychology (Rhine left Duke University in 1965) was forced to resign after the discovery that he had been interfering with automatic testing equipment. Among all this confused evidence, much of it unreliable, one must search very hard to find any test results which might indicate unmistakable evidence of ESP. When a subject who from time to time scores, say, 60 out of 200 in telepathy tests with ESP cards is held up as living proof of telepathy, because the odds are ten to the umpteenth power against him having achieved this by random guessing, it should not be forgotten that he guessed wrongly 140 times out of 200.

Despite all this it is evident that most people want to believe in ESP. They are easily persuaded by a demonstration, preferring to believe what they think they have seen rather than look for non-psychic explanations. The perfect example of this is the spoon bender Uri Geller, an Israeli who achieved world-wide fame in the mid-1970s. Geller gave many public demonstrations, including some which were televised, presenting various effects which he claimed to be the result of psycho-kinesis or clairvoyancy. Best known was his bending of metal objects (spoons, keys, etc) which were often too hard to have been bent by the fingers alone. He convinced his audiences of his genuineness, and even some of the scientific experts (including Professor John Taylor) for whom he performed under conditions of varying severity. Under very careful scrutiny he was unable to achieve much success. When comprehensively denounced as a fraud by the stage magician James Randi (among others), Geller claimed that he had been forced to employ occasional tricks to help out his genuine but inconsistent PK talent—and this was generally accepted by the public, who will probably continue to remember him as a true exponent of ESP.

Research continues in the USA and, perhaps surprisingly, in the USSR, and although there are occasional news releases referring to promising results no dependable practitioners seem to have been discovered, nor any totally convincing evidence for ESP's existence.[7] Why, then, does research continue? There are two logical answers. The first is that the military value of a person with any dependable ESP power would be so great that it would exceed any amount of money invested in the funding of research and testing programmes. Imagine the possibilities for espionage, for sabotage and for mental control over key members of an enemy government. The second answer is that all this continuously unsuccessful research is a bluff, that both the USA and the USSR already possess telepaths, clairvoyants and psychokineticists but that the information is classified for security reasons.

Once again, science fiction provides careful extrapolations of premises such as these. In Wilson Tucker's novel *Wild Talent*, the story of a young telepath (actually he has various talents, including some precognition and some PK) discovered in the US, credibility is increased by the story being set in the past—in the years 1934 to 1953. (It was first published in 1954.) The convincing bewilderment of the teenager who discovers he is different turns to cynicism when he finds that the US government is only interested in him as a military asset, as a unique and valuable machine, rather than as a person. The distaste of others, who are afraid that all their most initimate thoughts are being rifled, is well put across.

Many science fiction novels deal with the birth of ESP, with a lone telepath striving against public hatred. The initial manifestation of psi power is frequently shown as the product of necessity, as where a man is forced to teleport himself or die. One of the few successful novels dealing with a future society of which ESP is an accepted part is Alfred Bester's *The Demolished Man*. Those with psi power are in a minority there; they occupy an ambivalent position, both respected and disliked. Since a future human society may well include some people with ESP it will be as well to examine the possibilities. Because of the complexity of the human mind it seems highly unlikely that one's deepest thoughts and memories would be open to the scrutiny of any telepath. More likely only one's surface thoughts which are actually converted into words or unmistakable pictures would be readable, though if telepaths were in a minority they would scarcely be able to scan the minds of everybody. It is probable that they would form an élite, employed by the world's governments and largest corporations for security purposes. This could cause the disappearance of most forms of premeditated crime unless the use of telepaths was restricted drastically for reasons of personal privacy. Also, telepathy may or may not be subject to distance constraints. In *The Demolished Man* thought transmission is 'too faint to penetrate masonry', while in *Wild Talent* neither distance nor physical barriers pose any difficulty —thoughts can be received thousands of miles away. Whichever is correct, if any form of ESP does prove possible the chances are that it will totally revolutionise society. Those known to possess psi powers may be hailed as law bringers or set upon for being different; certainly they will not be ignored. It seems likely that if anything can trigger off the development of ESP in the human mind it will be one of the many lines of mind research being worked on now; so if ESP is possible at all it may be with us in a big way very soon.

Controlling the Mind

Much of the current research into the mind, or brain, consists of searching for better ways to control parts of it—or at least to control the activities caused by those parts. This is not such a sinister business as it sounds—not yet—because many of the controls are aimed at those who are physically or mentally ill. The aim is to find new ways of reducing pain without resorting to habit-forming painkiller drugs, and to control antisocial tendencies among the mentally ill not by locking them up or using the last resort of prefrontal lobotomy to quieten them.

One 'new' means of reducing pain is hypnosis. Although

it was first used for medical purposes just over two hundred years ago by an Austrian doctor, Franz Mesmer, it was generally neglected—relegated to the music halls—for many years, until about the middle of the present century. It was recognised by the BMA and the AMA as an accepted scientific therapy in 1958. Over the last twenty years hypnotism has become a fairly standard medical technique, a little less reliable in its results than BFT but more widespread nonetheless. Investigation of the hypnotic state—which is a state of trance somewhere in between sleeping and waking—has led to detailed classifications being made of people's susceptibility to hypnosis and of the depth of trance. One of the latter classifications lists fifty stages, many of these being parts or organic functions of the subject's body over which the hypnotist gains control by deepening the hynotic state. In this way the results of hypnosis can resemble those of TM or BFT, though instead of the subject taking conscious control of his own heart beat, blood pressure and so on, the hypnotist suggests that these functions should be altered in some way. In fact, there is evidence that more control over the body can be exercised via hypnosis than by means of TM or BFT. Most often used are post-hypnotic suggestions to achieve emotional and physical relaxation and to eliminate pain, particularly in surgery and dentistry. The effect is thought to be associated with the assumption of positive control over the cerebral cortex and its process of hormone secretion, which is thought to pass on instructions to the pituitary and hypothalamus, the normal control centres of the body's involuntary systems. In some cases hypnotherapy has been used successfully to reduce swelling, to stop bleeding, to alter the levels of blood elements, and to cause the regression of tumours. Even greater triumphs can be anticipated.

It is becoming accepted that many mental abnormalities which are not due to physical injury (and some that are) are the result of hormone imbalances in the brain and are therefore controllable, if not curable, by chemical means. Wherever possible it is desirable that the brain itself should be persuaded to alter its chemical balance (by hypnotism or BFT); in other cases hormonal treatment can be given. This does not just mean the prescribing of stimulants or sedatives. Careful analysis, including brain X-rays and the implanting of electrodes in the cortex to gain information of the patient's chemical needs, is followed by controlled doses of suitable drugs or hormones. The future development of this will not—it is hoped—be the control of the entire population's free will by an extremist regime, but will be the marketing of non-habit-forming drugs which the individual will be able to use for the control of his moods and emotions. People will be able to change their personalities whenever they wish to, and moods will be chemically altered as often as (and as easily as) changing one's shirt—perhaps several times a day.

Psychosurgery is defined (by the World Health Organisation) as 'the selective surgical removal or destruction of nerve pathways with a view to influencing behaviour'. It is frequently performed in many countries (though not the USSR or in most states of the USA) including Britain, despite widespread condemnation by doctors and members of the public. Although the practice of performing a prefrontal lobotomy (leucotomy) on any and every violent mental patient has now been stopped, it would appear that there is still a great deal of psychosurgery of different kinds being carried out with insufficient regulation and with little evidence that, in most cases, it is either justified or helpful to the patient. The most recent figures for Britain are that during the three years 1974–6 psychosurgery was performed on 431 patients though this figure did not include operations for the treatment of epilepsy or Parkinson's disease.[8]

The techniques are more precise than they were. Generally speaking, specific areas of the brain are destroyed or separated, though the results are in many cases not a cure or even the permanent alleviation of symptoms. Some knife surgery is still used in the performance of leucotomies on dangerously aggressive patients[9] but more common are the insertion of electrodes, wires or rods through narrow incisions to destroy fairly tiny sections of the brain. In the treatment of sex offenders who prey on children it has been found that finely controlled surgery on the sex centre of the brain (by passing a strong electric current through to destroy it) has been very effective; the offenders so treated seem to have had their unnatural desires removed without any harm being done to the remainder of the brain, and they have been able to achieve normal sexual relationships afterwards. While there can be no objection to such treatment in the case of pederasts it is important that controls should exist to prevent its application as a general normalising influence upon all those others who are considered not to be conforming, such as homosexuals, religious extremists, believers in free speech, and so on. There are other cases where the surgical removal of brain tissue which has become damaged or diseased is necessary for the welfare of the patient. New techniques involving the use of lasers—much finer and more controllable than the scalpel—are being developed for this.

Other treatments for the controlling or normalising of the brain are aversion therapy and electroconvulsive therapy (ECT). Aversion or revulsion therapy is akin to Pavlov's experiments into the conditioning of dogs; in other words it is a technique for the erosion of free will. Prophesied in 1962 by Anthony Burgess in his novel *A Clockwork Orange* for the treatment of violent criminals, it has since been tried as a cure for various types of crime and for the breaking of habits such as cigarette smoking. The subject is usually shown films of the activity for which aversion is intended, while at the same time he is fed or injected with an emetic. The association of the activity with physical sickness is intended to so condition the brain (through continual repetition) that any suggestion of resuming that activity will result in nausea. ECT is the process, used in most mental institutions at the present day, of passing an electric current through the brain. The immediate result is a series of convulsions very similar to an epileptic fit. It is recognised as a valuable treatment for several forms of mental illness, particularly schizophrenia, though some recently developed drugs, such as chlorpromazine, have been almost as efficacious, while the only solution for chronic schizophrenia is likely to be genetic engineering to clean up the genes which carry the tendency for it. The reason for mentioning ECT here is that it has, over the last forty years or so, given some indication as to connections between the electrical currents generated in the brain and the nature of epilepsy.

Mind control by psychological methods is a science which has sprung up very quickly over the last forty years, though propaganda—which normally includes psychological elements—has been in existence for much longer. Techniques developed for wartime interrogation have been adopted and refined for use by police forces all over the world. Although such techniques can amount to torture they do not embody physical violence, though they can be combined with sensory deprivation, the use of drugs such as amylobarbitone (sodium amytal —a hypnotic inducer), and long periods of questioning under bright lights to confuse and exhaust the subject. The psychological techniques themselves play on the subject's fears and hopes, attempting to show him how mistaken he has been in his strongest-held beliefs. Continual improvements are made, and despite the regulations governing the use of some of the methods in countries such as Britain it is generally possible to make anybody relinquish information or reverse their beliefs today, however strong willed they are. The only avoidance of such a result is where the subject becomes mentally deranged and can be of no further use to those holding him. Two prophetic novels which show personalities and outlooks being altered by this kind of cunning assault on the mind are George Orwell's *1984* and David Karp's *One.* The widespread control of people's minds in this way is now so easy that it is becoming an increasingly likely scenario for the future. In a small way psychology is already used to manipulate people's behaviour —through advertising. Even though subliminal techniques have been banned there is still considerable use made of the individual's hopes and fears in getting him to buy one brand rather than another.

The Electronic Influence

Just as limbs and organs of the body are replaced or enhanced by artificial parts, so there are plans afoot to aid the working of the brain by the insertion of non-organic parts. It must be stressed that the cyborg mind is still some way off in the future (as opposed to the cyborg body, which is already possible), though preliminary work has been carried out satisfactorily—much of it with animal subjects. The most important factor is that if the cerebral cortex is physically pierced by a fine wire or a very narrow gauge tube it is not significantly affected; memory and brain power are not diminished, nor is the subject hurt. This means that electrodes can be implanted in the brain itself.

The electrodes are very tiny—about one millionth of an inch in diameter—and are sited precisely, after preliminary

X-rays have determined the relevant part of the brain, by the use of micro-manipulative techniques. Even so, siting remains a process of trial and error for the best results to be obtained in each case. There need be no trailing wires leading out of the skull, for signals can be transmitted to the electrodes without any impairment of results. (The physical and social implications of implanting a computer terminal inside the skull are examined in chapter five.)

But what are the results? So far a long list of existing and potential benefits has been drawn up, but this list is bound to lengthen as research proceeds. In general, though, the planting of electrodes means that an external electrical signal can now be used to control almost any bodily function which the brain normally controls. The applications are as wide-ranging as the mind itself; they are similar in some respects to the effects which can be obtained from hypnosis or BFT, though electronic brain stimulation is much more reliable than either, providing the correct area of the brain can be located and the correct signals provided.

The suppression of chronic severe pain—such as in cases of advanced cancer—has been achieved in this way, though the electrode is generally implanted into the spinal cord for this purpose. The pain message is interrupted or jammed by the electronic signal without any loss of motor control and without risk of addiction to drugs. Safer anaethesia has also been achieved by electrical brain stimulation, though it is still regarded as an experimental technique. For this purpose the electrodes need only be attached to the outside of the scalp. Alternatively, natural sleep can be induced by the right signal. The intention here is not just to help insomniacs by providing an alternative to drugs, but to be able to select the type of sleep required—with or without dreaming. Obviously, dreaming sleep (REM sleep) is more valuable, and it may soon be possible by this means to induce a full night's worth of dreaming sleep without any non-dreaming intervals, so that the individual can wake fully refreshed after a total of perhaps two hours' sleep.

An application which is still at the animal experiment stage is the stimulation of limbs where they have been paralysed by a stroke. Where there is nothing wrong with the limb itself it seems hopeful that the damaged parts of the brain can be bypassed to restore the full use of arms and legs. As well as allowing the paralysed to walk, the blind can be made to see and the deaf to hear. The eyes can be bypassed by attaching a TV camera (or a pair for stereo vision) to the subject's head and feeding a signal to electrodes (perhaps eighty or a hundred of them) planted in that portion of the brain which interprets visual signals. Sounds can be fed to electrodes to bypass the ears in a similar manner.

Behavioural control via implanted electrodes is already a fact. Patients who would otherwise be locked away in mental institutions or prisons on account of violent acts committed during uncontrollable rages are being allowed to live normal lives. The signal to the electrode can be sent by the patient himself when he feels an attack of rage coming on, or by a third party who sees what is happening. Epileptic fits can be controlled in the same manner.

Some research in this area has indicated the possibility of recapturing old memories which had been thought long-forgotten, by causing a subject to relive past events through electrode stimulation. This seems far more effective than regression therapy through hypnosis. The implication is that perhaps no details of our past lives are ever forgotten—only filed away in a safe place—so that the correct command can bring them back to the surface of the conscious mind. As an offshoot of this it is known that particular states of mind and even bizarre, experience-based hallucinations (similar to normal dreams) can be induced by stimulating certain parts of the cortex in sequence. Perhaps it will eventually be possible to select one's dreams in advance by this method.

The pleasure centres of the brain can be stimulated, too, giving a variety of results (presumably dependent upon the exact siting of the electrode) ranging from mildly pleasant feelings to giggling and flirtatious activity. Rats similarly fitted with electrodes obviously enjoyed the stimulation very much indeed because, when left to control the frequency of stimulation themselves, they did so at the rate of 5,000 times an hour for periods of several days. Within a couple of decades it may be common for people to be fitted with pleasure centre electrodes so that they can, effectively, experience a long string of orgasms by doing nothing more than pressing the button on a control box.

Of course, this system of controlling the mind, above all, is susceptible to misuse by an autocratic ruler. A few electrodes implanted in the right places in each citizen's brain would make him a slave for life.

Taking the process of electrode implantation a stage further, would it be possible to make a human being into a robot by linking his every thought, function and movement to a complex control board, so that somebody else could operate him like a puppet? The answer is probably not, because there is a constraint as to the number of electrodes which may be implanted into the cortex without damaging it. But the research into brain functions which accompanies the implantation of electrodes is leading towards a better understanding of the mind as a whole. Within a century, at the present rate of progress, it may well be possible to enhance the brain's functions by means of plug-in electronic boxes, while totally artificial minds as complex and compact as the real thing will almost certainly have been built.

5 The Twenty-First-Century Schizoid Man

'No exaggeration, no hyperbole, no outrage can realistically describe the extent and pace of change. In fact, only the exaggerations appear to be true.'

Warren Bennis

The subject of future societies is a large and complex one. Even leaving aside man in space (which is covered in chapter seven) there remains a great deal that can be said about the concerns, occupations and organisations of mankind over the next century or two. It will be helpful to divide it up, rather arbitrarily, into the microfuture and the macrofuture, in much the same way as teachers of economics split their subject between microeconomics. and macroeconomics The microfuture concerns future man as an individual, interacting with society, and will be dealt with in this chapter. The macrofuture is concerned with international societies and whole-world scenarios, extending as far as the year 2200, and that is the subject matter of chapter six—The Limits of Extrapolation.

The microfuture is not at all a single future. It should, more correctly, be the microfutures, not only because of the many possible futures which can be attained but also because of different starting points and different attitudes towards change. A New York business executive of today is living a life which is, effectively, ten or fifteen years ahead of the life of, say, a British farmer, and his life in turn is perhaps fifty or a hundred years ahead of that of an Indian peasant. Whatever the future brings it will be a radically different future for each of these three, though they may be moving in the same direction and the year differences between their lifestyles will probably narrow until they become negligible (though not in the lifetimes of these three). This homogenisation of the human race is not necessarily a good thing, even if it does mean a considerable rise in living standards for the worse off, but it seems almost inevitable unless certain groups suppress change for religious, ecological or other reasons. Attitudes to the future or, to be precise, towards the increasing degree of change which the future brings, vary with the individual.

The three year-differentiated subjects used as examples in the last paragraph might seem to be unfairly chosen because of the economic and social discrepancies between them, though they were carefully chosen. The New York executive exemplifies the future which many millions of people—perhaps billions—will experience. He is a trendsetter; he lives at a fast pace; he is as near as one can get, in 1980, to a man of the future. His job most probably necessitates some travelling, and he will think nothing of flying to Chicago or Washington, or even London, for a meeting, returning the same day. *En route* he may work out costs or quantities on a programmable calculator and dictate memos into a cassette recorder. In order to reach his present level of management he will have had to change firms every two to five years and occupational function once or twice, each change necessitating a move of house. Additionally he may be into his second or third marriage. Almost certainly he will welcome the challenge of change. The British farmer, by comparison, will be less mobile geographically. He will live in the same county, possibly the same village, as he was born in, and will always have lived there except for a spell away at agricultural college. He may never have been abroad except for a fortnight's holiday at a hotel in Spain. Farming will have been his only occupation, though he may well have changed to different crops or animals over the years. He may or may not welcome change, though his farm will certainly be using scientific methods and electronic equipment which are improved year by year. The Indian peasant will almost certainly not have experienced much change—geographical, occupational or technological. His lifestyle has changed remarkably little over hundreds of years. Yet very soon it will change. The harbingers have been medical aid, a few television sets showing instructional programmes beamed down from a communications satellite and alternative technology (solar- and wind-powered cottage industries) in some villages. For him, two hundred years of industrialisation and economic growth will be compressed into half or a quarter of that time. The future will be that much faster and, in all probability, more traumatic, due to his more primitive starting point. This is not to suggest that in the future all the hundreds of millions of Indians will be able to live the life of the present-day New York executive in all respects. Although they should eventually achieve the latter's high standard of living in terms of food, housing and level of technology enjoyed, there will be some constraints because the world will have moved on. There will never be room on Earth for an extra billion people to work as executives, drive cars and travel a thousand miles in a day to a meeting. But when (or if) thirty per cent of humanity lives in orbiting space colonies there will be homogenisation of all their lifestyles to a very great extent, irrespective of their own occupation or of whether their late-twentieth century grandfather was a New York executive or an Indian peasant farmer. (See chapter seven for more on space colonies.)

Many books about the future concentrate on the future which can be anticipated for the New York executive, to the exclusion of the Indian peasant's future. This is partly because their authors assume (correctly) that more copies will be bought by New York executives than by Indian peasants, and partly because they assume (incorrectly, this time) that the Indian peasant's progression from stone age to atomic age will be smooth and uneventful.

Furthermore it is common for authors to dwell on the economic or technological aspects of the future while ignoring or at best understating the importance of psychological and sociological aspects—the impact of the future upon the man in the street. People are not robots, and to extrapolate trends into the future as if they are is plain stupidity. For a start, people do not always make rational choices, based on economic sense. They will not necessarily take a much better paid job at a different firm a hundred miles away, or welcome the introduction of new methods or advanced technology at work, even when it means increased productivity and more pay. Nor will they do what is proven to be best for their own health or pocket; most smoke and overeat, while few will buy the cheapest brand of any product (even where there is no difference between brands) if other brands are more widely advertised. Authors often expect the social system to be fundamentally unchanged in the future, whereas it is already evolving swiftly in some areas and coming apart at the seams in others. Unless a new society can be established which will enable man to cope with the future, human factors will act as grit to jam up the working parts of technological and economic progress. The year 2080 will not be, as economists seem to think, like 1980 only more so; there will be qualitative changes, too, and unless people are put first and treated as the fickle, fragile, irrational beings that they are, future civilisation may break down because the sub-systems which make up society are no longer functioning and people may break down because they can no longer cope with change.

The Causes of Trauma[1]

Societies have always been subject to change, but only for the last couple of hundred years—since the beginning of the Industrial Revolution—has the degree of change in western society been really noticeable, even over the course of a life-time. During the twentieth century the pace of life has visibly quickened. It is still quickening, accelerating, year by year, and even month by month. Ask anyone and they will confirm it. But how does one know that there is more change, faster change? There is no absolute measurement of change. One has to make do with various quantifications of growth and industrialisation such as increasing national income, increasing energy consumption or passenger miles flown. The length of time it takes knowledge to double would seem to be a valid and interesting (if somewhat vague) statistical indicator of accelerating change; at the moment the mass of knowledge is said to be doubling every ten years. Since geographical relocation is a type of change, statistics for house moving or urban growth are useful; both show increases, though urban-isation in western society is not rising as much as in the LDCs (Less Developed Countries) because people in the US or Europe are tending to prefer to live in rural areas and com-mute perhaps fifty miles to their place of work, while in the LDCs there is a much greater rural population still, giving a larger potential for urbanisation. Divorce is another factor relevant to change in society. It is on the increase in western society, to the extent that in the US it is accepted as normal. Technological innovation is increasing, too, though this is a little more difficult to quantify. Not only are there more frequent innovations but they are being developed and marketed much more rapidly—almost always within five years rather than having multi-decade gaps between invention and marketing as there used to be (in electric clocks and television, for example).

The primary effect of accelerating change is that life becomes much faster-paced. This is not just a quantitative effect which can be shrugged off and accepted. In a great variety of ways the increased pace of life is altering all the systems of society.

In the economic system—the world of jobs and occupations —change is the order of the day. Already it is unusual for anybody to spend their whole working life with the same firm or in the same type of activity. The movement of labour from basic agricultural and mining occupations to manufacturing industry has already largely finished in western countries, leaving a small stable workforce aided by machinery to run these primary industries. There is still a movement from the secondary (manufacturing) industries towards service industry. Whenever manual jobs are automated (whether it is by means of an automatic welding machine introduced on an assembly line or a computer system introduced for record keeping) there is technological unemployment. Workers are made redundant and must either seek unskilled jobs in other firms or engage in retraining. The latter is no guarantee of continual employment, though; more and more skilled workers are finding that their skills are no longer in demand. This is an increasing trend, and in the twenty-first century most blue-collar workers must expect to change occupations several times during their working lives, being made redundant and retraining every ten years or so.

Nor will this apply only to blue-collar workers. Professionals such as engineers, doctors and architects will need to learn new techniques. They will find that there are opportunities to move into one of the proliferation of administrative or service posts connected with their profession. Scientists and lawyers will have increasing difficulty keeping up with new developments in just a small area of work. They will be forced to specialise ever more narrowly. (Already most scientists find it impossible to keep up with the research being done in their own fields.

So many scientific papers are being published that even to read through the abstracts of papers which concern them would be a full-time job.)

Those who hope to become high-level managers and executives have discovered that it is not enough to stay with one firm and do a good job. This may eventually earn promotion but not soon enough. (It may be counter-productive; the good worker who sticks at one job and knows the routines perfectly may be branded as 'irreplaceable' and promotion may go to somebody less valuable.) For the budding executive to rise high before he is considered too old he must amass enormous experience. All the time he must be actively seeking an appointment with another firm, not just at a higher level but also, if possible, in a different managerial function. In this way he will move along every couple of years, from production to purchasing to sales to finance, and so on. He may take a year out to obtain a second degree or to teach management at a college or business school. But each time he changes jobs he will almost certainly move house also, losing touch with old colleagues and aquaintances and needing to establish new relationships of this kind. This puts a tremendous strain on the executive, and on his wife and family. It is no coincidence that the business world is known as the rat race. It is an accelerating race, and if any participant falters he is trampled on by those behind him.

At a less exalted level in the business world is the 'temp'— the temporary worker, often a typist, who is on the books of an agency and is sent out to work at different firms who happen to need extra or replacement staff. The need may last a day, a week or a year. Firms prefer this system because they will only pay temporary staff for the hours worked rather than having to employ them continuously, paying salary whether or not there is work for them to do and paying redundancy money if they eventually prove to be in excess of requirements. Temporary workers seem to prefer the frequent changes and the freedom to work or not on a particular day. This procedure emphasises the transient nature of the business world, though it is confined mainly to large cities.

In most firms and organisations today very little is permanent. Apart from high-flying executives and temps there is an increasingly high turnover of other employees. Even where workers would prefer not to change their job they are caught up in frequent reorganisations. Their department is merged or split up or relocated. Systems and procedures are altered, then, before everybody has become accustomed to them, they are altered again. The firm itself takes over another, or is taken over, or expands its business into new areas (economic or geographical). Centralisation and decentralisation of function alternate, normally according to the whim of transient chief executives. Partly, this continual reorganisation is necessary because the traditional organisational pyramid is unsuited to the swiftly changing demands of modern business. No single organisational structure can cope for long in this changing world, and flexibility via frequent reorganisation is the only hope. Alvin Toffler refers to this as 'ad-hocracy'—the creation of organisational structures for specific purposes, such as a particular project, then dismantling them as soon as that task is complete. This is a solution to organisation in a rapidly changing world. It will probably become the normal thing in the twenty-first century, but it will do nothing to reduce the pace of life, nothing to combat the disorientation of transience.

Turning from the economic system to the political system one is immediately struck by the lack of change. The British Parliament is an ancient institution bound by traditional rules and procedures. In the US the arrangement of independent executive, legislature and judiciary has existed for two hundred years, But this is irrelevant. Legislation is produced by bureaucrats in such huge quantities that Parliament has not the time to debate it fully, even in committee. In any case, the petty rules and regulations issued by government bureaucracies concerning every area in which government and people interact are rarely put through Parliament in the form of a bill but are simply variations of an existing act, approved by the relevant minister. Thus changes in the laws and regulations which every citizen should obey are so frequent (and often so complex) that even those responsible for administering them (whether it is the judiciary or some civil service department) are not always sure of either the current state of the law or the interpretation of its wording. Organisational problems exist in government; the civil service bureaucracy is largely unable to cope with changing circumstances by means of its periodic reshufflings of departments and staff. It, too, will need to adopt ad-hocracy if it is to survive the increasing change which will affect it during the next century.

The educational system is adding to the causes of trauma—adding to the schizoid nature of the twenty-first-century man —by *not* changing. Despite the provision of more higher education establishments and the purely cosmetic changeover (in Britain) to comprehensive schooling, the pattern of education has altered little over the last hundred years. There is still an overconcentration on past events, dead languages and out-of-date information. Neither at school nor at university is the student taught how to cope with life or what to expect once he leaves the educational system.

One area of stability remains to aid and protect the individual against the effects of this frenetic world: the family. When people change jobs and move house they leave behind familiar surroundings, possibly some relatives, and certainly acquaintances and familiar faces in the shapes of colleagues, neighbours, shop assistants, doctors, solicitors, and so on. Apart from furniture (which will probably be traded in for new every two or three years) and a few personal possessions, all that will remain unchanged after the move are the husband, the wife and their children, if any. Coming home to a family every evening does give a continuing reference point to an executive who has recently joined a new firm and knows nobody, or who has just had his department rearranged or has flown a thousand miles and back that day for a meeting. Yet in the US most marriages end in divorce. The rate is lower in Europe but is increasing throughout the western world. Most divorcees remarry in an attempt to recreate that haven of stability, but it is not quite the same, and the traumas of divorce proceedings (though constantly being simplified) and division of property and offspring have been added to all the other trauma-causing changes.

It has been suggested by many authors that the institution of permanent marriage will die out. After all, perhaps it is unreasonable to expect two people to remain together happily in a future full of massive changes, especially if they got married young, before their personalities had time to fully develop, or if they both live to a greater age than their parents (which seems quite likely). But what will replace marriage?

Agreed short-term marriages for just five or ten years are a possibility; they would be formal enough to provide stability but would allow for automatic parting at the end of the period (unless renewed) thus saving the cost and anguish involved in divorce proceedings. Informal liaisons (common-law marriages) may become more popular. Group marriages are supposed to be in vogue in some parts of the USA. The main feature of family groupings in the future will be nonconformity —almost any combination is likely to be tried, even to become popular for a while. A second feature will be flexibility; few people will live out their lives as a member of the same particular group or category of group.

A final sub-system of society which should provide a life-belt to which the change-torn individual can cling is religion or, to put it more widely, his choice of belief system. Areas of belief have fragmented in recent years, and in addition to the traditional western religions—Protestent, Catholic and Jewish —there are various ideologies (such as Marxism), there is belief in science and there are many new (and old) small religions, cults and objects of belief. Some are the revival of old forms, like faith healing or devil worship, others are connected with the introduction to western civilisation of Oriental religions. Out of Hinduism have come yoga and transcendental meditation, while the *I Ching* (the Chinese Book of Changes) has become popular as a prophetic system. Some of these religions are restrictive in their membership, such as Rastafarianism, the Jamaica-based black power religion. Some are new and artificial, like Scientology. The common factor of them all is that they have sprung up because there was a need for them; unimpressed by the remoteness and changelessness of established religions, people have increasingly sought something new to believe in which would promise them salvation, peace, freedom, spiritual well-being, or whatever else they needed. They will continue to proliferate, with some examples fading away and many more springing up to take their places. The adherants to each will probably not spend their whole life following that one belief but will change as one religion fails to live up to their expectation of it, or another suddenly becomes fashionable.

The transience represented by this approach—and by short-lived religions—is paralleled by many other elements of present-day society. Increasingly, nothing can be counted on as permanent any more. The most solid structures (skyscraper office blocks or apartment blocks) are sometimes demolished within ten or twenty years of being built. Virtually all organisations and occupations now have both men and women as members. In general the new and faddish has come to replace the traditional. It seems that the temporary, evanescent needs of the consumer are being catered for to an ever-growing extent. This affects every walk of life. Many products are designed to be used once then thrown away. Restaurants and hotels are tending to serve coffee in disposable cups. The paper tissue is replacing the linen handkerchief. Shopping baskets are giving way to flimsy plastic carrier bags (which can, themselves, give way before the shopper arrives home). There are disposable razors, disposable toothbrushes (sold with a single application of toothpaste), and ballpoint pens which do not accept refils. Where once people bought framed pictures for their walls now they buy posters which grow dusty and dogeared over a period of a year or eighteen months and are then thrown out to make room for new ones. Indeed, posters are one of the spearheads of the new fad or craze industry, which produces a host of (mostly) junk souvenirs connected with an event (the American Bicentennial, Queen Elizabeth II's silver jubilee), or a film (*Star Wars*), or a personality (John Travolta). Often these products are aimed primarily at the teenage market or at the parents of young children. Apart from posters they include teeshirts, sweets, booklets, ashtrays, cheap jewellery and toys. Also there are activity crazes unconnected with big events or personalities, such as skateboarding, which spawn their own junk byproducts. Essentially they are all short-term interests, initially over-promoted, and the idea is that the souvenirs, whatever form they take, should be discarded by the time the next craze comes along, six or twelve months later.

Where larger, more expensive products are concerned the economics of transition work a little differently. Consumers are encouraged to trade in their cars, furniture or washing machines for new models every year or two. Frequently such products are not made to last longer than five years, in any case. This is not done necessarily to force the consumer to replace them but in expectation of obsolescence.[2] Advances due to technological innovation and changes in fashion, need or, sometimes, government regulation, will tend to result in the replacement of such goods within five years, whatever their condition. The story about a rich African chieftain who bought and discarded several new cars over a very short period before he discovered that they could be refilled with petrol is probably apocryphal, but it does illustrate the fact that, with increasing affluence, many expensive goods will become disposable items.

The alternative, with expensive items, is analogous to the 'temp' idea—hiring or leasing. More commonly used by businesses than by private individuals, it is a system which enables almost any form of transport, machinery or tool to be hired and used only when it is needed, whether that is for a long or short period. The user is relieved of the long-term bother or involvement. He does not have to worry about maintenance. If the particular model does not suit his needs in practice he can exchange it for a more suitable one with minimal loss of time and money.

Transience has also entered the sphere of building construction. Apart from the early demolition of high-rise blocks, there are various forms of 'instant' building. Prefabrication has been around for decades but now there are 'Portakabins' which are delivered in one piece, can be sited (without foundations) on almost any ground and can be aggregated to provide any amount of office or classroom space very quickly. There are inflatable buildings, too, which can be swiftly erected to form offices or factories. An idea which has barely been put into practice yet is the modular high-rise block, where one-piece apartments are plugged into a central access-and-facilities core. The idea is that the whole apartment can be easily detached and relocated, either to a different position on the same core (for an improved view) or to a compatible core in another city. This may become the popular system of moving house in the twenty-first century.

All these aspects of transience, of accelerating change throughout society, result in a situation of continuous revolution. Fewer and fewer items remain familiar and every situation is tending to become a first-time situation. Material changes are affecting people's attitudes and values, and vice versa. The results, which may destroy society, are what Alvin Toffler has christened *future shock*.

The Manifestations of Trauma

A certain degree of change is good. It provides stimulation and combats boredom. It makes the world different from the mental picture of how it should be (ie of how it *has been*) which people carry around with them. As long as the reality does not deviate too much from the image, a human being can alter his image and cope with life. When the deviation reaches a certain size—due to too-rapid change in the environment or too-slow adaptation by the individual—there are increasingly serious physical, mental and (eventually) social consequences.

'Future shock,' says Alvin Toffler, 'is the human response to overstimulation.'[3] Future shock is probably the basic cause of much personal and societal sickness already, but its occurrence is bound to spread and grow more acute; it is the disease of the future.

It is known that there is a high level of correlation between psychological stress and physical illness. If one experiences a strong emotion—any emotion—there is a rise in the body's metabolic rate produced by a release of chemicals into the blood stream by the adrenal glands. This process is also known as stress. If its incidence becomes much more frequent than normal (for a particular individual) over a period like a year, there will be some physical change and illness becomes more likely. Life-change questionnaires have become a common feature in newspapers and magazines in recent years. Headed by provocative questions such as 'How Likely Are You To Have a Heart Attack?' or 'How Does Your Stress Level Measure Up?' they ask for details of the individual's most likely stressful experiences of the past year. These include the deaths of relatives or friends, divorce, house moving, job change, promotion, added responsibilities of various sorts, frustrations, etc. Points are given for certain answers and (usually) the higher the final score the greater the likelihood of physical (or psychological) illness in ensuing months.

The actual physical effects can vary enormously, which is why future shock is so difficult to diagnose. A tendency towards a particular form of illness—particularly high blood pressure or a weak heart—is likely to become manifest, and former problems (asthma, old spinal injuries) may reassert themselves. Ulcers somewhere in the alimentary system are a fairly common effect. So is depression. It is thought (though not conclusively proven) that almost any other type of illness may be brought on or exacerbated by future shock.

In addition there are mental effects. These can be fairly mild and difficult to pin down, like emotional outbursts, irritability or hostility towards one's colleagues or family. They can take the form of increased anxiety—worrying too much, usually over small things. The opposite reaction is increasing apathy, initially characterised by an unwillingness or inability to make decisions. Any of these states of mind can grow worse if the cause becomes more acute. Hostility can turn into unprovoked violence—chosen involuntarily by the sufferer because it simplifies his life, narrows his choice to a single channel of reality whatever the circumstances. Baby battering can be put down to this cause in many instances. Anxiety leads to either an 'escape route' (see below) or a nervous breakdown. Apathy may become anomie—an alienation from work and from life —leading to withdrawal into a world of one's own. All these final states—which are becoming more common—necessitate a spell in a psychiatric hospital. Extreme cases of trauma can bring results similar to those caused by shell shock—the sufferer becomes emotionally disoriented, cannot accept new information, fails to recognise his surroundings and is unable to cope with even the simplest of activities. Wartime refugees have often been affected in this way. They have lost their homes and possessions, been parted from family and friends (or seen them killed), and experienced the destruction of their whole world. The many thousands of refugees now escaping by boat from Vietnam are a case in point. Those who are given refuge in Britain or the USA will find every aspect of life different from what they are used to. However hardy they are some of them will die from future shock.

There exist several 'escape routes' which people use unwisely—in trying to avoid the mounting stress of life. Alcohol is one. Drug abuse is another—and this does not mean only marijuana, LSD and heroin, the illegal drugs. It includes sedatives—'mother's little helpers'—which are medically prescribed, most often to women, for the relief of anxiety and tension, or to induce sleep. These are the barbiturates, which can be addictive and have more serious withdrawal

symptoms than heroin. Everywhere, drug addiction is rising.
The number of registered drug addicts in the UK rose by
almost twenty-five per cent during 1978; the total number,
including those who are not registered, is now about 50,000.[4]

A very common escape route is psychosomatic illness, where
the subconsicous produces pain or disability symptoms rather
than face another day's normal routine. This is often something difficult for a doctor to discredit, like a migraine, a
gastric upset or back pain (though the 'sufferer' will almost
always believe he feels the pain). In severe cases there may be
some degree of paralysis, or perhaps loss of speech. Some
people, especially US housewives, escape from reality by
watching television all day. This is certainly cheaper than
alcohol or barbiturates, but considering the level of the programmes it may not be less damaging mentally.

A more deliberate, more calculated, escape route is to drop
out. This may just mean giving up the big business rat race
for a quieter, less demanding, less stressful occupation, which
will be less well paid but eventually more satisfying, such as
writing, lecturing or managing a country pub. But better known
are those drop-outs—often in their twenties—who try to live
entirely outside the economic system. This involves operating
a self-sufficient farm or smallholding, often by the use of
alternative technology. The hard work involved is mainly
physical and the degree of change can be held down to an
acceptable level. Successful examples of drop-out self-sufficiency exist in Britain and America. Although there is no great
rush towards this sort of life the numbers involved are expanding and it seems fair to predict that this will become a major
category of employment (or non-employment) in the twenty-
first century, as the levels of change and trauma rise.

There are other personal reactions to excessive change-
induced stress. Some older people, in particular, refuse to
accept more change. They object to any new products, methods
or arrangements on principle. Connected with this is the feeling of nostalgia for earlier, quieter times (though nostalgia is
currently being exploited not only in fashion, decoration and
music, but as a series of fads which destroy any tendency it
might have had to reduce the level of change). An alternative
reaction is to specialise madly. The theory is that if one cuts
down one's area of interest so that only certain small pieces

of the world intersect with one's life then the amount of change encountered will be reduced. Any change occurring in that tiny sector of specialisation can be assimilated; other change can be ignored. This works, but only if one is willing to become something of a hermit.

The wider implications for society of increasing stress trauma are potentially very disturbing. Increasing incidence of physical and mental illness will remove more and more people from the workforce, temporarily or permanently, and will place a greater burden on medical facilities, eventually leading to a greater proportion of the country's resources being shifted towards health and welfare at the expense of other sectors of the economy. Worse, considerably greater numbers of people will remain at work but will be less productive and more difficult to work with. Organisational and industrial efficiency will plummet. More housewives suffering from stress will seek solace in the nightmare worlds of barbiturates, alcohol or TV. Trade union militants will obstruct industrial and commercial changes to the extent of forcing their employers out of business, or else will demand enormous increases in pay and manning in exchange for the introduction of labour-saving innovations, which will have the same effect. Drop-outs— including a high proportion of graduates, whose contribution to world economic progress is important—will continue to leave the economic system. Violence will flare in many more situations among young and old, at work, in the street and in the home. This will result in widespread vandalism whenever large crowds gather; queueing will give way to pushing; car driving skills will deteriorate as tempers flare; baby battering will rise to new heights. Urban terrorism is bound to increase.

If these trends are allowed to continue, with the pace of change accelerating day by day and taking its toll of society as it does so, there will be mounting chaos culminating in a breakdown of western civilisation. And if future shock can have this effect upon our own way of life, what will a faster rate of change, a greater degree of trauma, do to the peasant societies of LDCs? Obviously ways must be found of reducing the impact of change upon mankind. Once these have been perfected in our own technologically advanced countries they can be exported, along with capital and technology, to the LDCs, to help them into the twenty-first century.

The Avoidance of Trauma

Just as change and the trauma it produces are man-made, so can man-made systems and approaches lead to its control. Even Frankenstein's monster is capable of being neutralised. Change itself cannot be prevented; we cannot justify any regression to the 'good old days' of a century or two ago, when medicine was in its infancy and three-quarters of the world was ruled by primitive barbarism. But there is no reason why change must result in future shock. There are many things which the individual and society can do to minimise the shock effect, some so simple that they are practised already, some which could be encouraged by firms or local authorities, and others which need the whole-hearted approval and funding of national government.

People usually learn for themselves how to cope with sensory overstimulation. A very large proportion of advertisements are ignored automatically because the brain recognises them for what they are and avoids concentrating on them. In general, adults are more resistant to new fads or crazes (though they may not be able to ignore them completely because of the reaction of their children). It is easy to become a specialist by taking in only certain types of information; despite the vast number and variety of newspapers, magazines, books, films and TV programmes, individuals will restrict their input to a few categories or favourite areas of interest. As external noise mounts they will shut out the unfamiliar, uneven pattern of sounds from outside by means of a familiar close-up noise such as a radio, a car engine or an air-conditioning unit (though a 'counter-noise' generator has now been developed which automatically emits sounds which complement, and thus expunge, most of the ambient sounds). In other ways people combat change by keeping to routines—this saves them having to make too many small decisions. If in doubt they do something the same way as before. 'Play it again, Sam' is now a familiar cry. Also they practise deliberately calming activities such as TM, yoga, listening to or playing music, reading, gardening, and a variety of handicrafts. Firms help this process by placing pot plants in offices and playing piped music in factories and big stores. To save themselves becoming bogged down in excess information more people are unconsciously cultivating short-term memories of the kind which successful waiters and shop assistants have always possessed. The essence of this is being able to remember instructions or requests perfectly for a few minutes or a few hours but forgetting them completely by the next day. This will have no detrimental effect upon the long-term memory, which will retain any important information all the better for being relieved of the burden of inconsequentials.

These more-or-less automatic measures can be extended by the refusal of the individual to allow certain aspects of his life to change—either at all or at the natural rate. Alvin Toffler calls these controlled aspects 'stability zones'. They provide areas of calm, which help to counteract rapid change in other areas of life. Examples are keeping the same car for several years, wearing older-style clothes, or furnishing one's home with antique furniture or original paintings which accompany the family from house to house. Any type of collection will provide a reference point—sometimes throughout life—whether it is of records, postage stamps or *objets d'art*. The author of this work owns a large collection of books which, following each change of residence, line the study walls to give a comforting sense of familiarity. It need not be a collection; almost any hobby or sport which is kept up over a number of years will form a stability zone, especially now that an increasing amount of time is made available for leisure activities by the shorter working week and more labour-saving devices in the home. This idea of familiarity, for better or worse, seems to have been taken up by many chains of big stores and hotels. They use almost exactly the same interior and exterior decoration in all their branches, presumably not to confuse people as to which town they are in but to encourage customers to patronise a familiar establishment in which they will no doubt feel happier.

An advance on stability zones is the concept of budgeting big changes so as to spread them out evenly over the years as much as possible. Obviously, death cannot be controlled but house moves, job changes, marriage and the birth of children can be, so as to minimise the likelihood of stress-induced illness.

Useful as they may be, all these methods of managing change are only temporary palliatives. They may stave off the worst effects of trauma during the remainder of the twentieth century, but unless they are supplemented by an institutionalisation of the management and absorption of change the man of the twenty-first century will indeed become schizoid. There are many things which can be done by the authorities at local and national level but the difficulty is going to be in persuading the relevant committees to take action soon enough.

There is a great potential for professional aid for those sections of the population who are in the process of undergoing exceptional personal change. Dr Herbert Gerjuoy, an American psychologist, has suggested 'situational grouping', which means assembling groups of people who are experiencing the same change at the same time. They can obtain preparatory advice from experts, meet others 'in the same boat', offer and receive mutual sympathy, and ask any questions necessary to help their transition and allay their fears. Schemes of this kind already exist for mothers-to-be and for those about to retire from work (though the latter are catered for only sometimes, at the whim of the firm employing them, and the time devoted to the scheme varies considerably). Although considerable quantities of advice are offered to those about to undergo other traumatic experiences, such as marriage, this advice is not always reliable (or even physically possible). Those about to move house, change jobs, become divorced, leave hospital, leave school, or who have just suffered the death of a spouse could all profit from the establishment of suitable situational groups in every geographic area. Membership would be temporary in each case, but attendance at six or twelve weekly meetings (or even fewer) could be of enormous value. In each of these categories there may be thousands of people at one time in Britain or the USA. They may not think of themselves as a category (house movers, for example) and just to realise that others share their problems and feelings may help. A difficulty is that some of these life situations keep people so busy that they will begrudge the time taken up by meetings—or even the time taken in finding out when and where they are held. If Dr Gerjuoy's idea works it might be possible to organise groups caught up in all kinds of other situations; for couples whose last child is about to leave home, for homosexuals about to set up house together, or for those about to buy a car of a particular make. The mind boggles.

These crises of life can be helped in various ways. Programmes can be established to provide intermediate steps which will allay the effects of extreme change. This is not a new idea. In certain cases it is used successfully for the sick (there are some convalescent and rehabilitation centres, though not enough), for young children about to start school (half-day nursery schools exist but not widely enough), for prisoners (the parole system), for school leavers (a few schemes exist to allow them to spend a day or two viewing or even working at local firms), and for mental patients (often allowed home at weekends unless committed). There is room for expansion. Those moving house should perhaps spend a few days in the new neighbourhood before they move (perhaps even before they commit themselves to moving there); job changers should spend a day or two at the new firm before leaving the old one; trial marriages should be encouraged.

Even if these major causes of trauma can be managed there are other occasions—becoming increasingly frequent—when a combination of personal changes or some other future-oriented cause produces a crisis which requires professional help. There will be a need for many counsellors of various kinds who do not exist today, either in numbers or speciality. Some will be general, able to offer advice to any future-shocked person, whatever the cause; others will have a limited area of expertise. There may be an extension of untrained help from organisations like the Samaritans.

Although there can be no halt to progress and no return to the past, it would be a valuable antidote to future change if the past could somehow be travelled back to; it could act as a quiet and peaceful haven of refuge from the present or future. Although the past is a 'foreign land' where they 'do things differently' (to quote L. P. Hartley) it is none the less a peaceful and comforting foreign land, so long as most of the idiosyncracies of its inhabitants (such as genocide, slavery and widespread human misery) can be ignored. If time travel ever became possible, trips into the past would certainly be enormously popular at any price. Many more people than ever lived in the past would queue up to travel back, spending their life savings on a few days' respite from future shock. Until then we shall have to make do by recreating the past through museums, historic buildings (often fully furnished as in past centuries), a few unspoilt villages and one or two throwback communities which have not allowed technology to infiltrate them. In the case of the Amish in New England the reason is religious; in Dorset in 1977–8 an Iron Age community was set up for scientific purposes and the results were shown regularly on BBC television. More often the reason has been to show people what the past was like—a colourful display for visitors. Perhaps there should be more reconstructions of this kind, not simply to instruct but to provide uncomplicated holidays 'in the past'.[5] The 1973 science fiction film *Westworld* portrayed a historical holiday town with separate Roman, medieval and Wild West areas, staffed by robots. Likewise, pageants and costume rituals help remind people of the past and demonstrate that not everything from previous times has disappeared.

The opposite of this—giving people a foretaste of the future —would also be very helpful. It would show them what to expect, allowing them time to get used to it. The idea of continuing progress could be put across. They would be able to learn how society will cope with ever more rapid change, see that 1984 will not really be like *1984* after all, find out who won all the big horse races of 1981 . . . But there is no time travel into the future either, at least not with a return ticket to the present. If we, here and now, wish to prepare people for the future we must learn to predict its course and then set up simulated future environments to train people in future survival.

It all comes back to the problem of predicting the future, set out first in the introduction to this book. How do we know what the future will be like so that people can be warned, trained, slowly adapted? Well, for most of the world's population the future will be much like our past, but faster. The people in LDCs who are caught up in this orgy of industrialisation must be helped through it with the minimum of trauma by means of a managed programme of counselling, teaching and preparation. They must learn how to filter out unnecessary sensory information (such as advertising) and how to erect their own stability zones so that the whole of their culture is not swept away at a single stroke. As for western society, we are the advance guard, moving forward into the relatively unknown territory of advanced industrialisation (passing through the tertiary, or service industry stage and going on to the quaternary or post-industrial stage, to use Herman Kahn's terminology). It is we who must map out the terrain, conquer the economic and social problems, and then go back and help the LDCs to advance across that new land. The transition is more swift for them, but the pitfalls are already marked. It is always the pioneers who have the most difficult task.

The problem can be put this way: how can the people of industrialised societies be trained and prepared for a future which is uncertain? The answer is that while it would be an advantage to be able to predict the future accurately and so be better prepared, *any* preparation at all will be valuable. By alerting people to the fact that the future exists, that it is approaching them at speed and that it will be different from and more complex than today, they will (it is hoped) be moved to do their own thinking about it. It is this creation of an awareness of the future which is the most important step. Something which is expected, even if that expectation is a little dim and blurred, is something which can be coped with, something which is not going to appear suddenly bearing a massive dose of future shock.

Very rarely does the future take everybody by surprise. True, there are occasional serendipitous discoveries, unforseen experimental results and unprecedented natural disasters, but these are unusual. Most often, discoveries, developments and events have already been predicted, either in serious prediction or in fiction. Scenarios will have been worked out and solutions to economic, environmental and social problems already prepared. But the ordinary person can help himself by skimming through popular science magazines (*Scientific American* in the US, *New Scientist* in Britain) and by reading some predictive science fiction. Of course, most of these past predictions will not come true; some become obsolete every day; but the fact of reading about them, of assessing them and of choosing those which one finds most attractive, will have better prepared mankind to face the real thing. Discussion groups should be set up all over the world where people can go along to talk about the future. A few are already in existence, in one guise or another; many more are needed. Young people, especially, should try to keep abreast of the future. After all, it will be their future rather than their parents'.[6]

While education about the future is important for adults

because they are more set in their ways, more resistant to change and less adaptable than children, that is no reason to neglect children entirely in this respect. Although changes are made fairly regularly in the educational systems of most countries, the idea of teaching children to cope with the future has been largely ignored. The present drawbacks are partly in the syllabuses and partly in the teaching. Taking the latter first, a decrease in class sizes would enable teachers to provide more individual attention (this is the perennial cry of all teachers), and more frequent retraining for teachers would make them more aware of changes in technique. Technology can be used to supplant the teacher in a few cases, such as language laboratories, and expensive equipment (for the showing of films or for scientific experiments) can be used to maintain pupil interest, but it would be a mistake to contemplate a wholesale switchover to teaching by machines, despite all the science fiction stories which show such schemes in operation.

Any major alterations to the syllabus will have to begin at examination levels, and what is required is not a once-and-for-all change but a greater flexibility of approach. To a certain extent the emphasis upon teaching the past should be reduced, which means cutting out the classics and much history; certainly pre-industrial history should be omitted. In the sciences, where discovery and refinement advance so swiftly that textbooks (particularly at higher levels) may well become outdated during the lag between writing and publication, there needs to be closer liaison between teachers and scientists. Perhaps this could be achieved through the medium of groups of interpreters, set up for the purpose by central education authorities. Obviously, this is a function which science journalists and the writers of science textbooks perform to a certain extent, but a more formal approach would help laymen and would-be scientists of all ages. It would be a step towards greater flexibility if, instead of teaching individual subjects, there could be more integrated studies, as in universities, with faculties of science and maths, social sciences, craft and design, etc. The range of specialist subjects taught in schools (at senior levels) has expanded considerably over recent years, giving a wide choice. This is a good thing, but there must be regular creation of new specialist subjects to keep up with the demands of the future. It would seem necessary that all children should be taught how to cope with the outside world of trauma, petty regulations, personal relationships, mortgages, work situations and inherent change before they leave school. In view of the rapidity with which facts will change in tomorrow's world, one subject taught should be information studies, so that all citizens will know how to find out information. A preview of the workplace should be provided by periods of work experience sandwiched in between periods of school for all children in their last couple of years of education.

The Technological Interface

The other major feature of life in the twenty-first century, apart from coping with future shock, is the pattern of change dictated by technological innovation. This has been referred to earlier and will be mentioned again. It is easy to predict improvements and breakthroughs, new theories and new gadgets. Predicting their effects upon society is much more difficult and, in fact, is seldom attempted with much imagination. Science fiction *at its best* has examined some possibilities, exhaustively demonstrating that even small and seemingly unimportant bits of hardware can have profound effects on future man. Few such inventions prove to be wholly good or wholly bad; most have a capacity for both, and the outcome depends upon the maturity, depravity or fiendish ingenuity of the consumer, the manufacturer and, quite often, the government. Governments are frequently responsible for applying technological innovations, or for the licensing or legalisation of their use.

A good example of a gadget which will revolutionise society when it appears is a little box, implanted inside the head, which monitors, calculates and advises. It has been used by quite a few science fiction authors. The details vary but the essential idea of an electronic assistant or guardian sharing one's brain has become common—just another piece of the background rather than a startling revelation.

In fact such a device is almost possible. Or to put that another way, many of the necessary prerequisites for its development have been achieved. Called a biocomp (short for bionic-implant computer terminal) it has been discussed by

David Langford in an article.[7] If the device is to be a calculator it can only be of moderate size due to the lack of room inside the head (which was not designed for such an addition), the power source problem and the difficulty of dissipating the heat produced by its operation. But there is nothing to prevent it from maintaining radio contact with large computers; such transmission-of-data facilities between calculator and computer already exist in some systems. Of course, there is very little need to have such a calculator buried in one's head. Carrying it in a coat pocket would be so much cheaper. It could be built into the frames of a pair of spectacles. It could even be implanted beneath the skin—say close to an ear—rather than within the skull, because the biocomp should be 'about the size of a postage stamp and a millimetre or two thick'.[8] The instructions could be subvocalised by the wearer and picked up by the biocomp via skull vibrations; answers would come 'via a voice-synthesiser to the sensitive bone behind the ear. The effect would be of a voice in one's ear . . . not audible to others.'[9]

Medical monitoring would be the only reason for inserting the biocomp inside the skull. Electrodes would be precisely planted in the brain and connected to the biocomp by fine wires. Heart cases could be told that their blood pressure was up; diabetics could be warned of rising blood sugar. In this case the computing facility would be just a bonus. The means of communication for an internal system would be direct interfacing between the machine and areas of the brain (not yet perfected, but it should be possible within twenty years). The possible applications of the biocomp are almost limitless. It could monitor every part of the body (via the brain's own nervous system, which connects up even the remotest extremities of the body). Injuries or potential damage due to high or low temperature could be notified. Almost any information could be obtained by a radio link with computer banks; communication would be possible with other biocomp owners; the brain's pleasure centres could be directly activated by the correct thought; the biocomp could even tell bedtime stories.

This all sounds marvellous—the very thing which society has always needed. But there are problems. Apart from the very high cost (reducible with a high demand for identical units, but not to the sort of ridiculous levels reached by pocket calculators, due to the cost of 'plumbing it in') there are possibilities of abuse. It would be so easy for the biocomp, instead of informing 'Your blood pressure is up to 190. It would be advisable to lie down,' to say 'You will vote for General X in our free and fair national elections, otherwise you will suffer a headache so severe as to make you wish you had never been born.' With all biocomps connected by radio control it would not be an empty threat. Citizens with biocomps could become slaves of the state. Particular actions could be demanded or prohibited. Thoughts of treason might be picked up and the thinker punished, perhaps by being made to torture himself. Any crimes, even minor infringements, could possibly be noticed by a central monitoring department. Not only would Big Brother be watching everything but his control would be farther-reaching and his reactions potentially swifter than George Orwell ever imagined.

Other possible and probable technological innovations of the twenty-first and twenty-second centuries and their good and bad effects are shown in tabular form:

ADVANTAGES	DISADVANTAGES
(A) Private cars forbidden in most/all countries due to over-use of roads and lack of fuel.	
No pressure to build more roads or more cars, or to use more fossil fuel. Saves money, space and energy.	Serious restriction of personal movement and freedom. Some countries would not conform. Difficult to enforce on private property.
(B) Nuclear engines developed for cars.	
Non-exhaustable fuel system.	Danger of widespread nuclear sources. Insufficient roads for all who want to drive.
(C) Cheap and foolproof individual flying kits.	
Fast personal travel for all. No need for extra roads.	Danger of collisions. Frontiers would be meaningless. Policing would be impossible. Either fossil or nuclear fuelling would be bad.

(D) International tunnel transport.

Fast. Electric powered. Great capacity. Not noisy.

High cost of tunnelling. Number of destinations restricted.

(E) Personal sound-negation devices.

Relief of stress from excess noise. Sleeping easier. Walls can be made thinner. Houses closer to roads and airports possible.

Possessors will probably raise their own noise level, forcing others to buy one. Telephone/doorbell problem. Low pitched sounds still felt as vibrations.

(F) Cheap power from solar satellites.

Cheap energy for all domestic and industrial needs. Faster industrialisation for LDCs.

Redundancy in fossil fuel production. High initial costs. Wastage of energy. Interference with radio telescopes.

(G) Cheap electric power from nuclear fusion.

Cheap energy for all domestic and industrial needs.

Danger of much nuclear material in existence—theft or leakage. Difficulty of providing power for LDCs.

(H) Some control of weather/climate.

Better agricultural conditions. Less storm or freak weather damage. Better public holidays.

Conflict over required weather for different purposes. Possible interference with the weather of other regions. Use as a weapon.

(I) Cheap, acceptable synthetic food.

No more starvation or undernourishment. Agricultural land for recreation or housing.

Losses by farmers. Competition between artificial and natural food. LDCs have less export potential.

(J) Man/machine hybrid intelligence.

Very high intelligence possible. All kinds of brain control systems possible.

Hybrids considered a race apart. Objections to hybrid suggestions or innovations.

(K) Solid 'REM' (dreaming) sleep developed.

Sleeping cut to two hours per night. Much more time per day/per week/per lifetime (thirty per cent more). Greater demand for leisure facilities.

More activity means more food required, more money spent. Possibility of exhaustion (rest needed too). Possibility of premature ageing.

(L) Easy answer to interstellar travel.

Fast export of people from Earth. No danger of overcrowding. Man can roam the galaxy for exploration and fun.

Problem of selection. Would Earth be left almost empty?

Transcendental Changes

Apart from the unexpected effects of technology there may be psychological changes in mankind over the next couple of centuries which will totally revolutionise society. Examples of such changes are the emergence of a major new belief system, the development of a greater seriousness of mind by a large proportion of humanity, or the achievement of one or more forms of ESP. The linking factor here is one of mental change; technology may play a part but the sociological repercussions will stem from different mental attitudes rather than from the introduction of new technology alone.

One possibility for a new belief system (or religion) is the millennialistic cult, a phenomenon discussed at the beginning of chapter six. But that will, by its nature, be short-lived. A belief system suitable for the atomic age does not yet seem to have arisen. Perhaps in predicting that it will take the form of a religion, with houses of worship and forms of prayer, one is drawing too much upon what has gone before. At all events, there seems to be something of a belief vacuum at present, which none of the new small religions seem capable of filling. If it could be filled, the spiritual improvement of mankind would most probably lead to a happier, more peaceful and more productive world order.

The concept of a greater seriousness of mind is necessarily vague. It means a new mental maturity; it may be a concomitant of a new belief system or of ESP, or it may come as a result of greater intelligence—chemically or genetically induced —or from an encounter with intelligent extraterrestrials (see chapter seven). There may even be no clear starting point. It cannot be denied that there is a need for something of the kind, for mankind to begin to consider its purpose in occupying this planet and its intentions in the centuries to come. A unified seriousness of mind such as this could bring about a streamlining of many areas of society. Frivolity and time wasting would give way to increased efficiency. Perhaps people's thoughts would be turned inwards, and there would be less development of technological innovation and less demand for its products. Society might appear to advance more slowly (it might appear to have ceased advancing) but it would be a more spiritually worthwhile society.

Perhaps it seems over-fanciful to suggest that some form of ESP could become widespread within the next couple of centuries, but predictions must be fanciful from time to time if they are to rise above the level of mere extrapolations. There does seem a possibility that either Biofeedback Training (BFT) or Transcendental Meditation (TM) will lead to the development of telepathy or telekinesis. There are many ifs and buts concerning the possible strengths of these powers and the proportion of the world's population which might be expected to learn them, though there is no denying the impact that any such breakthrough would have. Telepathy would mean instant communication, perhaps over long distances. It could put an end to all misunderstanding and loneliness. It might make crime and violence identifiable at an early stage, enabling them to be controlled. Lack of privacy could be a problem, depending on how easy it became to read the thoughts of others and whether any barriers (mental or physical) could be erected to prevent this. If only a small percentage were found to have telepathic talent they would presumably be controlled by governments (or would control the governments), and they would be a race apart. Telekinesis, if it included teleportation of oneself, could make all other forms of transport obsolete. It might lead to the redesigning of buildings, but it could present even more problems of lack of privacy. If there was widespread teleportation without telepathy there would be a potential for everything portable to be stolen. Certainly the whole world economy would be turned upside-down by the development of any ESP talent. Eventually this might lead to greater mental maturity, but the short-term problems could be disastrous.

6 The Limits of Extrapolation

'You can never plan the future by the past.'

Edmund Burke

This chapter is concerned with the foreseeable 'macro-future'. That is, the state of the world (or of significantly large parts of it) rather than of individuals, over the period which can be predicted by extrapolating present trends. As mentioned earlier, extrapolation is an extremely inexact process. Just because certain factors (population growth, energy consumption, life expectancy, mineral reserves, etc) are increasing or decreasing at particular rates it does not mean that they will continue to do so. Rising trends may peak and become falling trends. Reductions may level out and start rising. By the intelligent application of statistics it is possible to build up increasingly vague pictures of the state of the world over the next couple of hundred years or so—say up to the year 2200. This must be regarded as the furthest limit for serious extrapolation; long before that the possibilities of altered rates will have invalidated most predictions. Even now some statistical indicators are being used to predict that by the end of the twenty-first century future man will be inhabiting:

a) a high-technology, ample-energy utopia
b) a low-technology, overcrowded, energy-poor dystopia.

Before these possibilities are examined in detail a more likely and more imminent phenomenon requires mention.

The Cult of the Millennium

At midnight on the last day of December in the year 2000 not only will a new century begin but also a new millennium.[1] This event will have been heralded for several years by the expectation of better times, miracles, great changes and even the

Apocalypse—the end of the world. Many of those people who have become disillusioned with the world as it is will band together in chiliastic cults, cults of the millennium. Broadly speaking, these will be sufferers from future shock, particularly those who have (in their own opinion) been disadvantaged by the chaos of incessant change. There will be those who have been put out of work by technological innovation and who hope for a change of fortune, some who are disappointed that science has not already led them to the 'promised land' of unbounded affluence and are seeking a mystical replacement, others trying to find themselves by joining a trendy, popular group of any sort. Cults will spring up world-wide. National and international links will be formed. Figure-heads will appear—both those with a genuine belief in millennialism and those who are seeking fame or fortune. The cults will manifest themselves as ultra-fast-growing religious movements of the revivalist type, complete with open-air meetings, hymns, chants and mass hysteria.

Millions will join during 1998 and 1999. When the years 2000 and 2001 have come and gone, without miracles or apocalypse, numbers will drift away rapidly. Adherents will throw away badges, forget the chants and go looking for newer movements to join. The state of belonging, of having something to believe in and to hope for will have helped many of them cope better with future shock, despite the ultimate failure to deliver.

Technological Optimism

This is the most hopeful of all views of the future of the human race. It is not a passing trend like the millennial cult but a long-term standpoint expressing supreme confidence in mankind's ability to advance and prosper through technological innovation. Holders of this view are frequently American scientists carrying out a study of the future for some US university or institute. Books and papers by many such individuals or groups have appeared since 1945. Typical is *The Next Hundred Years* by Harrison Brown, James Bonner and John Weir of the California Institute of Technology, first published in 1957. It says:

In principle man has at his disposal ample material resources to permit him to provide adequately for a much larger population than exists today and for a very long period of time. The future, viewed solely from the technological standpoint, would appear to offer little excuse for starvation, for privation or for misery.

Best known of the institutions which seek to forecast the future is the Hudson Institute, New York, a non-profit-making policy research organisation. Its director is Herman Kahn, co-author of such works as *The Year 2000* (1961) and *The Next 200 Years* (1976), who has become the world's leading proponent of the technological optimist position.

The basic tenet of this position is that future man has almost unlimited potential—even on Earth—with no significant limits to growth. Investment-led growth will (it is alleged) lead to the solution of most problems, even those brought about by uneven growth or badly used technology. (In other words, even deforestation and pollution can be reversed.) All it takes is sufficient investment of capital in research and development and in the education and training of necessary skilled personnel. Sufficient capital investment and sufficient technology will, if the correct decisions are made regarding their application, result in continuous expansion.

According to the technological optimist there is no problem of a shortage of resources. Many resources appear to be in short supply, with only about twenty-five years' (or less) known reserves left when the anticipated growth in demand for them is taken into account. This includes petroleum, natural gas, silver, gold, mercury, lead, copper and so on. But to suggest that these minerals will be exhausted within that timespan and should thus be conserved or substitutes found is a misleading use of the figures. The *known* reserves of many commodities have always been fairly low. It does mining companies no good to locate additional reserves of a mineral if they are not going to be required for thirty years. Undoubtedly there are further undiscovered reserves in all those cases mentioned, even though extraction might be more difficult than before. (From seabed nodules, for example.) Alternatively, if the known reserves should drop below five years' supply or if extraction costs should rise excessively, two things will happen. Strenuous moves will be made to recover more of the mineral from scrap, and synthetic substitutes will be sought.[2] As a final resort, if the demand is great enough to put up the price to a very high figure, it will become economic to hunt for extraterrestrial sources. When these are brought into the picture (see chapter seven) it becomes clear that mankind need never be short of resources so long as a high level of technological innovation is maintained. The corollary of this is, of course, that available resources *must* be consumed with no thoughts of economising or of 'saving something for the future', because these available resources will all be needed if man is going to mount mining operations on the Moon and on other planets. In other words man must not slacken up on his use of resources or on his technological advance if he is to secure adequate future sources of minerals and energy (which will be necessary if future technological advance is to be possible). This is a very important point. The same argument covers the establishment of orbiting solar-power satellites as soon as possible, however high the initial cost. Prices of all these resources (minerals and fuels) will fluctuate in response to temporary variations in supply and demand, but a free market will lead to price correction eventually, even if substitutes or extraterrestrial sources are required.

Continued economic growth is an important part of the technological optimist thesis, for without it there cannot be a sustained increase in real living standards. For economic growth to exceed population increase there must be a more efficient use of resources—which can only come about as a result of technological innovation and improved organisation. No limits to such growth are recognised. Even population growth is seen as desirable, though this is expected to peak very soon, or already to have peaked, and for the extremely rapid acceleration of growth of the last couple of centuries to level off (as the LDCs become developed) leaving the Earth of the year 2200 with a total population in the region of twenty to thirty billion. (The current figure is about four billion.) Such numbers are regarded as being easily accommodated by a mixture of high-rise, undersea and orbiting habitats. Innovations in agriculture and the production of synthetic foods are expected to provide abundant supplies of food without difficulty.

It is recognised that mankind is not a homogeneous whole

but is composed of rich and poor, of industrialised and non-industrialised nations. Although the poor seem to be getting poorer as the rich get richer, the LDCs of the world are achieving higher rates of economic growth which will lead to widespread industrialisation, probably within fifty years. The lot of the peasant in Asia or Africa cannot be improved until he is weaned away from subsistence agriculture and learns to apply technology. Within the next couple of centuries it is anticipated that all countries have the potential to become wealthy.

The technological optimist points out that all the benefits of modern civilisation have come from industrialisation. Only the organised division of labour can properly lead to the exploitation of technology in this way; individuality will prevent industrialisation and will result in lives which are 'nasty, brutish and short'. A certain diminution of natural beauty and freedom is unavoidable. Industrialisation is, after all, a revolution, with a concommitant overturning of long-established traditions and values. There will be many difficulties and anomalies to be overcome, and those who think themselves worse off because of the change towards greater industrialisation will always complain about it. Most of the disadvantages of industrialisation are temporary. Pollution, however, is always disadvantageous in the long term because of its social costs (bronchial ailments, psychological problems, etc) and is an unnecessary part of industrialisation now that these costs have been proven. The diminution of the quality of life is dismissed by the technological optimist as meaningless—as an unquantifiable complaint by those who are afraid of the future.

The future is not expected to be perfect (at least, not in the short run) but the optimism of this view is expressed in its adherents' confidence that the future will be much better than the past or the present because mankind will overcome problems by the use of technology. It is never denied that there will be problems—the technological optimists are sufficiently realistic to know that the road to a high-technology utopia will be a difficult one—but many of these can be anticipated and contingency plans made for their solution.

If this route into the future is to be followed, what steps must be taken now? More capital should be invested in research and development activities. The US space programme should be pushed ahead, because sooner or later men will need both living space and mineral resources which are not available on Earth. International cooperation should be a feature of all this research, as no single nation will be able to take some of the necessary future decisions (on pollution control, living space, resource management and the provision of energy), and no single nation will be able to afford or have the capacity to undertake, some of the more ambitious projects which will be necessary. People must learn to live with increasing technology and not be afraid of change. Mineral resources should be used boldly, with no attempt made to economise, because there will always be access to alternative supplies if this is done. (This must not be taken as an invitation to profligacy but more as a statement of confidence in the Earth's vast wealth of resources and in mankind's ability to obtain and use them.)

And what sort of future will it be, two hundred years or so from now, if these policies are followed and if the technological optimists are proved correct? The answer could be radically different depending upon the amount of space activity which is engaged in. As this aspect is more fully covered in chapter seven, Man in Space, here the Earth-centred alternative will be considered, following the approach used in *The Next 200 Years* (of which, see chapter one). Kahn's belief is that, before the end of the twenty-second century, Earth will have made the transition to a quatenary or post-industrial economy, in which most human work activities are engaged in for their own sakes.[3] The implication is that virtually all primary and secondary activities will have been fully automated. There will still need to be some, perhaps many, people employed in tertiary activities, such as research, industrial planning, government, medicine and education. The majority of people will not be needed as a workforce or as an aid to the economy. The superabundance of energy and resources will enable the remainder to enjoy a very high standard of living. They will pass their time largely by engaging in what are regarded as leisure activities today. Some people will, no doubt, pursue educational studies in the hope of becoming sufficiently qualified to take a job in one of the service industries (though this will probably not bring them a higher standard of living, just greater prestige and self-satisfaction). Some will do voluntary work while others will devote themselves to cultural activities, or to sports or gardening. It may be necessary to manufacture jobs for millions of people in order to give them the satisfaction of 'doing something useful'. Or it may be necessary to employ hordes of workers—mostly unskilled—to 'supervise' automatic machinery because of the persistence of restrictive practices among trade unions and other labour organisations. This is where a major programme of space and interstellar colonisation would be invaluable; it could occupy very large numbers of people in development work on Earth and in construction and mission participation in space itself.

To these people of the late twenty-second century the Earth may seem a very calm and uneventful place—though there is always the possibility that boredom will lead to widespread violence, with terrorism becoming a popular sport. It will probably be possible to correct any tendency towards violent or antisocial behaviour by means of chemical or electronic adjustment of the brain. Certainly all physical and mental illnesses will be treatable, and the resources should exist for each person to be given all the medical care they need or want (including genetic alteration, plastic surgery, organ replacement and sex changes). Considerably increased longevity can be anticipated, resulting in a population twice as large as mentioned earlier—perhaps as high as sixty billion. But here, as in many other areas of life, governmental decisions and the level of governmental control in general can make a vast difference to the appearance of society. It may be decided —arbitrarily or by referendum—that increased longevity should not be available to all but only to those who are prepared to work for and with the government. By this time 'the government' will almost certainly be a single world-wide body with absolute powers which controls and regulates every aspect of life. This seems the only way of ensuring that all decisions are made responsibly, rather than to satisfy the profit motive. While all commercial operations will not necessarily need to be government-owned they will have to obey strict regulations regarding health and safety, pollution, product desirability and advertising. The frenetic 'ad-hocracy' of the twenty-first century should have been replaced by a new flexible bureaucracy which will be almost omniscient, extremely swift to operate and not at all cumbersome. Most decisions will be made by artificial intelligences (to speak of them as computers would be to give the wrong impression) working from precedent.

It would be easy, and almost certainly misleading, to attempt detailed predictions of environment and lifestyle. No doubt there will be a very high level of technology. Sophisticated control devices whose functions we could barely guess at will be in common use. When it is mentioned that all manual jobs will have been automated, the late-twentieth-century reader may imagine (for example) a humanoid robot going round the house with a duster and vacuum cleaner. This is direct extrapolation and is almost certain to be wrong. Instead, new materials will have been developed which reject all dust and dirt, or else all living environments will be kept dust free by systems of airlocks, air conditioning and by the use of non-dust-producing materials in furnishings and clothes. Similarly, the image of a family of the future loading up their space car for a weekend trip to the Moon is equally ludicrous. Almost certainly private transport of every kind will need to be severely restricted—if not abolished altogether—to prevent chronic overcrowding of roads, air lanes, space lanes and so on. It may be that even a complex public transport system will be unable to cope with billions of passengers at the same time, so unless an instantaneous matter transmitter is invented there may be very little long-distance travel except for essential reasons. Trips outside comfortable walking or cycling distance may need to be booked some time in advance. Perhaps agoraphobia will develop—or will be deliberately cultured by the government. Also, when considering that family of the future one should not imagine them as a father, mother, two freckled children and a dog (in line with present-day TV commercials). Although this format may not cease to exist (except for the dog; there may be no room for large pets in the world of the late-twenty-second century) it may become no more common than a childless couple, a single parent family, a homosexual couple (with or without children) or a group marriage consisting of several adults and several children.

The point must be made that many of these geographical and occupational restrictions will not matter to the people of the future, not just because they have grown up with them but because their concerns are more in the field of non-physical things. Having freed themselves from the necessity of physical work they may wish to spend their time developing their minds and personalities—searching within themselves for the soul and for the essence of humanity.

Malthusianism

Thomas Malthus (1766–1834) was an English economist who asserted in his *Essay on Population* (1798) that, in the long run, humanity would never achieve anything but unhappiness and poverty because of the tendency for population to increase geometrically while the means of subsistence (most importantly, food production) could only increase arithmetically. His conclusion was that population would always expand to the size which could just be supported at a subsistence level by the amount of land under cultivation, and would remain close to that figure, controlled by disease, famine and war. Although this theory is valid for pre-industrial societies (including LDCs at the present day) it does not operate in industrial societies, where technological innovation causes production (and real national income) to far outpace even potential population increase, while the actual population increase is slowed down by reliable contraceptive methods. However, the essential economic pessimism of Malthus has been adopted as a perspective of the future which is at the opposite end of the spectrum from technological optimism.

The Malthusians (or neo-Malthusians) foresee a future full of eco-disaster and poverty, brought on by the same trends that the technological optimists hail as mankind's greatest hopes. The emergence of this pessimistic view came in the mid-1960s with warnings of pollution. In 1968 the Club of Rome was set up, consisting of prominent scientists worried about the way man was misusing the Earth's resources. Its founder and chief prophet of doom was Dr Aurelio Peccei, an Italian industrialist. Under the auspices of the Club of Rome a computer study of the future was carried out in 1970–1 by Jay Forrester of the Massachussets Institute of Technology. A computer model was designed using five variables (food production, industrialisation, pollution, population increase and resource consumption) and almost a hundred relationships between them. The scope of this study was the whole world. Its results were unequivocal: world civilisation would collapse within a century—perhaps within half a century—unless immediate steps were taken to halt population increase, pollution and industrialisation. These findings were presented to the general public in *The Limits to Growth* by Donella H. Meadows et al, published early in 1972.

The most important ideas contained within this Malthusian position are that growth must not be allowed to continue and that all our resources are finite—energy supplies in particular. Whatever we consume today will not be available for out descendants to consume tomorrow: we are stealing their birthright and bequeathing them nothing but our problems.

The Malthusian view on resources is that Earth's finite potential is rapidly being diminished. Not only are fossil fuels being used up but metals are being converted into products from which they are difficult to retrieve, natural food stocks (particularly whales and some fish) are being reduced almost to extinction and the Earth's capacity for recycling pollutants is being diminished (by the decrease of forests, for example) and overloaded. The ecological balance of the Earth is obviously being upset and we do not yet know the results of our actions or whether the system can recover from our increasing assaults on it. (The idea of Earth's biosphere being a single complex system, almost like a living organism, is the Gaia theory, from an old name for Earth-mother. (See, among others, *The Quest for Gaia* by Kit Pedler.) Immediate decisions must be taken to conserve fossil fuels by means of rationing, while long-term alternatives are developed. It is from this expectation that the so-called 'alternative technology' approach has emerged, which urges, among other things, that natural, non-polluting energy sources should be found—solar power, wind power, wave power and geothermal energy (not nuclear energy because of the waste disposal problem); private cars should be powered by electric batteries while freight should be transported by rail or canal—that all waste products should be carefully recycled (methane from manure, etc), that all throwaway packing should be biodegradable, and that personal self-sufficiency should be encouraged. The Malthusian prophecy is that supplies of many important minerals and food items will have been exhausted within the next fifty years.

Any future growth, whether of population or of industrial-isation, will be catastrophic for our planet. The number of people is already greater than can be comfortably accommo-dated in the long term, and steps should be taken not just to control population increase but to reduce total population from its present four billion to three or three and a half billion. If this is not done world population will go on doubling every thirty-five years—more rapidly than food production—until the whole world is reduced to a bare subsistence level, though presumably there would be famine and warfare before that happened.[1] It is continued economic growth to satisfy unnecessary demand by the rich nations which is responsible for the profligate over-use of resources.

Because the Earth (often referred to by Malthusians and ecologically aware groups by the trendy title of Spaceship Earth) is already sick and out of balance, and because its management is so complex, it is unlikely that the correct decisions will be made to repair the damage and to achieve a reasonable future. Even using computers the correct course cannot be known. Even if it were known it would be impos-sible to get all countries to work together for a long enough period to put things right. Nationalistic chauvinism, party politics and the profit motive would cause agreements to be broken and would bring Earth back to the brink of disaster.

Innovation, that cure-all of the technological optimist, is seen by the Malthusians as little more than a temporary reprieve, and a dangerous one at that because of the false hope it brings. (This does sound suspiciously similar to the sentiment voiced by the Director of the US Patent Office in 1899, who begged President McKinley to abolish the Patent Office on the grounds that everything which could be invented had already been invented.) In any case, the effort and resources devoted to producing and developing that innovation will have depleted the store of resources even more. The view on industrialisation is similar, suggesting that the only outcome of greater industrialisation is greater pollution. On these grounds, conventional industrialisation of the LDCs should cease forthwith, though they should be given economic aid in the form of capital with a view to setting up economies based on alternative technology. This may reduce the gap a little between rich and poor countries, especially if those poorer countries who possess natural resources needed by the rich countries will increase their prices considerably. (This would appear to be the policy which the oil exporting countries are employing at the moment.)

The quality of life has already been seriously affected by excessive industrialisation and too high a population, and this can only get worse. Air pollution shortens lives in larger cities and is unpleasant in many areas. The pollution of rivers and seas has made swimming and fishing into dangerous hobbies. Noise pollution, particularly from road vehicles and aircraft, is a daily intrusion into our lives. The countryside has become a rubbish dump due to over-use and non-biodegradable packaging. The food we eat is full of artificial flavouring to disguise its poor quality and the presence of fertilising or weedkilling chemicals. Of the intended benefits of industrialisation, cars, so Ralph Nader has said, are 'unsafe at any speed', while drugs are not always tested as thoroughly as they should be before appearing on the market, with results like the Thalidomide tragedy. Hence it is only possible to live a satisfactory and wholesome life if one goes off to a LDC or to a remote part of an industrialised one.

The Malthusian view of the future is one of mounting misery. They have presented their warnings of doom unless immediate action is taken, and so far very little action has been taken except for the reduction of the US space programme and some token gestures towards controlling pollution and developing alternative energy sources in a few countries.[5] So their worst dooms may yet fall upon the world. If they are correct, pollution can be expected to grow worse and ecological disturbances will show themselves via freak weather conditions and the extinction of some species of plants and animals. Major catastrophes may not arrive for three or four decades until some particular mineral proves not to have any more locatable reserves and scientists fail to produce a suitable synthetic alternative or to recover sufficient quantities from scrap. Meanwhile the industrialised countries will apparently have been growing richer, though this will be an illusion because the quality of life will have been lowered in many respects. The LDCs will be in a dreadful state by that time, because their populations will have more than doubled without a corresponding increase in their ability to produce food. Although techniques exist to achieve a great increase in farming efficiency in those countries it will not have been possible to introduce them due to insufficient interest by the industrialised nations. The education and infrastructure will not be present to allow any new methods to become widespread. The world population (by about 2015) will be eight billion and the industrialised nations will be too busy feeding and housing their own people to bother with other countries.

There will be energy crises which will cut industrial production. Capital investment will decline in both industry and agriculture. Transport systems will collapse from fuel shortages, seriously affecting imports, exports and internal distribution. The standard of living among industrial nations will fall rapidly as communities are forced to support themselves. From this point onwards the decline of civilisation will be swift. The populations of cities will, in many areas, starve. In rural areas, small communities will be able to weather the storm, providing they can protect themselves against gangs hunting for food, and these communities will eventually emerge to repopulate the former industrialised countries.

But at the same time some serious effects of pollution should have become unmistakable. The build-up of carbon dioxide in the Earth's atmosphere, due to the high levels of fossil fuels used and to the decreasing areas of green plants remaining, will result in infra-red radiation being trapped within the atmosphere. This will raise the global temperature, melting the polar ice caps and possibly bringing on a runaway greenhouse effect, thickening the cloud layer and raising the temperature even further until life on Earth is exterminated. Alternatively, the use of freon (the propellant in aerosol sprays), combined with the increasing numbers of supersonic aircraft, may deplete Earth's protective ozone layer, allowing more of the Sun's ultra-violet rays through. These can cause skin cancer in man and can kill off some plant species. Although both these effects are scientifically verifiable as having begun, there is a dispute as to how long it will be before either (rising temperature or lack of ozone) has a critical effect upon the Earth. Naturally, the evidence already gathered is interpreted in different ways by the Malthusians and the technological optimists. (A recent study has found that the carbon dioxide released into the atmosphere by man has tended to counteract the depletion of the ozone layer. See *New Scientist* 12 July 1979, p87.) The Malthusians also expect that the next thirty or forty years will bring widespread pollution of most rivers, lakes and seas, resulting in the extinction of life in them, and in the near-impossibility of providing uncontaminated water for domestic use. Many strains of insects will appear which are immune to existing pesticides. Leaks of radioactive waste will render many spots unsuitable for human habitation. Falls of corrosive rain (as already experienced in Scandinavia, resulting from Western European industrial smoke) will grow more frequent with greater concentrations of pollutants. If only a few of these predictions come true the Malthusian future will be grim indeed.[6]

It seems unlikely that a stable, controlled Malthusian world will exist at the furthest limits of extrapolation—in 2200—but it is worth examining as a total contrast to the 2200 of the technological optimist. The assumption here is that decisions are made now, in line with *The Limits to Growth*, to cut world population and to limit industry, pollution and the use of scarce resources. A necessary condition for any of these would be agreement between all national governments on both the ends and the means. An immediate programme of sterilisation would need to be implemented for all women who had borne two or more children. Eventually this would be replaced by a chemical sterility treatment which would be chemically reversible, but the limit would remain at two children per mother. The consumption of petroleum would be limited to essential users, probably the police, armed services, emergency services, food distribution and other special cases, as designated by the government. Some areas of industry would be immediately shut down and the workers redeployed in food production or in helping to clear up the accumulated mass of pollution. In countries like Britain, where most food is imported, agricultural production would need to be stepped up several hundred per cent in order to relieve the LDCs of the burden of growing food for others, and to save the fuel used in transportation. Certain areas of industry would have to be retained, but their output of smoke, noxious gases and poisonous wastes would be suppressed. Wherever possible, waste products would be contained and recycled to useful forms, even if the cost in terms of manpower or energy seemed excessive. Energy would be mainly electrical but generated as far as possible without recourse to fossil fuels. Natural power sources would be developed as quickly as possible, and private motoring would not be permitted until battery-powered or liquid-hydrogen-powered cars reached a high level of efficiency.[7]

It will not have escaped the reader's attention that such measures as these would be impossible to introduce and enforce except by a very strong government backed by considerable numbers of armed police and troops, and supported by similarly determined governments all over the world. In other words an international autocracy (or dictatorship) would be necessary, and any dissenters would have to be executed in order to 'encourage the rest'. Indeed, such a state of affairs, even if well-intentioned, seems highly improbable.

But if it is extrapolated through to 2200 one can imagine Earth as an idyllic, largely unspoilt planet housing a population not exceeding three billion (but possibly only half that if the dictatorship had met with open rebellion and war had ensued), living in spacious conditions, with every family encouraged to keep a smallholding and to be at least partly self-supporting in food and power. Both the idea of the smallholding and the restrictiveness of governmental control will have encouraged the traditional family structure to be retained, perhaps with a return to the older arrangement of extended and joint families in some cases. Innovation will not have ceased, although a lack of capital investment will have slowed it down. Highly sophisticated power units and energy collectors will exist, though industry will be localised and little automation or gadgetry will exist—perhaps less than today. There will be no real shortage of energy or resources, due more to a tight control of supplies and to recycling than to the extensive development of technology able to give unlimited power or to locate and mine new resources. The level of technology will be limited, probably by industrial capacity rather than by knowhow. For example, the construction of orbiting power satellites or colonies will be outside their capacity. On the other hand they will be enjoying many benefits—spaciousness, tranquillity, clean air, wholesome food—that would be welcomed by the people of today. And by that time the whole world population will be fairly well homogenised in terms of lifestyle, level of education, level of technology and income.

At some stage—perhaps before 2200, perhaps after—a swing back to industrialisation will occur. But this second industrial revolution will be a clean one, accomplished without fossil fuels (because they will have run out). It will usher in an age of automation and with it will come a high level of change such as will not have been seen for two centuries. By that time people will, hopefully, be sufficiently mature to maintain the world population at a stable figure, or else to develop space colonies and interstellar travel as a means of dispersing the surplus.

Intermediate Scenarios

Between any pair of extreme positions there are many moderate points. In extrapolations of trends into the future these in-between predictions are probably more likely to come true. Kahn, in *The Next 200 Years*, examines two intermediate scenarios, guarded pessimist (moderate Malthusian position) and guarded optimist (moderate technological optimist position). The guarded optimist future is one in which the growth of the world economy continues rapidly. Resources are adequate, though means of population limitation need to be found, particularly in the LDCs, if their standards of living are ever to reach western standards, and if western standards of living are to markedly increase. Technological innovation and continued industrialisation will help solve current problems but will sometimes create new ones. The poorer countries will grow richer and their populations move away from bare subsistence, but income gaps between rich and poor nations may not decrease much because of continual innovations in the rich countries which are only applied to poor ones after a time lag (or not at all). In the quality of life there will be more gains than losses. Overall there will be progress though not without difficulties, and the situation by 2200 will not be the post-industrial bed of roses suggested by the technological optimist; problems and inequalities will still remain.

To the guarded pessimist the future is at best uncertain. The twenty-first century will be full of major problems, many of them handled badly. If the LDCs are wise they will learn from our mistakes and not industrialise. Continued growth of industry and population will probably bring disaster but it is uncertain when or in what form. Innovation may defer the environmental crunch but cannot do so for ever.

Three key issues exist which will determine just where on this spectrum between technological utopia and eco-disaster the world will be by 2200. These concern population control, international cooperation and the nature of innovation. All other aspects of the macrofuture are either implicit in these or else are relatively unimportant.

On population control the issue is not whether the Earth could be made to support a population of twenty billion or thirty billion or forty billion (it probably could, but see chapter eight for methods of coping with huge Earth populations) but that all aspects of life in the twenty-first and twenty-second centuries will be simpler and better (however one defines 'better') with a lower world population rather than a higher one. There is no advantage to be gained whatsoever from a higher population. There are many disadvantages. The higher consumption resulting from a growing population might seem to help some firms in the short term, but this would be very marginal because the greatest population increase would be among the economically disadvantaged, who would not become additional consumers of manufactured goods or services but additional peasant farmers or recipients of state benefits. And in the long term any growth in population makes future planning and resource management more difficult while reducing the effect of growth obtained by technological innovation. (National income grows rapidly but national income per head grows less rapidly.) There is a relationship between population increase and income, or, to be more precise, between family size and family income—as income rises so family size falls—but this is not a simple relationship. Religious factors, educational factors, traditional factors and time lags are all involved, making quantification difficult. However, official UN population projections suggest that the present increase rate of two per cent per annum will be reduced by between five and twenty-five per cent during the 1980s and reduced again round about the turn of the century to give a stable population thereafter. This is, perhaps, wishful thinking based on the widespread acceptance of birth control in the LDCs plus a considerable rise in *per capita* income there. It is important to realise that zero population growth is no real hardship. It means that each family is allowed to have two children—to replace itself. The sooner this state of affairs comes about the greater the benefit to the human race.

International cooperation, leading to international government (rather than a powerless international debating chamber like the UN) will become essential within the next half century. If it does not come about, Earth's economic growth may be slowed, technological innovations may be impracticable and Earth's biosphere may be irreparably damaged as a result. There are some areas of advance in which even the largest and richest nations will find it difficult to proceed unaided, such as the construction of orbiting space colonies and power satellites (see chapter seven Man in Space), and in pollution control. In other cases the lack of international agreement prevents the exploitation of resources or the control of their exploitation. Almost twenty years of discussion have failed to come up with a formula for the sea-bed mining of metallic nodules (to which a group of LDCs object because they lack the technology or capital to participate in what they regard as a very profitable venture), and some species of whale are being made extinct by excessive hunting on the part of Russia and Japan, even though other countries have agreed to reduce or halt their whaling activities. Innovations such as supersonic passenger aircraft have been obstructed by some countries' refusal to allow *Concorde* to overfly their territory, without scientific excuse. Governments generally think in narrow, nationalistic terms rather than trying to do what is best for the world as a whole. They endeavour to please the people who elected them rather than pleasing the faceless billions who live elsewhere in the world or the countless billions who are yet to be born. Their attitude is, as George Bernard Shaw put it, 'What has posterity done for me that I should do anything for posterity?' Even worse, these national governments must seek re-election every three to five years. (Many countries never hold elections, or else prohibit opposition parties, but that sort of government is no more likely to consider the state of the world than is a democracy; probably less.) Very often, in western countries at least, there is a change of government and any earlier agreements on international action or plans for the future are overturned. The US congress can always reverse previous decisions, and no British parliament need be bound by decisions of a previous parliament. Thus, as things stand, there can be no lasting international agreements and no firm long-range planning. This is a major reason why no extrapolations can be expected to be valid for more than a few decades ahead: no final and authoritative decision-making procedure exists.

Technological discoveries and innovations are pretty common these days and becoming more so. Most can be foreseen because they are refinements, practical applications of existing theories or more efficient methods of doing the same job, while a few come out of the blue with no warning and make the imaginations of science fiction writers seem limited. Again, most are fairly unimportant to the majority of people and will have no bearing on the shape of the future, but a few will be so important that they will set the whole future society of mankind moving in a different direction. These are predominantly unforseen. One can be fairly sure that a certain number of innovations of worldwide importance will occur per decade or per century (the frequency is increasing) but one can never know when (or if) the answer to any particular problem will be found. And even when a solution is found it may produce new problems, previously unconsidered (as shown, with examples, in chapter five). No major innovation is likely to be devoid of side effects; there will be many thorny issues to decide. Those who claim that technological innovation will solve all mankind's problems are being too hopeful. The answers will come eventually but they may not come when they are needed and they may be more problematical than the problems they are meant to solve.

In the light of these points, how will intermediate scenarios of the future look? In general, economic growth, consumption of resources and industrialisation will all continue undiminished, except that progress will never be smooth, The increase in population will slow down over the next half century but it will not reach a point of stability, of zero population growth, because certain nations (and particular groups within nations) will never agree to limit their families. They will be steadfastly supported by some religious and political leaders. The lengths to which the more responsible nations will go in imposing sanctions upon these minorities is not something which can be forecast by extrapolation.

Generally, decision-making will be a farce. No international unanimity will be achieved on any subject of importance before 2050 and the situation will improve only gradually after that date. Worse still, very little long-range planning will be possible due to the vacillations of national politicians, who will continue to consider the scoring of party points much more important than the long-term prosperity of the world or even of their own countries. The few politicians who are exceptions to this will only escape quick defeat and obscurity by the overthrow of democracy.

But in general national policies are likely to pull against each other: as one country succeeds in clearing up a particular type of environmental threat so another country will aggravate it. This will be obvious, too, in the use of resources. Industrialised countries will not willingly limit their consumption of fossil fuels or raw materials, but the actions of LDCs (particularly of the Arab oil producers) will undoubtedly cause artificial energy shortages worse than anything experienced so far which will persist during the rest of the twentieth century, causing some slowing of economic growth. By the year 2000 or 2010 alternative energy sources should be perfectly adequate, probably with a few orbiting power satellites in operation, while cars and aircraft are powered by liquid hydrogen.

By and large industrialisation will continue, but there will be opposition to this from nations and groups who will support Malthusian theories to the point of committing Luddite-type acts of terrorism. A few countries will ban industrialisation or exploitation of any natural reasources they happen to possess. In many other countries Malthusian groups will set up communes, aiming at self-sufficiency but ending up at a subsistence level, thus proving that Malthus was right. For most of the world, innovation and greater industrial efficiency (stemming from greater capital investment) will gradually raise the standard of living. In the LDCs progress will be particularly uneven, with many setbacks. Inexorably the countries which wish for continued industrialisation will draw away from those of a Malthusian outlook in terms of *per capita* income.

Most forms of pollution will be overcome but many plant and animal species will become extinct first. Vast areas of sea and shore will be sterilised by oil spillages and industrial wastes. During the twenty-second century much capital and effort will go into trying to repair the ecological damage caused between 1950 and 2050. Forests will be replanted and attempts made to regenerate lost species by genetic engineering. The quality of life will improve dramatically from a very low ebb.

By 2150 there will be a considerable degree of homogeneity throughout the world in the matter of lifestyle. Drop-out groups may have been enticed back into the rat race. The western nations will probably still be slightly ahead of the rest of the world in such things as income, sophistication and technological development. Any really large projects (orbiting colonies, undersea cities, etc) will have been undertaken by one or more of these nations (the US, EEC countries, Japan) or by private enterprise corporations. All the problems of the late-twentieth century will have been solved or forgotten but newer problems will have taken their places.

Nuclear War

Although Herman Kahn has called large-scale nuclear war 'the unthinkable' it must be thought about.[8] For over thirty years the USA and the USSR have both possessed nuclear weapons, so the possibility of nuclear war has existed. It has become an accepted part of man's life. Each technological advance in destructive capacity or ease of missile delivery has been received with stoicism rather than hysteria. True, a little hysteria has affected mankind; in Britain the Campaign for Nuclear Disarmament was the real in-crowd scene of about 1960 and its curious symbol, daubed in white paint, seemed to appear overnight on every brick wall throughout the land. Yet interest in disarmament has waned, even as nuclear stockpiles have grown and increased sophistication of delivery has ensured that no part of the world can be considered safe from a direct hit. People have learned to stop worrying and, if not actually to love the bomb, at least to tolerate or ignore its presence. It has become another future shock factor for the individual to integrate within himself, but a minor one. The threat of nuclear war has come very close on occasion, particularly during the Cuban missile crisis of 1962, but it has always receded. Probably most people have come to the conclusion that because several nations now possess efficient nuclear weapons and the degree of overkill is enormous, only an insane government would instigate a nuclear war, whatever the provocation.

This is true. Any nuclear attack by a major power would be instantly answered by retaliation, perhaps even before the initial missiles exploded. There could be no hope of destroying all of the enemy power's launching sites, because some at least would be mobile. Thus any attack would be suicidal. All major powers have too much to lose to try such a thing. In other words the possession of such power by more than one nation is in itself a safeguard against the use of it by any of them. Besides, the current state of *détente* between the USA and the USSR makes the occurrence of a situation which could escalate to the contemplation of a nuclear war between them very remote. Herman Kahn's scenarios of various escalation ladders leading inexorably to a full-blown exchange of total nuclear fire-power between East and West would appear to be defunct; highly improbable, anyway.

There are other possibilities. An insane chief minister might order a nuclear attack; an insane general might press the 'unthinkable' button; a flight of birds might be mistaken for missiles; a technician might test a firing button while it was still connected up. The crew of a Polaris submarine might mutiny and use their nuclear missiles as bargaining counters.[9] These, too, are all remote.

The only real likelihood of nuclear attack at the present moment comes from the existence of groups of extremist terrorists. They—and only they—have nothing to lose by constructing a nuclear bomb and using it to kill their political enemies. The construction of a device would be fairly easy. The obtaining of enough fissionable material would not be impossible. (Apparently, most of Israel's fissionable material was obtained by stealth.) No large and complex missile would be necessary. The bomb could be planted by hand, with a self-contained timing device, in just the same fashion as bombs employing conventional explosives have been planted in most world capitals during the past decade. While such a device would undoubtedly be of low power—of no more than a few kilotons —it could still demolish a large building (the White House, the Falace of Westminster, etc). Even worse than the initial devastation would be the possibility of retaliation in a similar vein against any country which sheltered such terrorists.

The destructive capacities of nuclear weapons and the precise means by which they kill and maim people are not relevant to the scope of this book, but David Langford, in *War in 2080*, provides horrifyingly detailed descriptions of the effects of heat flash, shockwave and radioactive fall-out.

However unlikely, a future in which there is nuclear war must be examined, because it remains an alternative to the possibilities of exponential growth or steady slide into eco-disaster. Although stockpiles of nuclear weapons are so huge that their destructive power is equivalent to about ten tons of TNT for each man, woman and child on this planet, the initial loss of life if all warheads were used would perhaps be no more than ten per cent of world population. This is because the aim of war would not be to deliver ten tons of TNT to the immediate vicinity of each member of the human race, but to destroy utterly all the most vital economic and military sites of one's enemy. To this end an excessive number of missiles would be despatched towards the enemy's missile bases, major cities, ports, largest industrial complexes and armed forces establishments. Even allowing for a considerable degree of missile interception, most of the targets would be pulverised. Yet rural areas would initially be untouched.

Detailed studies of the effects of a nuclear war have been made in the USA. Two congressional committees (the Holfield Committees) have produced figures for death, injury and damage, and so has Herman Kahn in *On Thermonuclear War*. The findings were that even in all-out war only a third to a half of the American population would be killed and that within forty years the country would have recovered fully. Although the studies were carried out about twenty years ago, since when stockpiles have grown and the neutron bomb (which kills more people but does less damage to property) has appeared—at least in blueprint form—the findings have not been totally invalidated. A nuclear war between the USA and USSR might leave half the population of both countries dead and all major urban centres destroyed, but it would not 'wipe out' those countries completely. Recovery might be measured in centuries rather than decades, but it would be possible. Other countries might not be attacked at all.

The only doubt is over fall-out. Initial casualties caused by the heat flash and blast wave can be calculated quite accurately; the possibility of lethal amounts of radioactive dust being liberally distributed around the globe by the world's wind systems cannot be ruled out. This is why reference is made, above, to 'initial' loss of life. Secondary deaths from fall-out, from contaminated food and water, and from all the causes which spring from a breakdown of civilisation, might reach totals almost as great.

Science fiction has dealt thoroughly with a variety of post-atomic-war situations. Sometimes the survivors are dying slowly from the effects of radioactivity in their submarine (*On the Beach* by Nevil Shute) or subterranean shelter (*Level 7* by Mordecai Roshwald). Sometimes the survivors are not themselves threatened but have been genetically damaged so that their few offspring are hideous (*Twilight World* by Poul Anderson). Some very bizarre civilisations have been forecast for the twenty-first and twenty-second centuries following a twentieth-century nuclear war. There are telepathic societies, high-technology societies, barbarism and dictatorships. In a few cases mankind has been driven from the Earth's surface and lives underground, under the sea, or elsewhere in the Solar System.

Both Herman Kahn and Professor J. B. S. Haldane have suggested that a nuclear war could result in the rise of an authoritarian world state. This is a logical extrapolation. If today's major world powers were temporarily crippled by the effects of nuclear war some lesser nation might easily be able to establish total world domination.

But, as Adrian Berry stresses in *The Next Ten Thousand Years*, if it seems difficult to exterminate the human race in a nuclear war, it would be next to impossible to make Earth devoid of all life. Probably some animals and plants would survive even the worst possible holocaust or the heaviest fall-out, to evolve again into an eventual intelligent species. Scorpions can withstand radiation levels two hundred times higher than humans can.[10] Perhaps they could form the next civilisation on Earth?

7 Man in Space

*'I must go/Where the fleet of stars is anchored and the young
star-captains glow.'*

James Elroy Flecker

Mankind will—indeed, must—leave Earth and go out into
space in large numbers. These numbers should not be in tens
or hundreds, but in millions, and the time to begin the mass
exodus is as soon as possible, with significant quantities of
people living and working in space before the end of the 1980s.
The alternative is an unbearably overcrowded Earth with ever
dwindling stocks of raw materials (especially food and energy),
causing living standards to deteriorate to the point of economic
collapse on the part of the industrialised nations.

Shifting millons of people off Earth will benefit those who
go and those who stay. Firstly it will provide more living
space, for this must be a one-way movement; those who leave
Earth will not be able to return. Herein, too, lies the necessity
for hurrying: for every man who is transported off Earth in
the year 1990 it will (assuming mankind continues to double
itself every thirty-five years, as at present) be necessary to
transport two by the year 2025 to have achieved the same
proportional reduction in the world's population.

A second benefit, which will bring more tangible short-term
gains, is that the presence of a few thousand technicians in
space can lead to an early solution to Earth's energy problems.
This solution is the construction of solar power satellites,
which will gather the Sun's rays with great efficiency, convert
them to microwave energy and beam this down to receiving
antennae on Earth.[1] The amount of power available is limited
only by the size and efficiency of the satellites, and all Earth's
electrical energy requirements could be met by this approach.
It is believed that the overall cost, admittedly enormous,
could be recovered over thirty years through the sale of
electrical power—which would almost certainly be cheaper
than that produced by any other process. The only disadvan-

tage would be the production of so much interference that radio-astronomy would probably become impossible from Earth and would need to be sited elsewhere, possibly on the far side of the Moon. No interference with normal radio or TV signals is anticipated.

The third category of benefit would stem from having access to vacuum and zero-gravity conditions, and would manifest itself in terms of scientific research possibilities, improved astronomical observation and greater ease of certain manufacturing processes.

As man moves further out from the world of his ancestors so he will be changed culturally, mentally and physically by the strangeness of his new environment, or will need to be changed in order to survive it. Such changes are the subject of this chapter.

Orbital Colonies

These could be constructed from the mid-1980s, initially as 'construction shacks' for those building solar power satellites. All the parts—for the power satellites and for the colonies—will be lifted into a fairly low Earth orbit by heavy lift launch vehicles (HLLVs) similar to the existing space shuttle, and assembled there. The investment required is comparable to the cost of the Apollo project, say $8–10 billion per annum (at 1980 price levels) over twenty years. Later space colonies will be built of materials mined on the Moon, and should be both larger and less expensive.

Various sizes and shapes have been proposed for orbital colonies, particularly by Dr Gerard K. O'Neill, who can claim to be the main originator of current interest in the subject. The most important design criteria are that each colony should have an Earth-strength gravity in at least some areas and that this should be provided by a rotational spin of no more than one revolution per minute. There are important physiological reasons for these rules. The experiences of the Skylab astronauts have shown that zero-gravity conditions produce motion sickness (though this wears off after a few uncomfortable days), a drop in red blood cell count (though this eventually levels off and reverses itself) and a loss of bone calcium of approximately half a per cent per month (only reversible by a return to Earth gravity). The rule about spin is to avoid Coriolis effects—the sideways swirling of gravity due to rapid rotation, which can result in nausea and in the deviation of falling objects. These requirements mean that any colony would need a diameter of just over a mile, and in response the Stanford torus has been designed.

This is effectively a gigantic version of the archetypal space station, as depicted by Chesley Bonestell during the 1950s— the cartwheel shape. Its circumference is about four miles, but its width is only four hundred feet, and it is joined to the hub (with non-rotating docking point) by six spokes containing transport facilities. Above the colony (assuming the wheel to be lying flat) is a large circular mirror, well over half a mile in diameter, which will reflect sunlight into the colony. It is intended that such a colony would be virtually self-sufficient, providing living space for 10,000 people. This will consist of more-or-less conventional houses of two or three storeys situated around the rim (ie with the rim as 'down' and the hub as 'up') under the ceiling some two hundred feet high. (This is not high enough for cloud formation and natural weather.) The colony must grow all its own food, and this will occupy a minimum of sixty acres—just under a third of the surface area of the rim. Such intensity of agriculture will only be possible because every factor of the growing conditions will be rigidly controlled. There will be no seasons; crops will be grown in particular sequences with considerable intercropping, and any stems or inedible portions will help to feed livestock —particularly goats, for a fresh milk supply. Also, chickens will be kept for their egg production and fish (*Tilapia* species) for their meat. The idea is to provide a varied and nourishing diet of fresh food not too different from that enjoyed on Earth. The reason for this is not simply physiological, to maintain good health, but also psychological. Breaking all one's ties with Earth and adjusting to life in space will be very traumatic, and the presence of some familiar aspects of life, such as foodstuffs, will help to alleviate this.

The location of Stanford torus colonies needs to be in a stable orbit within easy reach of both Earth and the Moon. Although the stable Lagrangian points L4 and L5 in the Moon's orbit (but 60° ahead and behind the Moon) were though to be ideal, more recent studies show that a better situation for purposes of rendezvousing with material sent up from the Moon would be in a so-called 'resonant' orbit around Earth (see FIGURE). So the colonies will probably orbit Earth every two weeks, at a distance varying between 100,000 and 200,000 miles; they will approach to within 50,000 miles of the Moon. Perhaps the first such orbit colony should be named Laputa, after the flying island of that name visited by Lemuel Gulliver in Swift's *Gulliver's Travels.*

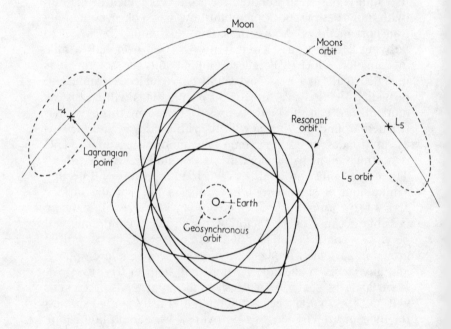

The colonists themselves will be young—probably under thirty, because their working lives in the colony will be that much longer—and skilled in some aspect of heavy construction work (for power satellite construction) or in a relevant scientific, technical or planning discipline. Single people and married couples will be employed (if both are suitably qualified) but a rough equalisation of the sexes will be necessary in any case, because there will be no return to Earth. These will not be short-term 'overseas' jobs, but lifetime moves away from Earth. The colonists will be the first true 'space-men'—men of space. In many ways their lives will be little different from those of people living in any industrialised society back on Earth. They will be able to marry and have children, to work at their jobs and hope for promotion, to relax by watching TV, reading, gardening, swimming, walking in the park and going out to a restaurant or cinema. Each colony will resemble a small town, with its residential areas, industrial areas, cultivated land and parkland. Accommodation will range from bachelor apartments to large family homes. But the differences from Earth will always be present. People will be living in the closed environment of the colony (except for those who work out in space on construction projects, though they too will forever remain in a closed environment of some sort, whether it is a deep space shuttle or a spacesuit). They will probably never again experience weather such as a fresh morning, or a rainstorm, or see a cloudy sky. It is unlikely that many of them will return to Earth even for a holiday, though Earth will frequently be visible to them—a very large object, clear in the 'sky', with its continents and islands all tantalisingly discernible. So they will never meet relatives again, though they may be allowed to talk to them quite often over picture phones. Very few Earth-made products will be available to the colonists because of the high cost of freighting them up to the colony, though detailed plans will be obtained and facsimiles built in the colony whenever possible.

To live in such a colony, far removed from the dirt and squalor of Earth, many seem idyllic. Certainly there will be some advantages, including cleanliness (the lack of air pollution will be noticeable; it will also be essential to ensure maximisation of crop yields) and a lower incidence of accident or illness than on Earth, resulting in an improved lifespan.[2] But there are potential problems to be faced, with which none of the literature of space colonies attempts to deal. Who will govern them? Will it be some faceless bureaucrats in Washington or Whitehall or Brussels, or will it be a board of directors, more concerned with profit than with people? It must not be forgotten that, even though a space colony might have the population of only a small town, many colonies will exist, with a total population running into perhaps tens of millions before the end of the twenty-first century. Perhaps the space colonies, or a group of them, will become an additional state of the USA, or a country within the European Economic Community. It could be that they will need to fight for their independence, with the tricentennial of 2076 being marked by declarations of independence from America's own colonies.

Each space colony is likely to have a small police force to maintain law and order, and an elected council, in the manner of a small town anywhere, but what solutions will they find for a proven murderer, for a person who refuses to work, for a mentally deficient child? The colony will not be able to afford to support many pairs of idle hands, so will all these categories be shipped back to Earth (which would not want them) or will they simply be executed and their bodies recycled as fertiliser? Come to that, what will happen to a colony forty years after its foundation, when all its original inhabitants have reached retirement age or are no longer able to do their jobs? By that time there should be space-born children who have grown up, trained and are already taking over from their parents, but there will not be enough room in a single Stanford torus colony for enough of them. An environment designed to contain and feed 10,000 people will not be able to hold 15,000 or 20,000, and the solution will be for the colonists to duplicate their colony every generation, or even more frequently. Then the more aged members of the original colony could be split between two or three separate toruses, with the numbers being made up by a combination of the space-born and new settlers from Earth. Birth control—or the lack of it—is another important consideration. Perhaps there will be sufficient room amongst the colonies for people to have as many children as they wish. But if space constraints existed (no pun intended), what remedies would a colony have against a couple who insisted upon having a child every year—forcible sterilisation, euthanasia for the children?

Hopefully the answer to some of these problems lies in the construction of very large colonies. These could be cylindrical, twenty miles long and four miles in diameter, each supporting a population of up to ten million, living across the whole of its inner surface, except for the window apertures. Here there would be enough empty space inside for clouds to form and for natural rain to fall, though the 'sky' would normally appear to be blue if one looked across the cylinder. Although such colonies are already being designed they could not be built until perhaps the 2020s or 2030s, by which time much experience in space construction will have been gained and certain technical problems overcome. The main reason for having colonies of this size will be to provide living space for a significant proportion of the world's population. One of these cylinders—and particularly two linked together but rotating in opposite directions to provide a zero overall spin, as suggested by T. A. Heppenheimer—will not be so much a colony as a fully fledged nation in space. The high frontier will have become a settled land.[3]

On the Other Worlds of the Solar System

Some of the existing planets, moons and asteroids of the Solar System will provide a home for the overflow of humanity, but in very few cases will they be as suitable for colonisation as purpose-built habitats in Earth orbit. The problems are both physiological and positional; often they are severe. This does not mean that man will find it impossible to establish bases on any bodies in the Solar System, just that most bases are unlikely to become colonies.

The Moon, as our nearest natural neighbour in space, will undoubtedly acquire a population running into thousands, perhaps hundreds of thousands, but these will be contract workers rather than colonists. The main disadvantage of the Moon is its low gravity, only one sixth of Earth's. Even though the long term effects of low-g living are uncertain, they will not be beneficial. The loss of bone calcium has already been mentioned; the atrophying of some muscles might reasonably be expected. The other major problem is the Moon's two-week night, when lights would have to be used and solar power would not be available unless beamed down from an orbiting satellite. Probably workers would spend no more than one year in four or five working on the Moon. Why would they be needed there? Well, the Moon is a very convenient source of ores containing aluminium, iron and silicon, from which the space colonies will be constructed. With escape velocity at only 1·5 miles per second (as compared with Earth's 7mps) the launching of loads of ore into space from the Moon will be relatively easy.[4] Much of the accumulation and despatching of ore would be handled by automatic machines, but even so quite a few operators, maintenance men, planners and back-up service workers would be needed. Also, the far side of the Moon is the perfect location for astronomical purposes, so a large observatory is likely to be established there.

Venus, the closest planet to Earth, was long considered by writers of fact and fiction to be a second Earth—a watery planet full of primeval monsters. Not until the mid-1950s was it suggested that the planet's surface temperature might be very high—in the region of 300° to 500°C, and this was confirmed by space probes during the 1960s. Venus is now known to be a dry inferno beneath dense clouds of carbon dioxide (at a very high pressure) which allow the Sun's heat in but prevent it from radiating away. But there is hope that this situation may be changed. Professor Carl Sagan has asserted that if Venus is seeded with algae they will break down the carbon dioxide to produce free oxygen. A thinner barrier of carbon dioxide will permit the heat to escape. Eventually water vapour will form and, when the temperature has dropped sufficiently, rain will fall. By that time the planet will have a breathable atmosphere and the temperature will be no higher than Earth's. A laboratory simulation bears out this theory: the terraforming of Venus is a workable proposition. The time period involved is uncertain but could be in terms of decades rather than centuries. Although Venus is slightly smaller than Earth, it has no oceans (though these might form naturally after terraforming) and therefore more land area.[5] It could offer a partial solution to mankind's population pressure, except that it rotates extremely slowly, having a day and night each almost sixty Earth days long. This would cause temperature and crop-growing problems and might force colonists to build totally enclosed cities. Or possibly a gigantic orbiting mirror may be built to reflect the Sun's rays down onto the dark side for alternate twelve-hour intervals.[6]

Mars, with its supposed canals, has a fictional past as romantic as Venus's. Edgar Rice Burroughs called it Barsoom—the planet where John Carter of Earth fights red and green men and many monsters, marries a princess of Mars and continues to be embroiled in fantastic, blood-thirsty adventures. Numerous authors imitated Burroughs, though even he was not the first to set a heroic tale there; all any of them got right was the planet's colour. The real Mars is a dead and desolate world with below-zero temperatures, no free oxygen and no discernible life forms. Its gravity is on the low side for permanent colonisation (just under forty per cent of Earth's) but it has no other disadvantages. As a last resort it would provide about fifty-six million square miles in which colonists could live under domes. An interesting recent novel is Frederik Pohl's *Man Plus*, in which an astronaut is physically adapted to survive under Martian conditions without a heated suit or breathing mask. He has been partly cyborgised, though the accepted term for altering man to fit a new physical environment is pantropy. To do this at a cost of millions of dollars per individual is a clear waste of money in terms of research value because it will not help mankind to survive on Mars—just one man. It is justifiable only in terms of national pride.

The asteroids present a range of possibilities. Lying between Mars and Jupiter, they range in size from about six hundred miles in diameter (Ceres) down to, presumably, microscopic dust. Although many thousand have been identified their total mass is only equivalent to about one per cent of Earth's. Science fiction dwells upon the miners of the asteroid belt (the 'belters') who are always searching the vast emptiness of space for asteroids of solid gold, or platinum, or uranium. There is just a grain of sense in this, for if lumps of carbon dioxide or ammonia several miles across can be found—and they should be present—they will provide the fastest means of filling a large cylindrical space colony with a breathable atmosphere. Some asteroids may be suitable for use as space colonies. They will be hollowed out as much as is necessary for living space, and propulsion systems will be fitted to them. As Konstantin Tsiolkovsky forecast as long ago as 1912, 'We shall one day learn to ride the asteroids as today we ride horses.'

The major planets out beyond Mars are generally unsuitable for permanent colonisation. Jupiter has too high a gravity (150 per cent higher then Earth's) and all of them are remote, frigid bodies which receive insufficient solar radiation for this to be a source of power. Some of the moons of these outer planets are large—Jupiter's Io is similar in size to the Moon, while Ganymede and Callisto, together with Saturn's Titan and Neptune's Triton, are even larger, all with diameters of

more than 3,000 miles. They may well be used as bases, particularly for astronomical purposes, but there seems no reason
for people to live out their lives there when space colonies
in the vicinity of Earth are so much more attractive. Eventually
these outlying major planets may be incorporated into a Dyson
sphere, which is dealt with in chapter eight.

Starships

It was Thomas Carlyle (1795–1881) who looked up at the stars
and commented, 'A sad spectacle. If they be inhabited, what
a scope for misery and folly. If they be not habited, what a
waste of space.' The time will come, probably within the next
century and a half, when a manned expedition will set off for
another star with the hope of finding habitable planets in orbit
around it. Unless an unexpected breakthrough has occurred
by then (enabling man to travel instantaneously from one solar
system to another, for example) an interstellar voyage will be
a lengthy operation. Excluding the Sun, the nearest star to us
is Proxima Centauri, about 4·3 light years distant.[7] The time
taken will depend upon the percentage of the speed of light
which the starship can attain. If a propulsion system could be
developed which would provide a constant acceleration of one
g, just a year of this would boost the starship's speed up to the
speed of light; this would reduce the one-way journey time to
under five and a half years. But current best estimates of a
conceivable propulsion system suggests a maximum attainable
of ten per cent of the speed of light which, allowing for acceleration and deceleration, would mean a journey time of forty-
five years to Proxima Centauri. So far neither of these possibilities can be built, and a Saturn V moon-rocket would take
30,000 years to travel the distance.

In fact, Proxima Centauri is unlikely to possess any habitable planets, so more likely stars, slightly further away, will
probably be visited instead, making the trip even longer. This
illustrates the futility of despatching anything, even an
unmanned probe such as the proposed Daedalus, to another
star, until we have the technical capacity to make it travel at
a respectable fraction of the speed of light. It would be farcical
if (as in A. E. van Vogt's story 'Far Centaurus') a starship
were to take hundreds of years to reach another star only to

find that mankind had already colonised the planets there because improved technology had reduced the travelling time to a few months, or even a few hours.[8]

But inevitably there will be a first attempt, and when it is being planned there will be queues of applicants miles long who want to join the crew. To the members of the earliest unmanned expeditions the long journey time means they will almost certainly never return to the Solar System, though their descendants may. There are several approaches to this problem. In the first place, no starship crew will consist of three male astronauts in cramped conditions, like the Apollo missions. Instead the starship may well be similar to a Stanford torus but with engines attached. To allow plenty of space for a nuclear power plant (the amount of solar energy available in the enormous gulfs between solar systems is insufficient to keep even an undemanding bacterium alive), sufficient spare parts and various exhaustable stores, including those for children born during the expedition, the initial number of people would need to be less than ten thousand—probably only one or two thousand. Even so, this would be a small town in space. The tasks of food production, maintenance and scientific observation would need to sustain them all over a period of ten or twenty years at the minimum, and the population might double in this time, with many people being required to help with the process of education.

Outlook and social structure might be expected to change during a voyage, perhaps quite radically. Without being unduly metaphysical or mystical about this, the fact cannot be ignored that the existence of Earth beneath one's feet has a normalising influence. The presence of millions of other people, of custom and law and religion, of centuries of history, inhibits us and keeps our behaviour within bounds. Space colonists in Earth orbit will not escape this feeling; the planet of their fathers will be visible, its cities and its people will only be as far away as a telephone. But out between the stars things will be different. Earth will no longer be visible. Radio contact will be slow, with conversations spread out over years, like postal chess games by second-class mail, and becoming less real all the time. The starship colonists will have severed the umbilical cord between themselves and their planet of origin. One can imagine that the family structure and belief in conventional religion may disappear to be replaced by forms of grouping and belief more suited to an isolated community in deepest space. It is not possible to predict whether these changes will unfetter the imagination and lead to scientific innovation or increased happiness, or whether they will force some colonists to retreat within themselves, or have other adverse effects upon the mission.

In multi-generation starship voyages of science fiction the colonists have a habit of rebelling, reverting to savagery and forgetting that they are on a ship at all.[9] Certainly there is some likelihood that over four or five generations, when all those of the original complement have died, the objectives of the mission might be altered and, through accident or design, some important knowledge lost for ever. As an alternative fictional means, humans are transported across the interstellar gulf in a state of suspended animation. Either the crew keep continuous watch, with each man (in fiction, spaceship crews are almost inevitably men, though more recent examples sometimes include a token woman) being out of suspended animation for one year in ten or twenty, or else they too sleep through the entire multi-decade voyage, being woken automatically only if a problem occurs which the computers cannot handle alone.

Even if the crew of a starship were to stay awake for the whole of the twenty-year voyage, so long as the ship's speed was a substantial proportion of that of light, time would speed up for them. This is part of Einstein's theory of relativity. To those back on Earth the starship's voyage would last twenty years; to those aboard (even to the clocks aboard) it might be five years, or perhaps only five months, depending upon the ship's closeness to the speed of light.

It has been suggested in other stories that, to save room, human eggs and sperm might be carried frozen rather than whole adult humans. Perhaps it could be argued that single cloned cells from five thousand of Earth's finest potential colonists (or five million; let us not be pennypinching about this) together with a complete memory record of each one, would be an even better starship payload. Unfortunately neither human cloning nor memory recording has yet been perfected, but by the time it has perhaps large-scale imperialism will be back in fashion and ships bearing such packages will be despatched in sufficiently huge numbers for mankind to conquer the galaxy.

Meanwhile, a Stanford torus starship with two thousand adults and a horde of young children on board is heading out towards one of the nearby stars. Which star will it be? It is hoped that by setting up a really large optical telescope on the far side of the Moon the presence of planets around suitable Sol-type stars such as Alpha Centauri, Epsilon Eridani, Tau Ceti or 70 Ophiuchi will be detected. A distance of twenty light years from Earth is not unthinkably far if one possesses the capability of accelerating up to a large percentage of the speed of light, and there are fifty-nine stars within that radius of us. Estimates of the proportion of stars which possess planets and of the proportion of planets where life is expected to occur change frequently with little evidence to support them. At present only Barnard's Star, the next nearest after the Centauri group, has shown unmistakable evidence of having planets.

The starship personnel have a number of choices, though most of these will have been decided for them at the mission planning stage, decades earlier. They can begin decelerating as much as a light year away from their target sun, aiming to be travelling sufficiently slowly as they enter its solar system to be able to *rendezvous* with and orbit any particular planet. Or they may not decelerate but speed through the solar system *en route* for another star, either gathering information as they pass or else dropping off small robot data collectors. These will be able to slow down, locate and possibly orbit all planets, and the data will be beamed to the retreating starship, or straight back to Earth. The starship will go on to a second star, either decelerating or turning in a multi-light-year curve to head back to Earth. Where the ship decelerates and goes into orbit around a planet it may carry out a survey and return or it may be intended as a one-way mission with insufficient fuel for a return journey, in which case the colonists will be faced with the final choice of whether to try colonising the most suitable planet in their vicinity or to stay in their Stanford torus. They would not need to remain in orbit for ever, though. The possibility would exist of procuring fresh supplies of whatever fuel was required (by mining on a nearby planet or perhaps by gathering atmospheric helium from a gas giant similar to Jupiter) so that the starship could continue its journey. It might be found that some, even many, of the colonists preferred to travel on hopefully from star to star, imbued with an updated 'frontiersman' spirit. They would build a new starship from local materials whenever they needed more room for their expanding population, but would never actually settle for good on a planet. They would have adapted so well to starship life that they would be content to remain space gypsies for ever.

The men and women who make up the complement of starships will have been selected and trained with great care and forethought. Psychological testing will be used to ensure compatability. Most ship control routines will be so complex that they will be handled by computers, but it may still be necessary for a few crew members to be surgically altered to enable a full man-machine interface to be achieved. Ideally this would mean running a multi-filament cable from the ship's computers or control systems into a specially prepared skull socket, so that information could come in and questions or orders go out without the need for speaking or button pressing. This development will probably be available by the time the first manned starships are sent out—say by the year 2075 or 2100. Indeed, there may be no crew members as such, just one or two disembodied human brains with minimal life support equipment controlling every aspect of the starship. This is a more speculative prospect, not because of any extra technical difficulties but for moral reasons. It may be that some people, especially those with crippled or paralysed bodies, would welcome the opportunity to join a starship in this fashion.

Terra Nova

A new Earth is what all colonists will hope to find—a planet of suitable gravity and temperature with a breathable atmosphere, accessible mineral deposits and no intelligent indigenes. Such worlds are common enough in science fiction but probably very rare in fact. Still, even if a perfect planet is never found, some sufficiently Earth-like ones will be. A few points of difference, such as gravity up to twenty-five per cent high or low, or surface temperatures ranging from $80°F$ upwards, or an excessively long or short rotational period, can be endured. Also, any planet with abundant vegetable life is almost bound to contain some species which are inimical to man, and which will, given the slenderest of opportunities, poison him, invade his body microscopically with devastating results or simply ingest him. Ditto for non-intelligent animal species. (Intelligent species will be considered in a later section.) Probably these difficulties and dangers will be overcome much as they have been on Earth—with a few fatalities at first, then the eventual triumph of man over nature.

So many bizarre dangers have been encountered by humans in science fiction stories set on alien worlds that it might be a good idea to analyse them all by computer with the intention of producing a checklist of potential dangers for intending colonists. Obviously, the colonists will take care, sending down robot vehicles first, then perhaps laboratory animals, sterilising all items before they re-enter the starship and allowing ample time for quarantine. Equally obviously, the most dangerous factors will be the most subtle, the most insidious. While large carnivores can be exterminated with relative ease, a microscopic airborne organism which takes a year to kill its host might decimate a colony before it could be isolated and its effects counteracted. It will have to be remembered that nothing on an alien planet will necessarily behave, or have developed, in the same way as on Earth. Life may not be based on the hydrogen-carbon-oxygen combinations with which we are familiar. Even the natural laws of physics may not still hold there; instead they will be shown up as special cases of more fundamental laws.

It is very likely that most planets discovered and surveyed will not be immediately suitable for human colonisation. But some of these will be suitable candidates for terraforming—as mentioned earlier in connection with Venus. There will be many planets of the right size, density, rotation and temperature but without life: they may be barren, rocky worlds with empty oceans—rather like Earth was some 3,000 million years ago. These conditions can be changed to give a suitable atmosphere for mankind by the introduction of bacteria—the species used being dependent upon the existing atmosphere. The starship will need to carry freeze-dried spores for a range of species for this purpose (for turning ammonia into nitrates and nitrites, hydrogen sulphide into sulphates, hydrogen into water, carbon monoxide into carbon dioxide, methane to carbon dioxide, etc). After any poisons have been removed from the atmosphere and the seas (or at least changed into forms which can be absorbed by plant life) algae will be introduced to oxygenate the atmosphere. When conditions are suitable, arable crops, meat and dairy animals and fish can be added. None of this is speculative; the bacteria and algae already exist; the entire process is similar to what happened naturally on Earth. The only uncertainty is the time period. Depending upon the amounts of bacteria released it could take centuries for atmospheres of ammonia and methane to be broken down into the sort of compounds (nitrates, carbon dioxide, etc) which could be handled by plants. But if a starship began this process of terraforming once every ten years, say, it could leave in its wake a stream of planets which would be suitable for colonisation by a wave of starships perhaps a century later.

On some alien planets the process of terraforming would mean not just bringing life to barren rocks but the destruction of an existing ecology. It is reasonable to predict that there will always be some opposition to this on conservationist grounds. These colonists will probably have witnessed the disruption of Earth's own ecological systems and the extinction of many of its species of flora and fauna for reasons of expediency, human error or fun. They may be reluctant to impose the same dreadful sentence upon a whole new world which they do not understand, and which has never done them any harm. But we are a selfish race, putting survival ahead of everything else. If it is deemed necessary to destroy alien environments in the process of terraforming worlds for humanity to live on, it will be done.

Once begun, the outward urge from Earth to space and from space to new worlds will continue. Millions of people will be transported across interstellar space. The means by which this will be accomplished do not matter; these are hardware problems which man's ingenuity will solve in ways which we cannot even guess at. What is important is the software—man himself. These settlers on alien worlds orbiting alien suns cannot and should not be thought of as early pioneers in America or Voortrekkers in nineteenth-century South Africa. They will not cast off the advantages of twenty-first- or twenty-second-century technology as soon as they arrive there and begin living in log cabins or ploughing the soil by hand. Right from the start they will have ample solar-derived electric power. Sophisticated automation will be employed in constructing towns and cultivating crops. There will be no need for technological regression. Undoubtedly some settlers will be closer to the soil than previously because the vast, empty tracts of land around them will be a lure. If the world has not been extensively terraformed there will be unknown species of plants and animals to discover and catalogue; if it has been there will still be minerals to be sought, cave systems to be explored and mountains to be climbed. Some settlers may prefer to live away from towns, like the pioneers of the American West, feeling crowded if they have neighbours within ten or twenty miles. But they will not be able to escape from the web of civilisation. A radio-telephone system, probably with viewing screen attachment, will help keep them in touch with everybody else on the colony world. They will be less than an hour's flying time from the nearest city. All their automatic machinery for domestic purposes, ground clearance, ploughing, sowing, fertilising and harvesting will need regular maintenance visits. Computers will keep account of their contributions to colony production and their withdrawals in terms of goods and services. Overhead satellites will, if necessary, keep a check on the exact whereabouts of every colony member by means of heat sensing. Membership of a relatively small high-technology community will be a different kind of existence from anything yet experienced by man, conferring some of the benefits enjoyed by first settlers in any new land (particularly almost unlimited territory) but also making demands on the individual for the sake of the community. Such a colony will be large and small at the same time. Its most precious resource will be people.

Some colonies will prosper; others will fail. They will not be able to keep in regular contact with Earth, nor with each other, unless there is a scientific breakthrough which permits faster-than-light communication or faster-than-light travel. Most likely they will receive occasional radio messages beamed at them from Earth, including details of scientific and technological advancement—already a decade out of date when they arrive—and even more occasional visits from passing starships. Each colony world will acquire a distinct flavour. They will diverge from each other in customs, speech, dress and ways of thinking. If a colony is wiped out (by plague or volcanic activity, for example) it may not be missed for decades, and when its loss is confirmed no tears will be shed; there will be too many people around on Earth, in space and on colony worlds for a few thousand or a few million to make much difference.

After a few generations the colonies which have survived will have grown apart almost to the point of mutual unintelligibility. They will have progressed at different rates and by different means, though their scientific advance will probably have lagged behind Earth's. In some instances there will be civil war within a colony, which could lead to technological regression. Other colonies will build starships of their own and send expeditions to nearby solar systems. But in all cases the alienness of the environment will be assimilated by the colonists. Mental and physical evolution will come much sooner for them than for those still living on Earth. Spontaneous genetic mutations will occur more frequently and accumulate more quickly. It is safe to predict that the initial successor to *Homo sapiens sapiens* will be an inhabitant of one of these colonies, though the accumulation of sufficient physiological changes for a new species to arise naturally may not come about for thousands of years. More will be said about this in chapter eight.

Pantropy

To change man to fit a particular planet is the other side of the coin from terraforming. It has been suggested in science fiction that this could be done by genetic engineering so that different races of mankind could settle almost any type of planet. The most notable treatment of the theme is by James Blish in his novel *The Seedling Stars*, though Olaf Stapledon mentioned it thirty years earlier in *Last and First Men* (see chapter eight for a detailed description of this novel). Within a relatively few years (perhaps fifty, perhaps only twenty) it may be possible to alter the genetic package of a fertilised human egg very precisely so that the child will develop with fully operative gills or with the ability to thrive under high-gravity conditions. It may be possible, but will it be worth doing?

In the first place man does not need to settle on all planets found, whether or not they are Earth-like. Before the 1960s the opposite view was held. Now that orbiting space colonies, starships and Dyson spheres (see chapter eight) are all accepted as possible by the scientific fraternity there is no such vital need for planetary living space. In any case, if it became necessary for humans to live on a hostile world (such as Venus during the period of terraforming) our unaltered bodies could be protected quite satisfactorily from the temperature and atmosphere by technological barriers.

But let us suppose for a moment that pantropy were to be considered. There are objections to it on both moral and practical grounds. Morally the altering of human genetic material before birth in such a way that a small number of children are set apart from the rest of humanity for ever would be indefensible unless it was being done to promote the survival of the human race as a whole. As an experimental technique it would probably result in the infertility, crippling or early death of many subjects. The impracticality is best appreciated by trying to imagine the difficulty of either simulating the eventual planetary conditions on Earth while the foetuses develop and the babies are born, reared and educated, or else carrying out the whole process on an alien world where the technicians and teachers are continually working in a strange environment, hampered by protective clothing which may prevent them from ever actually touching the children, skin to skin. However it is approached, the creation of the first generation would be extremely difficult, and costly. Also, once created, the altered race will always be overspecialised, less adaptable than man, unless the genetic tampering can be reversed.

There is one way in which pantropy could be used to man's benefit. It is clear that many people in the future will spend their lives in space—in orbital colonies, on construction jobs and in the vicinity of low-gravity spaceships or planetoids. Frequently it would be helpful if man were better adapted to zero or low-g conditions, because the necessity of causing colonies and ships to rotate in order to simulate Earth gravity is sometimes a disadvantage. Under these conditions prehensile feet (or even a prehensile tail) would be invaluable, as would an immunity to bone calcium loss and resistance to dizziness and nausea at all levels of gravity and degrees of spin. If the

prehensile feet, in particular, cannot be arranged genetically
they will probably need to be grafted on surgically, as in
John Varley's story 'Gotta Sing, Gotta Dance'.

Alien Contact

Any form of contact between mankind and a race of intelligent
extraterrestrial beings is bound to affect man's future. Even if
we knew for certain that such beings existed this knowledge
would need to be taken into account in our planning and
predicting of the future. A public opinion poll survey carried
out in 1979 (in connection with the publication of *Extraterrestrial Encounter* by Chris Boyce) found that if it were
announced authoritatively and beyond a shadow of a doubt
that intelligent beings existed 'out there', less than twenty per
cent of the population of Britain would be alarmed. So far
there is no such evidence. The 'proof' of UFO sightings and
books (which seem to outnumber the sightings) such as George
Adamski's *Flying Saucers Have Landed* and Erich von
Daniken's *Chariot of the Gods* are at best inconclusive and at
worst deliberate attempts to make money out of falsehoods.[10]
The claims that whales and dolphins possess high intelligence
is another matter entirely, and one which is outside the scope
of this book.

In fact there is reasonable optimism among scientists that
extraterrestrial intelligence does exist. Our galaxy, the Milky
Way, consists of some 250 billion stars. (There are possibly
as many as a hundred billion other galaxies, too, but they are
all an awfully long way away and can be ignored.) Of these,
only a certain proportion have planets, only a few planets
can support life, on only some of these planets does life
actually appear, in a smaller number of instances does it
become intelligent, only a fraction of cases of intelligent life
ever reach the level of interstellar communication or travel,
and none of these interstellar civilisations exist for ever. This
logical diminution of the original 250 billion is very difficult
to quantify because none of the proportions are known.[11]
Despite this some scientists have made guesses of between
100,000 and one million civilisations which are at least as
advanced as ourselves existing in our galaxy at the moment.

So where are they all? Nobody knows, but certain explanations have been proposed. It could be that advanced civilisations are much rarer than this, either that we are the only one or that the few in existence are too widely spread to be able to make contact. After all, it is only just over twenty years since we made our presence known by deliberately beaming radio transmissions towards other stars, and the Milky Way is 100,000 light years across; perhaps nobody else has noticed us yet, but that as soon as they do they will reply or come to visit—arriving in a thousand years' time. Or it may be that other civilisations are not interested in us, because they have turned their thoughts inwards as a consequence of maturity, or because we are still too primitive to be worth contacting. It may even be that other civilisations are trying to contact us but we are not sufficiently intelligent to notice. The corollary of this is that as soon as we pass the galactic intelligence test we will find ourselves surrounded by extraterrestrials wanting to welcome us to the club (or at least to sell us a membership). This does not exhaust all possible explanations.

Although plans were put forward during the nineteenth century, before the advent of radio, for contacting the inhabitants of the planet Mars by forming vast geometric figures with canals across the Sahara desert or specially planted forests in Siberia, nothing came of these. During the 1920s Marconi believed that occasionally he had picked up radio signals from Mars or some other extraterrestrial source. The first serious attempts at interstellar communication, as part of the Search for ExtraTerrestrial Intelligence (SETI) date from 1959. Several astronomers and physicists proposed at about the same time that radio signals should be sent out and a radio watch kept on the 21cm (1420 megacycles) waveband, because this is the frequency emitted by individual atoms of hydrogen—which occur throughout the known universe and should be recognised by all civilisations as the lightest element. Initially this was done at the US National Radio Astronomy Observatory at Green Bank, West Virginia, in spring 1960; the exercise was known as Project Ozma. Although other radio telescopes have done much listening in to this waveband (and others) while aiming their receiving equipment at specific stars (including Tau Ceti and Epsilon Eridani) no definitely artificial signals have been heard. Since 1974 the world's largest radio telescope, 1,000ft in diameter, at Arecibo in Puerto Rico, has been sending out messages to other stars, and even to other galaxies.

The language in which it is hoped to communicate with alien intelligence is, unsurprisingly, science. The proposals for message forms vary from simple arithmetic progressions, though scientific formulae and binary-coded pictures to Lingua Cosmica, a mathematically based language purpose built for interstellar communication and developed by a Dutchman, Hans Freudenthal, in 1960.

But all this cleverness will be wasted if we cannot recognise an alien intelligence when we (eventually) see it. It is always possible that some almost entirely disregarded phenomenon on Earth is really an attempt by unlikely aliens to attract our attention. Starships entering new solar systems will have to look very hard to ascertain whether or not intelligent life exists there, especially as the aliens may not communicate by sound, light, radio waves or even body movements. One is reminded of the cartoon showing a starship approaching a new planet. Bubbles of thought from inside the ship read: 'Ah, a colony world!' Bubbles of thought from the planet (yes, from the whole planet) read: 'Ah, food!' Certainly the aliens will not be human or even humanoid, and any such appearance can safely be assumed by the colonists to be an artificial image intended to fool or comfort them. Aliens on the covers of science fiction books and magazines are frequently depicted as being roughly humanoid in appearance, though with the proportions distorted or an unhuman skin tone or an extra pair of arms. This represents an acute lack of imagination. The human arm and hand may not prove to be unique throughout the galaxy, but its distinctive and complex skeletal arrangement of one bone (upper arm), two bones (lower arm), many bones (wrist) and sets of five bones (fingers) is highly unlikely to appear by parallel evolution.[12]

Alien intelligence may take almost any form—most of which we cannot imagine. Almost certainly it will not be mammalian. If it is an animal it will not be of a type which fits neatly into our system of classification because it will be the end product of a different evolutionary progression in response to a different set of environmental pressures. For example, its brain will not necessarily be protected by a bony skull; instead it may be deep in the middle of its body. It need not be an animal at all but may be of plant origin or, due to a different body chemistry from anything terrestrial, not classifiable by any of our standards. It may be insubstantial—a gaseous or electromagnetic intelligence. It may take drastically different forms at different stages of its life cycle. Its size may be less than ours or very much greater.[13]

However mistaken man's prediction of the shapes of intelligent aliens might be, predictions of their attitudes and motivations are likely to be even less accurate. The most important point about them is their alienness. Any fictional attempt to imbue them with arms and legs, wives, cities, a religion, or avaricious desires for the planet Earth or its women are anthropomorphism. As Chris Boyce warns in *Extraterrestrial Encounter*, it is unwise to anthropomorphise aliens to any degree at all. It should not be assumed, he says, that any intelligent aliens possess advanced technology or understand the meaning of science. While our consciousness is the product of reason, symbolism and perception, alien consciousness may well lack one or more of these basic factors.

First contact between human and alien is a popular theme of science fiction. Best known though not the earliest is H. G. Wells' *The War of the Worlds* (1898). The Martian invaders of the Earth in that novel have become a prototype for all aliens—emotionless killers and would-be enslavers of mankind—which was rarely deviated from for fifty years afterwards. One must hope that war will not ensue from first contact, however repulsive the alien intelligence appears to us. Probably the repulsion will be mutual, and it may be, besides intelligence, the only thing human and alien have in common. If contact occurs in space—particularly following some form of radio communication—it can be presumed that both sides welcome the meeting and have achieved sufficient maturity not to retain aggresive intentions. If contact occurs through aliens visiting Earth or vice versa there can be no certainty that this is not the advance guard of an invasion force, so friendly relations may be more difficult to establish. Uncertain intentions work the other way, too: can we be certain that an alien spaceship landing on Earth today would not be attacked by local inhabitants or fired on by anti-missile defence systems even if it acted in a perfectly friendly fashion? Alternatively, intelligent extraterrestrials may, for their own inscrutable reasons, ignore totally any humans who land on their planet. This may exacerbate the problem of recognising an alien intelligence on a planet which we wish to colonise or terra-form. The aliens may be identified as creatures of some sort by survey parties (or they may not) but if they persistently ignore humans the problem of classifying them as intelligent or otherwise will be a thorny one.

Undoubtedly the road to stable human–alien relations will be paved with misunderstandings. If both sides wish to com-municate it will be possible to achieve a certain basic level of dialogue via mathematics and science, but to put across abstract concepts (love, hate, envy, pride, etc) to a being whose civilisation, physiology and whole manner of thinking are totally different from one's own may not be possible. Both sides will appear irrational to the other, because the systems of logic will be different. For example, a remark which, when translated into English, becomes 'You look nice enough to eat' may be a compliment, a warning of attack by a hungry alien, or just conceivably an insult. Even without an excess of xenophobia, mankind is likely always to be very wary of intelligent aliens.

What will man and alien find to talk about? The possible options have been catalogued by S. Golomb under the cynical headings *help*, *buy*, *convert*, *negotiate*, *work*, *discuss*.[14] Some of these are self-explanatory, though *vacate* (we want a planet they are occupying or vice versa) and *work* (they look a good source of cheap labour to us or vice versa) are unduly aggres-sive. *Discuss* means that we share no common environment with them and thus can be no danger to one another. 'Only in such a case does the history of our species offer encouragement for the prospect of free mutual interchange of ideas, experi-ences and scientific theories,' says Mr Golomb. In fact this is not necessarily a complete list. Several science fiction authors have suggested that mankind—ever obsessed by the exotic and bizarre—will lose no time in establishing sexual relations with aliens.

The assimilation of alien culture is bound to have a pro-found effect upon humanity. On the surface there will be a few—perhaps many—fairly obvious changes brought about by the introduction of alien products and alien technology. It is difficult to predict the nature of trade items. Whatever the relative levels of scientific advance between mankind and a particular alien race it would be surprising if each had not developed a few areas of technological expertise which the other had never contemplated. (They might have developed matter transmission but not space travel, for example.) There is a danger not only that our culture may be altered beyond recognition but that the human race may wipe itself out by the inept handling of alien technology. Although there may be some basic goods such as drugs or foodstuffs which one race wishes to buy from the other, these will be few. A much more fruitful sphere of exchange will be in luxury goods. The more affluent members of mankind have always sought to emphasise their wealth by buying rare imported goods, and this is certain to continue. Alien gemstones, plants, *objets d'art* and trinkets —in fact almost anything unmistakably alien—will be in great demand, with prices rising to (as one might say) astronomical levels due to high freight costs and an excess of demand over supply.

As alien products become more commonplace on Earth and in the various orbiting and planetary colonies, and as alien methods and scientific ideas come to be taken for granted, so the theories and viewpoints and lifestyles of the alien race will come to occupy a niche in man's civilisation. Some aspects of our own culture will be ousted—lost for ever—while others will be altered or complemented. Those aspects of the alien's society which meet with public appeal will be welcomed, others ignored. However hesitant or ephemeral our contact with an alien race, something of them will rub off on to us. By way of an example, think of the way in which foreign cultures have left their mark on the English way of life, particularly through the medium of foreign additions to the English language. (But think, too, of the Tasmanians, a race of mankind which was wiped out within living memory by cultural contact with Europeans.) The assimilation of various aspects of alien culture will bring benefits, tragedies through misuse, a sense of wonder and a sense of disillusionment. But mankind will never quite be the same again. For better or worse the alien influence will have become a part of us.

Will future man ever manage to live in the same community as members of an alien race? Presumably there will come a time when diplomatic representatives are exchanged, when trade delegations or technical experts pay visits to each other's home planets. (Of course, there may be barriers to this, resulting from mutually incompatible planetary environments or deep distrust.) But when man is able, or at least willing, to live peacefully with aliens he will surely have rid himself of all bigotry and racial prejudice and will be demonstrating his maturity. There are many changes to be made first, but change is something the future will never be short of.

Interstellar Man

The process of leaving Earth in spaceships, bound for the stars, has been compared with a baby leaving the womb (and even with an orange being squeezed so that the starships are equated with pips—seeds of Earth). Just as a baby continues to develop in all respects after it has left the womb, so will man in space. Of course there will be cultural change; it may be either faster or slower among relatively small, isolated groups of colonists or space travellers from that on Earth, but it will be change of a different order—in different directions, for different reasons. With it will come philosophical change, a continual revision of all man's standards, ideals and ways of looking at life. This may not express itself overtly in the formulation of new philosophic doctrines or the founding of new religions (though both are possible) but it will colour man's approach to the universe at large. It will, of course, have been caused by man's exposure to the universe at large. Travelling across the abyss of space between stars and visiting alien worlds will have broadened man's perspective. These will be trancendental experiences. Contact with aliens and the physical results of exposure to different environments will produce further mental and physical changes.

Interstellar man will not be a new species—not at first—but he will have been altered by his experiences and will be better suited to colonial or space-borne life in the future. This difference in outlook will be passed on to children as part of the socialisation process. It is interstellar man who will journey across the galaxy. It is he who will thrive far away from Earth, he who will learn to live with other interstellar races.

In time interstellar man will come to outnumber all the stop-at-homes who have remained on Earth or in its immediate vicinity. He is the future of our race.

8 When Man Becomes Not-Man

*'The day will come when there will be no people, only thought.
And that will be life eternal . . . None of us now believe that all
this machinery of flesh and blood is necessary. It dies. It imprisons
us on this petty planet and forbids us to range through the stars.'*
G. B. Shaw *Back to Methuselah*

In less than a millon years, perhaps less than a hundred
thousand, *Homo sapiens* will have evolved naturally into a new
species. This is not speculation, but inevitability. Man is a
developing evolutionary line, a work in progress rather than
an over-specialised end product. Leaving aside for the moment
the effects of deliberate alteration of human genetic material
and the results of living elsewhere than on our own planet,
natural evolution is very gradually bringing about changes
in the human mind and body. We may not be able to identify
any of these changes within the next ten thousand years
(though some may begin to appear much sooner; when evolution does occur it can do so quite rapidly, at least in geological
terms) but we can be sure that they will come.

It seems likely that those parts of the human body which
are no longer necessary will atrophy and disappear. There is
no certainty involved here, but the most likely candidates
would seem to be the appendix, the smallest (outermost) toes,
all toenails, tonsils, wisdom teeth and most remaining body
hair (though not that in the armpit or genital regions—as
already mentioned—where it performs the sexual function
of absorbing and retaining the natural sexual scent). A small
adaptation which seems logical has been suggested by science
fiction writer Larry Niven. This is the human body's gradual
adjustment to a higher level of carbon dioxide in the air we
breathe, so that the present-day level would be insufficient to
trigger the autonomic nerves into causing a breath to be taken,
and a man from the more highly polluted Earth of 3000 AD
who managed to travel back to our time would faint because
his involuntary breathing mechanism would not operate.

Assuredly there will be no regression in the future, towards our remote ancestors such as *Australopithecus* or *Ramapithecus*; evolution is a one-way process.

The action of natural selection, which has ensured the survival of the fittest among all species, including man, ever since life appeared on earth, is now being thwarted—or, at least, is operating in a different manner upon humans. With the general availability of medical services today almost all babies survive to become adults and have children of their own. This includes those children who possess genetic defects resulting in deafness, blindness, haemophilia and imbecility. Whereas they would have died young (or, in some societies, would have been killed deliberately) they are now kept alive and allowed to pass on their bad genes to the following generation. But this will not automatically lead to the degeneration of the human race, generation by generation. The way in which natural selection operates today (and will probably continue to operate for a century or two at least) is by differential fertility. Instead of an even distribution of births throughout the world there is a skewed distribution, whether families are considered geographically or on the basis of income or education.

More children are born, per family, in the less developed countries of the world, and in all countries the poorer and less educated have more children, on average, than the richer or more educated. Or, to put it another way, 'genetically based ability and reproductive rate are today negatively correlated'.[1] The reasons for this state of affairs are obvious—notably knowledge of birth control (more widespread among the better-educated), custom (the expectancy of a high infant mortality rate even though this has been drastically cut) and the reluctance of many educated couples to start families in this uncertain present-day world. The long-term result will be, as Professor J. B. S. Haldane has observed, that the meek will inherit the Earth simply by being good at nothing except breeding.

Archetypes

In considering the more positive physical and mental changes, especially those of the far future, several millions of years ahead, one must proceed with care. This is the realm of science fiction and fantasy, where the majority of scientific predictors fear to tread. There are too many unquantifiable factors for any statistical extrapolations to be valid; one cannot imagine Herman Kahn ever writing a book entitled *The Next Two Hundred Million Years*. It is easy (as well as unduly sensational) to refer to supermen. The immediate public response is a mental picture of a creature with an enormous domed cranium and a wizened, tiny-legged body, rather like Dan Dare's arch-enemy, the Mekon, though without the green skin. *Homo megacephalus*, as he might be called, has become a cliché of future man even though he represents bad science and bad fiction alike. Such a creature could not evolve naturally because it could not be born. Anything more than a very marginal increase in skull diameter would make normal childbirth impossible, and a significant broadening of the female pelvis would be most unlikely to occur because this would have radical (and largely detrimental) effects upon strength, balance, posture and leg articulation, in addition to being aesthetically objectionable. There are at least three alternative means by which greatly increased skull size would be made possible, but none of these could occur by evolution—they are all artificial methods. The large-headed babies could be born by caesarian section or they could be developed by ectogenesis from the time of conception, in an artificial womb—both of which suggestions necessitate a continuing high degree of technology. The third method would be post-natal surgery to increase skull capacity (and brain size), which would not be an inheritable genetic change at all.

But this whole train of argument is based upon the false premise that future man will need more brain capacity within his cranium. As chapter six has shown, the human brain seems to possess tremendous unrealised potential. Portions of it are apparently unused or at least under-used. In any case, long before the brain becomes overfull and inadequate to cope with the extreme complexities of future life, electronic accessory brains will be available which will plug into the human brain, augmenting all its functions. (See chapter five.) Or it might be that the brain will be surgically removed and replaced by a more sophisticated artificial unit—though at such a stage the recipient's identity and essential humanity would be open to question. Once again it seems that the changes man makes to himself will come sooner and be more far-reaching than the effects of evolution.

Well, if the *Homo megacephalus* prediction must be thrown out as totally ridiculous, what about other popular conceptions of the superman of the future? The idea that, due to ubiquitous mechanical transport, man's legs will be unused and will gradually atrophy is as fatuous as the gigantic heads on tiny bodies archetype (and, indeed, often accompanies it). It was a byproduct of the upsurge of the automobile in the USA, which occurred contemporaneously with the upsurge of the science fiction pulp magazines, and it has remained a purely science-fictional notion, never seriously entertained by scientists. In fact, if mankind did begin to rely on machines heavily enough for a long enough period to allow the legs to atrophy it would be firm proof of man's decline; his extinction would soon follow. No, any evolutionary change will help man to coexist better with his environment and will never (unless that environment changes very rapidly) become a liability or a disadvantage. (It must not be forgotten, though, that future man will largely be controlling his environment.)

Juvenal, writing almost nineteen hundred years ago, recognised the need for a healthy mind in a healthy body, the point being that one cannot, in the long run, have one without the other. Modern scientific medicine has—perhaps to its own surprise—shown this to be true. Athletes need to discipline their minds in addition to training their bodies, while chess masters (to pick a sedentary form of competition almost at random) play better when they are physically fit. Hence one can expect future man's evolutionary advance to aid both his physical and mental states or, at least, that an advance in one state will not adversely affect the other.

An increase in physical size proceeding simultaneously with an increase in intelligence would seem likely. This is a fairly obvious prediction to make (indeed, several scientists have made it) since man's height has about doubled over the last twelve million years (since *Ramapithecus*) and cranial capacity has more than trebled. But it is too simplistic to expect trends of this kind to extend *ad infinitum* into the future. There are constraints to man's growth in body size which will prevent this from happening. For example, if over the next fourteen million years man slightly more than doubles his present height while retaining his present proportions he will stand thirteen feet tall. Or rather, he will lie thirteen feet long, because he will be unable to stand up without breaking his legs. This is because his weight will have increased tenfold while the cross-sectional area of his thigh bone will have increased only about four and a half times.[2] The answer to this is that if man is to achieve any considerable increase in size it must be accompanied by a more than proportional thickening and strengthening of his skeletal form—particularly the leg bones. It might be necessary for him to revert to a four-legged stance, moving about on very broad feet. (Think of the elephant.) But any such thickening will add yet more weight and will greatly increase man's clumsiness without affording him any obvious advantages, except the dubious one of being able to support a head with a larger cranial capacity, so that it would be a negative survival characteristic and evolution would not follow that path. Apart from anything else, the doubling of man's height would give rise to heart and lung problems soluble only by a complete redesigning of the human body into something not at all human. There is obviously an optimum size, which man has not yet reached (it may be seven or eight feet in height, with proportions unchanged) at which the extra weight does not become a drawback.[3] Similarly, there is scope for a modest increase in cranial capacity, though not much more than in proportion to the increase in body size. At the same time it must be remembered that cranial capacity is not everything. Neanderthal man, not noted for his intelligence, had a slightly larger cranial capacity than we have (about $1,500cm^3$ as compared to our $1,350cm^3$ on average). He died out.

At any rate, if man survives long enough on this planet to achieve a twenty-five per cent increase in height through natural evolution (over a period of two or three million years, perhaps) he is likely to change in other respects, too. The jaw, that important sorter-out of the men from the apes, will diminish in size and will contain smaller and probably fewer teeth. This is because the mouth is no longer used for grasping and tearing at food, as it always was until comparatively recently (perhaps the last twenty thousand years). The tongue, palate and larynx, though, are more likely to increase in size and become more perfectly adapted to rapid complex speech (unless telepathy becomes universal, in which case the larynx may well begin to atrophy). The nose will become increasingly truncated and nominal because the scenting of prey (or predator) has long been unnecessary, and even the function of the nostrils in warming air before it enters the body is being rendered redundant by the spread of central heating. The ears, too, have become less important and may gradually signify this by a reduction in size (or possibly an increase in number, depending upon the future development of systems of musical reproduction). Turning away from the face, it has been suggested by H. G. Wells (in a tongue-in-cheek article, 'The Man of the Year Million', first published during the 1890s) that the hand will become larger and more dexterous due to the increasingly subtle uses to which it must be put, and that the gastric system will wither away due to the artificial mastication and digestion of food, the resulting slop doubtless being injected or drip-fed. The former is a reasonable contention but the latter would require a consistently high level of technology over a very large number of centuries, with any breakdown of civilisation resulting in the extinction of the species by starvation.[4]

Like most of Wells' articles, he used its theme later in a science fiction novel. The novel in this instance was *The Time Machine*, but future men he portrays there—the Eloi and Morlocks of the year 802,701—are not at all like those in the article. It is clear that neither the childlike, almost fairy-like Eloi, who live useless lives in a kind of paradise, nor the repulsive, troglodytic Morlocks, who mind machines in the darkness and prey on the Eloi for meat, were intended as serious predictions of the future. Their inspiration is Marxian rather than Darwinian theory and they are intended as a sharp comment on the class divisions of late Victorian England—the idle rich and the disadvantaged workers. But in an earlier version of *The Time Machine*, 'The Chronic Argonauts' (written in 1888 but neither completed nor published except in an amateur journal), he describes a man of the future, Dr Nebogipfel, as having a phenomenally wide and high forehead, though otherwise appearing human.[5]

Yet *The Time Machine* does ask one question which is worth considering here. Why should there not be two or more differentiated species of future men in existence simultaneously? Some early species of man seem to have coexisted for periods of millions of years (see chapter one) so there is a precedent for future differentiation. The obvious way in which this may occur is in the case of human colonies in space or on other worlds, especially where there is no contact with Earth for many generations. (See chapter five.) On the face of it, it seems highly improbable that there will be a sufficient degree of geographical isolation in the future to allow differentiation to occur on Earth itself. Yet it may be that for religious, political or cultural reasons groups will cut themselves off via unusual habitats (sea-bed cities) or technological gimmicks (the impenetrable force-field) for long enough periods. It is difficult to believe that any such isolation will persist for tens of thousands of years, but the future is a long time.

Another factor is the long-term effect upon evolution of our experimentation with human DNA (see chapter seven). This surely will reach a peak in the twenty-first or twenty-second century and may leave behind it some extraordinary but true-breeding freaks of humanity. Thus there may, for many thousands of years to come, be a great variety of human types (unless all genetic packages are at some stage cleaned up by more genetic engineering). It could be that men with blue skin or green scales or snake-like hair will become a common sight. Even if it were to achieve nothing else for mankind, such variety would be certain to kill off racial discrimination, because nobody is going to object to a man with a black or brown skin when there are genetically altered people around who look far from human. Besides, to alter one's appearance, whether genetically, surgically or by chemically acting forms of make-up, will eventually be so cheap and easy that no inherited characteristics will be ineradicable. There will be fashions in bodily colour and form, which some will follow and others ignore. Perhaps black skin will be in vogue for a while, or transparent artificial hands, or feathers growing from the scalp. Whatever the imagination can come up with, future technology will be able to provide.

A third archetype of far future man is the cold, unemotional figure who has sacrificed all physical passions for increased mental ability (and mental stability). He is a solemn thinker, totally humourless, (a sad price to pay for enhanced mental attributes, for without humour the world would seem very dull and without emotion one could not even derive joy from one's triumphs of thought) who proceeds through life on a course set entirely by logic. Though he may coincide with *Homo megacephalus* he may alternatively be human in appearance—a tall stately person with a sour expression—though it is not his appearance which is important here; his greater mental abilities and unsmiling logical approach are the yardsticks by which he is measured. Often he may possess awesome mental powers. Like all archetypes, though, he is unconvincing as a norm of future man. It is possible to imagine one man like that running a country or a planet, with the rest of the population being held in mental bondage (though the setting-up of such a situation would be tricky), or else running around in the same frivolous, emotional way as we always have.

A type of far future where the background is important is the pastoral, sparsely populated one, based somewhat loosely on ancient Greece. The inhabitants, wandering around in white robes, tend to be of the cold, unemotional type, but are not always thus. W. H. Hudson's *A Crystal Age* is perhaps the most carefully developed example of this archetype; it will be examined at length later in this chapter. George Bernard Shaw's play *Back to Methuselah* has one of its parts set in such a future: in the year 31,920 'they have taken the agony from birth' and youths and maidens, all apparently seventeen years of age, spring fully formed from large, hard-shelled eggs. For four years they concern themselves with emotions and with unimportant physical things before their minds mature and they become serious, unsmiling adults.

But what if everybody had enormous mental power and an unemotional (and presumably unyielding) approach to life? The answer is that a classic situation would exist of 'too many chiefs and not enough Indians'. The outcome would be either all-out warfare or, if they had managed to abolish or re-channel violence, a kind of anarchistic *impasse* where each person did what he thought was the right and proper thing.[6] It is just possible, though, that there would be general agreement, that their minds would merge to form a greater, more powerful entity than its sum.

This greater entity, particularly where the number of individuals is small, is a gestalt. Where the numbers are very large it becomes effectively a hive society. Although hive members are normally represented as being of very low intelligence individually, like ant and bees, there is no reason why they should not be of superhuman intelligence provided that each is subservient to the concerted will of the whole. The hive society, as applied to future human cultures, is an intriguing possibility. A telepathic network would link all members all the time. Their thoughts and opinions would be individual, to encourage initiative and new ideas, but their actions would always coincide with the majority view and would always be for the greater good of the hive, even at the expense of one or more members. Any local deviation from the generally held opinion would be swamped by the weight of the majority, but its existence would have been noted by the totality of minds and it would be considered as an alternative in the future, possibly tempering the will of the majority. Obviously, in a hive of a million people there could not be total omniscience by each of all the others' thoughts and doings, though any deviation would stand out boldly. Although most of us would probably shrink from joining, unwilling to surrender up totally the privacy of our thoughts and most intimate actions to a million strangers, there is much to be said for such a society. Without doubt it would be egalitarian with no class or racial prejudice. It would also be the most efficient system possible, with a complete absence of any form of waste and without crime, though there would need to exist safeguards against the elimination of the original thinker, as well as some means of allowing informed opinion to carry more weight than uninformed opinion (unless it was possible for the majority to tap the mind of the expert in every instance). It is presumed that, due to variations in local conditions and local needs, a single hive covering the planet Earth would not be practicable, in which case inter-hive relations would need very careful handling to prevent conflicting interests from leading to hostilities. Although the hive society is such a logical extension of the telepathic society and is more logical than many other possibilities, it has received very little attention from either serious forecasters or science fiction writers. (It may indeed be a perfect example of Pierre Teilhard de Chardin's 'noosphere', but is hardly what he had in mind when developing the concept.)

Limited Predictions

So far this chapter has examined some of the broader aspects (and particularly the misconceptions) of mankind's physical and mental shape in what may be termed the medium long-term future—far enough ahead for natural evolution to have made *Homo sapiens* into 'something else' but not so far that man has yet attained his final fantastic shape (whatever that may be). It is fun to pick on certain lines of physical or mental development and suggest that this, that or the other trend will become more important than all the rest. This is the game played by many science fiction writers, who ask the question 'what if?' by extrapolating a single aspect of life or society (quite often an aspect which has some particular bearing on the period at which they are writing) while holding all other factors in stasis. Hence there are stories set several hundred or even a thousand years in the future in which everybody owns a private aircraft (the air traffic control problems would be prohibitive, but these are never mentioned), in which there is no natural vegetation left on Earth (but there is no provision for air renewal, either), in which a state of open warfare has existed for dozens or hundreds of years at a stretch (only likely if mankind has de-civilised itself by nuclear warfare and is back at the stage of fighting with chipped flints), in which there has been no scientific advance for hundreds of years (even if advances were not made generally available they would still occur and be used by the élite), and in which everybody needs to work for only three hours per week (most people would be unable to cope with so much leisure, besides which this would represent a vast under-utilisation of labour as a natural resource. In fairness to the writers concerned (and some are still hard at work, earning a living from this approach) there is frequently an element of social satire intended, sometimes as the *raison d'être* of the story and sometimes as no more than an occasional frill by which to vary the mood. At any rate, such references will date a work of fiction; many lessons can be learned from them, particularly lessons in how not to go about predicting a believable future.

Too often the men of the far future are not the product of careful thought but merely Americans of the 1940s or 1950s dressed in funny clothes and accompanied by anachronisms such as unconvincing banks of mechanical instruments and manual switches—the cockpit of a World War II aircraft seen through extrapolating spectacles. They prove themselves not to be future men by their contemporary hang-ups, by their 1940s American opinions on war, sex, politics and religion. All writers are, of course, constrained by their upbringing and environment. They tend to write about what they know, just changing the names and locales when they intend it to be science fiction. But it takes great inventive effort to work out the details of a convincing far future. Unless its primary intent is to satirise the present, science fiction of the future is best written without reference to the conventions, attitudes and institutions of the twentieth century. The reasons why so many authors ignore this is that it is easier to write and easier to read something which relates to the present—but this is not the best way of producing a prediction of the far future. There are many examples of novels in which man has spread out and occupied most of the galaxy (to the extent that Earth's name and location have been forgotten) but has somehow managed to remain the same. Among the best known of these is Isaac Asimov's *Foundation* trilogy, where humanity inhabits thousands of worlds without a bit of alienness or deviation in any way from the human values, family structure, motives, hopes or fears of 1940s America.

Very often a far future is presented to the reader by the 'stranger in a strange land' approach. A contemporary hero (or small group including a heroine; sometimes a ship or aircraft crew) is pitchforked into the far future, giving an excuse for the future's inhabitants to explain their world to him and for the reader to be given the benefit of his mid-twentieth-century reactions. Sometimes these men of the future, who tend to resemble one of the previously mentioned archetypes, will gravely show their visitor or visitors round, explaining that they have evolved from good old white Anglo-Saxon Protestant stock over the intervening million years or so. Not infrequently, though, the masters of the future are an unfriendly bunch who do their best to kill the temporally displaced hero, achieve carnal knowledge of his girlfriend, and so on. In these cases the WASP image has been replaced by a distinctly alien one: the future men have evolved from inscrutable orientals or cannibalistic blacks (as in Robert Heinlein's *Farnham's*

Freehold). Thus colour prejudice and poor scientific prediction go hand in hand.[7]

Equally questionable are those predictions of the remote future where man's shape has not altered. Although it will be possible for geneticists of the future to maintain man in his twentieth-century form, or to revert to this should changes occur, it seems highly unlikely that they would want to, or that particular men should wish to keep their shapes. *Homo sapiens*, though a handy form, is by no means perfect. There can be few people who have not, at some stage of their lives, wished for a slightly different physique, an improved constitution or more acute senses, and such things are just the start, the thin end of the wedge which leads to a major restructuring of body, mind and temperament. It seems most unlikely that future geneticists will be able to resist the temptation to play god; even legal strictures will not prevent some from building supermen. So when one finds a novel like Arthur C. Clarke's *The City and the Stars*, where the human form has apparently not altered at all over a period exceeding a thousand million years, one is sceptical. (A thousand million years ago, by comparison, the only life on Earth consisted of algae.)

It would be wrong to suggest that science fiction deals only with man evolved into superman or man unchanged. In a few cases man is replaced as lord of the world by some other species which evolves faster or farther. One such story is William Tenn's 'Null-P', in which a routine medical check-up reveals George Abnego as America's most average man. His averageness is taken up as a national symbol. Abnego becomes president and is renowned for never making a decision except by precedent. His calm placidity is adopted by the rest of the country and then by the whole world. All orginality and innovation are discouraged. With an Abnego as world president there is a gradual tendency for all humans to aim towards the mean in all things—with the result that the mean becomes depressed, particularly in the case of intelligence. The members of *Homo abnegus* regress for a quarter of a million years, until they are surpassed by a group of evolving dogs—Newfoundland retrievers. These begin to breed men for their ability to throw sticks, even causing new types of men to appear who are more specialised for the task, with longer arms. At length the retrievers develop machines which are even more efficient throwers of sticks, and man disappears altogether.

Although we cannot know the future, and so can neither promise that any particular event will happen nor be certain that it will not, there are certain considerations to be born in mind when attempting to predict the far future, in order to avoid making a fool of oneself. (And here the far future is taken to include everything beyond the twenty-second century, admittedly an arbitrary choice.)

These considerations are:

(i) No extrapolations are going to be valid. This is because trends will have plenty of opportunity to reverse themselves. Certain likelihoods exist but there are too many factors—some of which are currently unknown and unguessable—capable of intervening.

(ii) A greater part of today's advanced science will eventually be proved wrong. In some areas the proportion will be as high as ninety per cent. This indicates not the shortcomings of today's scientists but the relative infancy of many scientific disciplines.[8]

(iii) The future will be a very alien place and its inhabitants very alien people—even though they may look (beneath the evanescent excesses of fashion) exactly like us. This is really a *caveat* concerning the pace of social change. It is not impossible that change will gradually slow down to the rate found in pre-industrial centuries; highly improbable, but not impossible. Much more probable is that the pace of change will accelerate, with continual revolution affecting most institutions (in the widest sense) until the only thing one can count on to remain, day after day and year after year, is the condition of future shock. This is not to say that a time will not come when this trend reverses itself and eons pass without significant change, for it will. But by then life, and man, will already have become alien.

(iv) The future is big enough for anything to happen, and presupposing the survival of the human race (or its descendants) almost everything *will* happen. (This is so trite that many predictors of the future overlook it completely.)

(v) Assuming continuous scientific progress for several more centuries the only limits to man's powers and capabilities will be natural laws—and some of these will undoubtedly be shown to have been only special cases rather than universal laws. In other words, very little will eventually prove impossible.

The significance of those considerations is that man's future will be very complex and very strange. Our recorded history goes back over about 3,000 years and our industrialisation over about 200; just as a man from the year 1000 BC would not understand our culture and a craftsman from the late eighteenth century would not understand the means of manufacture, or even the purpose, of many of our artefacts, so would these aspects of our future—200 or 3,000 years ahead—elude us if we were to be shown them. How can we, then, hope to understand anything about our remote descendants, ten thousand or a million years removed from us?

To emphasise the point about very little eventually proving impossible, consider this list of 'impossibilities' from the point of view of a man living only a century ago: travel to the Moon, heart transplant surgery, instantaneous communication with any part of the world, programmable calculators for the price of a meal, an airborne weapon capable of destroying a city at a range of several thousand miles. Now, who would be rash enough to assert that all of the following, currently impossible, will still be impossible in a hundred years' time: faster-than-light travel, instantaneous matter transmission, time travel, personality and memory transfer from one body to another, widespread telepathic communication? But whichever of these do become fact they will at least be understandable; they will be accompanied by many other scientific achievements which would be as incomprehensible to us as that programmable calculator to the ordinary person of a century ago.[9]

But the important aspect of all this is, as Aldous Huxley says in his foreword to *Brave New World*, 'not the advancement of science as such; it is the advancement of science as it affects human individuals.' This final chapter, as with the book as a whole, is concerned with future man himself rather than with his scientific achievements or gadgets. On the other hand, if man's technological capacity becomes almost boundless there will be enormous repercussions upon society, so that even while he physically resembles the man of today future man will have aspirations, concerns and occupations which will set him apart from us. And the more unlike us future man becomes the more alien will be his application of all that boundless technological capacity, which will cause even greater changes in society, leading to even more feedback . . .

Writing in about 1930 on the future of leisure, C. E. M. Joad said:

> We have no right to judge the pursuits of the future by the tastes of the present; the amoeba would probably fail to enjoy a modern football match, while the delights of sitting in a bar, a theatre, the House of Commons or in church would probably leave our comparatively recent ancestor, the lemur, cold.

He goes on to suggest that future man perhaps should and will concern himself (in his leisure activities, at least) less with material things and more with the abstract (beauty, thought). With more than half the populations of western countries now spending (ie wasting) their evenings watching television it is evident that man's concern for the material world has, if anything, increased.

Environment

This is one of the most important factors of change; it will be both a cause and an effect in the increasing alienness of future man. The problems of overpopulation and pollution on Earth and of trying to live elsewhere than on the Earth have already been considered (chapters five, six and seven) but only in the short term. Longer-term solutions—to overpopulation in particular—all require technological ability which mankind does not yet possess but which should be within his capabilities by the time they have become urgent. All these solutions will entail considerable restructuring of the environment, a high degree of governmental control and extremely close international cooperation.

The great unknown at the centre of all this is the rate of population increase. If Herman Kahn's optimistic assumption in *The Next Two Hundred Years* is incorrect and the population growth rate fails to peak until, say, the year 2000; or if it fails to fall as rapidly as it rose; or if world population fails to level out for any other reason (religious, political, increased longevity, etc) before the end of the twenty-first century—then prompt international action will need to be taken to prevent widespread starvation. Producing eight or sixteen times as much food as at present would be an enormously difficult task. Even with more acreage ploughed up, more intensive methods, new crop strains and marine farms (for fish and seaweed, plus the harvesting of untouched food sources, such as krill) is would only be possible if there was international cooperation on an unprecedented scale. The solutions chosen will depend upon the distribution of the population increase. The USA, for example, could probably cope on its own with a tenfold increase in population over the next two to four hundred years by housing them in massive high-rise blocks. Industry and commerce could be partly integrated into these blocks and partly situated on floating marine platforms or in non-agricultural areas (mountains and deserts). In many less-developed countries the problem is more acute. In Latin America and Africa the current rate of increase will bring about a doubling of population every twenty-five years—a sixteenfold increase by 2080—which is roughly three times as fast as in the USA and Western Europe. There is no way in which the less-developed countries, acting alone, can cope with this rate of increase. The bulk of their populations live in villages and could not easily be transferred to high-rise apartments, while their agriculture is relatively inefficient and would be incapable of supporting (in most cases) even a doubling of population. This illustrates the heterogeneity of mankind.

Supposing that world population does continue to increase into the far future (and in the long term increased longevity seems a far more likely cause of this than any other factor), how will they all be housed and fed? Science journalist John Gribbin has suggested about twenty billion (about a fivefold increase on the present) as the maximum number who could inhabit the Earth by using conventional means.[10] However, if the population was totally homogenised by being rehoused in tower blocks a mile or two in height, and if *all* other land was to be used for agricultural production, then that maximum could be more than trebled to about seventy-five billion. (This is the background for Robert Silverberg's *The World Inside.*) Or course, this would necessitate the destruction of all present-day buildings, of all (or almost all) roads, and of most species of animal and plant life (with far-reaching effects on Earth's biosphere). An alternative would be to move the entire population into undersea cities (first suggested by W. D. Hay in 1881), or into cave cities which would fill mountain ranges, thus leaving the entire land surface free for crop production.

Although the idea of undersea cities may at first sight appear to be an elegant and logical solution to man's lack-of-space problems it seems doubtful whether it would meet with the acceptance of most people. Their stated reasons for objecting might vary considerably, from claustrophobia to an inability to swim, though the basis of it would be psychological. To return to the sea—the spawning ground of life itself—would seem like evolutionary regression, like a return to the womb. 'In my beginning is my end'— as T. S. Eliot put it in 'East Coker'. But most people would not accept this, preferring either the retention of the status quo or progress. Those in favour of undersea life would try to sell the idea as the conquest of a new frontier; the objectors would view it as an ignominious retreat. While frontiers are popular and give a *raison d'être* to life, the real frontier of man is space. Other planets and other solar systems are frontiers. The sea is not. Besides, the bulk of mankind would never again get the chance to see the stars; and the stars are an important symbol of hope and potential conquest.

A final solution (suggested by Professor John Fremlin of Birmingham University) is to roof in the entire planet, so that it would become, in effect, a single tower block, as high as was necessary (perhaps several miles) with a ground area of 197 million square miles (Earth's land and sea area together). This would not need to be built up from the ground, but could be constructed in orbit and lowered into place. Air pressure would support it above the ground. Probably it would need to be constructed of material of extraterrestrial origin, and the size and complexity of the project seems daunting at this time (not least the problem of what to do with Earth's burgeoning billions while assembly is taking place), but there would be no need for anything of this nature within the next five hundred years, and once built it would house several hundred billions. Food would need to be either artificially produced or imported from extraterrestrial sources.

Parallel developments will be the construction of living space in Earth orbit. Initially this will consist of clusters of colonies orbiting the Earth. (See chapter seven.)

The logical extension of this process of building orbiting space colonies is the construction of a Dyson sphere. Named after Professor F. J. Dyson, who first suggested it, this consists of an almost continuous sphere so vast that it encloses *every-*

thing within the Earth's solar orbit; in other words it is a hollow construction 186 million miles in diameter with the Sun at its centre. An ultra-lightweight structure of this size would be useful only for gathering up all the Sun's energy output (instead of the one part in 500 million which is all that is naturally received by the Earth). A more sturdy 'sphere' consisting of millions of separate planets and planetoids would provide potential living space equal to a million or so Earths. The material for such a project would have to come from elsewhere in the Solar System—partly from the disassembly of the planet Jupiter and the relocation of as much as possible of its mass in Earth's solar orbit. Although it sounds as fantastic as anything that ever appeared in the science fiction pulp magazines, this seems to be a perfectly feasible idea and of great benefit to mankind, except that we are unlikely to possess sufficient technical capacity to carry it out for a thousand years or more.

The effects of such technological achievements upon mankind will be threefold. Firstly, the possession of sufficient power to take Jupiter apart will confer immense responsibilities (and possibly temptations) upon those who wield it. This same power could be used to destroy the Earth, or at least as a bargaining counter to obtain whatever its possessor wanted, whether personal gain or some political end. (Because many branches of future technology will be applicable as weapons if their possessors are sufficiently daring or insane it is possible that this type of blackmail will be attempted. While the human race might be able to adjust quite easily to the autarchy of a 'Solar Emperor' who was formerly a technician involved with the demolition of Jupiter, most would not be around to adjust to the aftermath of an uncontrolled fusion reaction on or in the close vicinity of Earth.) Secondly, the provision of almost unlimited living space (and ready supplies of almost unlimited solar energy) by some form of Dyson sphere would bring profound changes in the way mankind looked at life. There might, indeed, be a renunciation of all forms of birth control and an unlimited population explosion. Certainly human culture and outlook could not remain unchanged while habitat changes of this nature occurred. People living in a totally built-over Earth would grow used to being enclosed. Those born in an O'Neill cylinder millions of miles from Earth would never feel or be quite like those born on Earth. Thirdly, the solving of technical problems associated with a Dyson sphere project (or even an O'Neill cities-in-space project) would provide spin-offs applicable to everyday life, in the same manner as the Apollo programme did—and perhaps some of these will have the same world-shaking effect as non-stick frying-pan coatings.

Any human culture which has utilised atomic power for, say, two thousand years, which is able to break down and reassemble planetary masses, which has perhaps half its members living elsewhere than on the Earth, would seem alien to us. Along with these capabilities they will have developed many others, including one or two from that 'impossible' list a few pages ago. Space travel will be cheap and commonplace —like transatlantic jet travel today—though there may be no demand for it; man's approach to life and his scale of values will be different from our own. As the Nobel Prize winner Dr P. B. Medawar has said, 'One of the lessons of history is that everything one can imagine possible will be done, if it is thought desirable; what we cannot predict is what people are going to think desirable.'[11] There may well be faster-than-light travel or matter transmission, bringing the other planets of the Solar System within easy reach. Energy, whether from solar power, atomic fusion or some source as yet undiscovered, will be abundant. The totality of human knowledge will be readily available to anyone, providing they know what they want and clearly enunciate the correct code within hearing of their (presumably portable) computer terminal. Every aspect of the environment will be under man's tight control. This is not to suggest that there will be no problems. On the contrary, life will be astonishingly complex, far more so than it is today. People will be able to change their faces and physiques as frequently as we now buy a new suit of clothes (assuming they can afford to), and they will live lives several times longer than ours, unless prevented by legislation. Some of them will possess mental powers undreamt of by today's foremost yogis. In short they will have more powers than the ancient Greeks ascribed to their gods. With any luck they will have rechannelled their aggressive instincts. If we could meet them we should not understand them. They might or might not appear human to us, depending upon the fashion that month, but we would be unable to communicate satisfactorily. Even setting aside the language barrier (for in a thousand years' time they will have the means of getting round any language barrier) little they said would have any meaning for us and little we said would be of any interest to them. Imagine the difficulties of trying to hold a conversation with a Roman from the time of Julius Caesar; the differences between us and the man of two thousand years' time will be far greater because more changes will have taken place.

Three Notable Predictions

As long as science and technology continue to advance there will be increasing change. (Even if there is a pause, perhaps for religious reasons, or a regression due to war, it is likely that the accumulated difference between our time and any particular point in the future will continue to grow; regression to a facsimile of medieval society is a common fictional theme but only a remote possibility in fact.) As the degree of alienness of future man from just the year 4000 AD would make communication and mutual understanding very difficult, so the increased alienness by the year 10,000 or 100,000 would make it impossible. The beings which we would be trying to understand would not be men, in the sense of *Homo sapiens sapiens* from 1980, though they would probably still be *Homo sapiens*. The corollary of this is that most fictional forecasts of far future man are illogical. Even the best, which have taken into consideration a great many avenues of change, have underestimated the swiftness of social change and technological advance, thus reducing the degree of alienness.[12] Despite this almost universal failing it is worth examining in some detail the far future portrayed in three novels. Besides being among the most interesting and successful of their type they are widely separated in terms of the date of first publication, scope and treatment.

A Crystal Age by W. H. Hudson is a pastoral utopia which first appeared anonymously in 1887. It is among the earliest of novels to embody the ideas of Darwin and is debatably the first to portray an evolved future man.[13] The scene is a sparsely populated world more than ten thousand years after an unspecified catastrophe. Various oblique references to the madness of men's minds preying on their bodies and to a 'sort of mighty Savonarola bonfire' suggest either divine intervention or else a violent reaction by church militants, aimed at cleansing the world of those who 'hoped by knowledge to gain absolute dominion over nature' and of all their works. The only survivors—'a small remnant', 'men of an humble mind' —have spread across the Earth, establishing a series of widely scattered houses where they live in extended family groups which are normal to them but odd to us and to Smith, our narrator, the late Victorian stranger who serendipitously finds this strange land. Rather like Rip Van Winkle, he oversleeps, waking to find almost everything changed. But this is only a convenient device—a one-way time machine—for bringing present and future together; the fact that these people of the year 12,000 or so speak in perfect Victorian English is another such device. Not that this shared language makes it easy for Smith to understand his hosts, for they have never heard of any of the cities, countries or great men whose names are so familiar to him, while their philosophies are for the most part antithetical to his own.

Smith is a young man of twenty-one, of good class and education, and rather brash. Almost at once he falls in love with Yoletta, the beautiful daughter of the head of this household. She appears to respond, but in that society all love is of a brotherly, sisterly kind and is freely given. The only marriage or sexual contact is between the Mother and father (note the upper-case, lower-case distinction, for this is a matriarchy) of the house. The father is obviously selected as the fittest to sire the next generation, and he chooses from the daughters of the house one whose 'brighter excellence' makes her most suitable to be the Mother. This system of eugenics has, over the centuries, led to great improvements in the race, most startling of which is their apparent youthfulness. The father of this house is white-bearded but sprightly and imposing; he is almost two hundred years old. Yoletta appears to be still in her teens ('a fine graceful girl about fourteen years old' is how Smith first describes her) and when she tells him that she is thirty-one our Victorian protagonist is scornfully unbelieving. These future men have also improved stamina, eyesight and voice control, but it is their spiritual qualities which are most alien to us. They possess a 'crystal purity of heart' and are placid by nature. Yet they demand the very highest standards from the members of their society: any favour—such as feeding or clothing a visitor—must be repaid by much hard work, and their penalties for minor infringements seem harsh. With them illness, if preventable, is a crime which must be punished (though this may be no more than an intentional satire by Hudson on Samuel Butler's *Erewhon*, in which crime is an illness).

This future civilisation is nicely alien and has a permanence which aids its credibility. Everything it produces—clothes, artwork, buildings—is made to last far longer than its late Victorian equivalent. This, together with the personal longevity and the rigidity of codes of conduct, lends an impression of stasis. Yet it is clearly a dynamic society in the long term because of its assumption of Darwinian evolution. Not only is these people's eugenics programme improving their own bodies but they are also exercising similar techniques in the case of animals. Their dogs and horses are very intelligent—perhaps as much so as the dog Sirius in Olaf Stapledon's novel of that name—and are able to carry out precise orders with great exactness but seem incapable of direct communication.

That mention of Stapledon leads neatly to his novel *Last and First Men*, first published in 1930, which is arguably the most important book ever written about the future. One critic has described it as 'probably the only fully developed evolutionary utopia, and . . . by far the most ambitious and sustained attempt to create an "evolutionary bible" '.[14] Its scope is astonishingly vast—an ever-accelerating future history of the human race right up to its extinction almost two billion years from now, as told by a member of the Last Men, the final form of civilised humanity. The most that there is room for here is a brief summary of the more crucial twists in man's development, together with descriptions of some of those races of men (seventeen in all) which follow *Homo sapiens*.

An Americanised world state founded in the twenty-third century survives for some four thousand years, becoming slowly more regimented and more rigidly stratified. A chronic power shortage leads to psychological depression and a breakdown of law and order. The result is descent into a new dark age of semi-barbarism which persists for 100,000 years (too long a period to be believable). At length civilisation re-emerges in Patagonia, which now enjoys a sub-tropical climate and is connected to Antarctica by a new continent extending up into what was the Atlantic Ocean. The Patagonians are still basic-ally First Men (Stapledon's name for us) though very short-lived; they are middle-aged by fifteen. Yet they spread across the world, regaining the former high level of science and technology. After half a millennium of searching they discover the secret of unlimited atomic power. Their society is based on ability but its stratifications harden; the offspring of the less able are almost inevitably less able themselves; mobility ceases between the élite and worker classes. Eventually there is a worker revolt. An atomic power unit is exploded by them and the succeeding chain reaction destroys their whole civilisation. All are killed—'burnt, roasted or suffocated'.

That is, 'all but thirty-five, who happen to be in the neigh-bourhood of the North Pole'. Stapledon's melodramatic preci-sion is at times comical. Habitually he focuses down on to a few individuals for half a chapter, only to skip ahead by a thousand or a million years in the very next sentence. These survivors degenerate but after ten million years their descend-ants have become the Second Men—much taller and sturdier, with greater than proportionate cranial capacities and large 'but finely moulded' hands. They lack appendixes and tonsils, have joined-up toes and live to about two hundred years. Despite their physical and mental advantages they are slow to develop and pass through several cycles of advancement and decline over a period of about a quarter of a million years. (Once again Stapledon's timespan is suspiciously long; perhaps he felt that this would be more credible to his readers, but the reverse is true; too often he seems to have been at a loss as to how to fill the enormous time period between First Men and Last and has resorted to adding excessive noughts to the pass-age of years, almost at random.)

Nevertheless, his Second Men are a logical development and show an alien temperament. Their civilisation is plagued by invasions of cloud-intelligences from the planet Mars, and only after an enormously protracted struggle lasting over 30,000 years are the invaders wiped out by an artificial virus which almost exterminates the Second Men, too. (The super-intelligent Second Men never develop space travel; perhaps

Stapledon never thought of it.) For the next thirty million years
the Second Men stagnate, not progressing and not even seem-
ing to change, At the end of this time some of them develop
relatively quickly into the Third Men.

The Third Men are only half the height of their prede-
cessors, with massive ears and large six-fingered hands. They
raise music to the status of a religion and are skilled at the
biological control of other animals. This ability leads them
finally to create the Great Brains (who are the Fourth Men).
Developed from normal foetuses, these creatures have vast
brains many feet across but otherwise retain only their hands,
the rest of their bodies being vestigal. Their senses are a combination of natural and artificial organs; they are practically
immortal. Gradually they learn all the secrets of the universe
and become the masters of the Third Men, but discovering
their own limitations—the lack of emotions and human values
—they design a successor race for themselves, combining the
best of everything that has gone before.

The resulting Fifth Men are 'more than twice as tall as the
First Men' with muscles and bones of new, stronger materials.
The basic human shape has been retained, though with larger
brains and six-fingered hands (plus an extra tiny pair of fingers
and thumb on the sixth finger, for fine work). A form of
telepathy is also possessed. They are at first subject to the
tyranny of the Great Brains; there is war between them, and
the Fifth Men are triumphant, going on to found a very
advanced civilisation which endures for millions of years and
fulfils their creators' greatest expectations. Discovering that the
Moon's orbit is beginning to swing in towards the Earth, with
which it will collide in about ten million years, they begin to
plan ahead by searching for another planet of the Solar
System on which to live. (Stapledon fails to consider other
solutions which seem obvious to us, fifty years on, such as the
repositioning or disintegration of the Moon, the construction
of space cities, or the search for Earth-type planets in other
solar systems. Ten million years is an awfully long time in
which to prepare for anything.)

Venus is chosen and partly terraformed, but as its only
land surface proves to be a chain of relatively small islands
the numbers of the Fifth Men are allowed to diminish (over
the centuries) by a factor of a hundred so that there will be

room. But the Fifth Men are never happy on Venus. Due to the climate and to various diseases and a chronic racial guilt feeling they begin to deteriorate. After some millions of years variations appear including seal-like submen and a barbarous human type—the Sixth Men. These have a long (two hundred million years) and varied existence upon the islands and emerging continents of Venus, with civilisations appearing and vanishing without reaching any great heights. Their one lasting achievement is in designing and breeding the Seventh Men, who are pygmy flying men. (It should be made clear that by this point Stapledon's future history has accelerated to an undetailed gabble, a hundred million years passing with each page.) They possess leathery membranes like bats and are lightweight and streamlined. Bothering little with science or anything material, they enjoy a carefree life in the sky for a hundred million years. At length it is the non-flying cripples of their race who develop the sciences and cause progress to be resumed.

The Eighth Men appear—physically more substantial than the flying men—but whether they occur naturally or are laboratory products the author does not say. They predict an astronomical collision between the Sun and a gas cloud and realise that the only escape is an outward migration to the planet Neptune. (The more remote Pluto was discovered in February 1930, about five months before the first edition of *Last and First Men* appeared.) To this end a new species is bred capable of surviving there—the dwarfish Ninth Men. These do survive but only by degenerating to beasthood. Over the following eight hundred million years another nine types of man succeed each other on remote Neptune, though few of them resemble *Homo sapiens*. Throughout cycles of achievement and collapse there is a trend towards spiritual fulfilment.

The Last Men—the Eighteenth Men—are a sturdy species but extremely variable. Greatly advanced scientifically and philosophically, they possess telepathy and a group mind facility, and they are virtually immortal. Just as all good things must come to an end, though, so they know that they are the Last Men because they will soon be consumed by a kind of supernova from which they are powerless to escape. They feel proud to have lived rather than sorry to die. Although limited in some respects, this book still retains its grandeur after half a century. If Stapledon had cared to borrow ideas from the science fiction pulp magazines of that time—ideas such as time travel, undersea cities, planet-smashing and faster-than-light travel—he could have increased credibility at several points. Yet he was probably as ignorant of the pulps as their readers were of him, and certainly he was no scientist; It was the philosophy of future man which interested him, not the science.

Nor is the last of our three novels the work of a scientist. It has been strongly criticised on scientific grounds[15] but remains the best novel to date of a dying Earth. This is Brian W. Aldiss's *Hothouse*, from 1962, which is better served by its US titling, *The Long Afternoon of Earth*. It is an adventure story set against the vivid backcloth of an Earth teeming with evolved plant life, much of it ambulatory and dangerous to the few remaining animals. This is 'the long age of the vegetable', two billion years in the future. Man still exists but is diminished in size (to little more than a foot high), in numbers (to a few scattered bands) and in intelligence. For the most part his shape remains human, though under certain circumstances a winged form develops.

Earth's rotation has slowed so that it has one face always towards the Sun. This hemisphere's land masses are covered by forest—mostly vast banyan trees which can span a continent—in which the small humans live their brief, precarious lives, many falling to vegetable or insect predators before reaching maturity. They live in and on the trees, never descending to the forest floor and only rarely venturing up to the strange world of the 'tips' (the treetops).

The Moon, too, has ceased rotating and has receded to a Trojan position in Earth's solar orbit. But members of a curious whale-sized species, the traversers (presumably of animal extraction), travel regularly between the Earth and Moon, pulling themselves along the enormous silken strands they spin. It is a custom of the remaining humans that when they begin to feel old they 'go to heaven' by sealing themselves inside the large airtight seed pods of a particular plant, which is then attached by friends to the lowest part of the web and adheres to the traversers—just like a burr to a dog's coat—when they visit the tips. These pods are carried across the void to the Moon, which now has a breathable atmosphere. The combination of chemicals inside the pod and hard radiation out in space causes the human inside the pod to develop wings —like a caterpillar inside its chrysalis—and he emerges as a flying man.

The author lets it be known that this far future Earth is soon coming to an end. It is in a winding-down phase; nature is devolving; the differences between animal and vegetable, and between species, are blurring. This may not be in accordance with evolutionary theories, but it never claims to be so. It is one man's personal, emotional view of Earth's last era, of man's final form, and as such is just another prediction, no less valid than those of Wells or Stapledon.

The Final Shape

The final topic of this final chapter is a swift glance at that least scientific, most far-reaching predictive area of all—the final shape of future man. What will man be like after he has spent millions of years exploring all that science has to offer, after he has remade his mind and body, after he has roamed the galaxy? Brian Aldiss's tiny forest dwellers are perhaps too human in their reactions and outlook. Olaf Stapledon's Last Men, for all their alienness, seem too disappointingly impotent in the face of oblivion, considering their mastery of science. The suggestion by H. G. Wells of a large-headed mankind which retains only hands out of all its bodily parts, and which plunges and floats in a basin of amber nutritive fluid, is sufficiently off-beat to make one pause for thought.[16] Later on in that article he says:

> And so at last comes a vision of earthly cherubim, hopping heads, great unemotional intelligence, and little hearts, fighting together perforce and fiercely against the cold that grips them tighter and tighter. For the world is cooling—slowly and inevitably it grows colder as the years roll by.

And one realises that this is not intended as a serious prediction at all but as a piece of tongue-in-cheek sentimentality by a twenty-six-year-old journalist aimed at the readers of a weekly newspaper.

It is probably safe to assume that if mankind survives and

continues advancing scientifically for another million years no single factor—be it an astronomical disaster or a clash with an alien race—will completely exterminate him. Part of the reason will be man's interstellar distribution, part his perfection of technological defence systems, and part his own mental and physical power. In the long term the act of eating will prove a hindrance and will be replaced by the direct absorption of energy, perhaps in an electrical form, derived from a solar or nuclear source. (The pleasure obtained from eating food may well be retained, though, by means of an electrode implanted in the brain or through self-hypnosis.) This will be a step towards the elimination of the physical body, leaving man as a sphere of force, able to travel across the galaxy—or even the universe—at will. In this form he will presumably be invulnerable (and immortal) since he will have no material needs. But it will be important for him to retain the ability to manipulate physical things (by electrical energy or telekinesis) so that he can have almost unlimited power over the natural world. If one pursues future man to 'the limit of imagination' as Northrop Frye does, one may imagine 'a universe entirely possessed and occupied by human life, a city of which the stars are suburbs'.[17] To assume anything less than this as a final form of mankind is to do a disservice to the inventiveness of our remote descendants and also to the power of evolution.

If this suggestion of an enormously powerful non-material being seems rather godlike, this is no coincidence. It could be that the idea of man being made in God's image refers to man's final shape rather than to his present one. In any case, a non-material body coupled with enormous powers seems a suitable shape for man as he makes himself master of the universe.

Only time will tell.

Notes

Introduction pp 7–11

1 See *The Next 200 Years* by Kahn, Brown and Martel, where chapter IV gives ample evidence that improved location techniques have led to large increases in known reserves of most minerals since 1950—see their Table 8. They also make the point that it is uneconomic for mineral companies to invest in exploration for new reserves until only two decades' worth of known reserves remain.

2 Except for fossil fuels few minerals are destroyed by usage. In some cases they can be recovered or reconstituted easily and reused, though in most cases they are thinly spread and recovery is prohibitively expensive.

3 In fact only the literate end of science fiction has managed to escape from this image. The Buck Rogers/Flash Gordon tradition—especially fast-moving adventure on other worlds or in other times involving spaceships, aliens, ray guns and a lot of dubious gadgetry—is being perpetuated by films (and books) like *Star Wars*.

4 Alvin Toffler makes this last point in a brief essay in *Science Fiction At Large* edited by Peter Nicholls.

Chapter One pp 12–28

1 Such a categorical statement as this may well bring on apoplexy in many of the world's leading cosmologists. There are almost as many hypotheses for the origins of the Solar System as there are specialists on the subject, and they agree on remarkably few details, except that the part-formed Sun gained, by the process of accretion, much of the material of which the planets are now composed, and that planet formation was completed in only a few thousand years. Most of the evidence connected with the creation of planets is open to more than one interpretation, and some of it (but which elements?) must be ignored as irrelevant. The old idea of a close encounter between the Sun and a passing star causing a huge linking filament of hot gas to be emitted by the Sun, which condensed to form the planets, has been discredited and is no longer current. Generally speaking, all present theorists may be classified as 'dustmen' or 'electricians'. This depends upon whether they accept the condensation of matter into planets to

be entirely the result of gravitational attraction or whether they postulate the ionisation of particles, forming plasma, and then, under correct conditions of temperature and pressure, the direct formation of crystals from the plasma, which coagulate and accrete into planets. For the current position see 'Cosmogony Now' by Jon Davies in *New Science in the Solar System* edited by Peter Stubbs.

2 The specific gravity of the Earth as a whole is 5·417, but the specific gravity of its crust is only 2·7 and that of the central nickel-iron mass is thought to be 16.

3 It is notable that Charles Darwin was unwilling to commit himself on the subject of the origin of life.

4 In *Diseases From Space*

5 A late Cretaceous paramomyid, *Purgatorius ceratops*, seventy-five million years old, is the earliest suggested pro-primate. *Human Evolution* by B. A. Wood.

6 G. H. R. von Koenigswald in *Anthrop Pap Amer Mus Nat Hist* 43, 294–325, quoted in Wood, *Human Evolution*.

7 *Not From The Apes*.

8 J. T. Robinson, *Early Hominid Posture and Locomotion*.

9 For example, M. H. Wolpoff, *Amer Anthrop* 70, 477–93.

10 *Human Evolution*, p50.

11 Observed by Dr Kurten in *Not From The Apes*, p134.

12 *The Beginning Was the End*.

13 *Not From The Apes*, p118.

14 *Journal of Human Evolution* 5, 488–95, quoted in Wood, *Human Evolution*.

15 *Future Shock*, chapter 1.

16 Dr Jack Eddy of the Smithsonian Observatory, Mass, has deduced that the Sun is shrinking by about ten kilometres per annum—*New Scientist* 21 June 1979. It is not known whether this is a long-term trend or merely a small fluctuation which will reverse itself. Earth's ice ages may be explainable in this manner.

Chapter Two pp 29–37

1 Not Darwin's own phrase, though it suits his theory beautifully, it was coined by the philosopher Herbert Spencer in 1867.

2 Brian Stableford, 'The Marriage of Science and Fiction' in *Encyclopaedia of Science Fiction* edited by Robert Holdstock.

3 This calculation is sometimes ascribed to Archbishop Ussher and, in any case, different authorities give different precise dates. Could it possibly be that they were not, after all, certain about it?

4 *For Her Own Good: 150 Years of the Experts' Advice to Women* by Barbara Ehrenreich and Deidre English.
5 See Brian W. Aldiss, *Billion Year Spree*, chapter 4.
6 According to Professor I. F. Clarke's *The Tale of the Future* 2nd ed (1972) there were twenty books set in the future published in Britain from 1801 to 1859, and only seven altogether before that. From 1860 to 1900, by contrast, there were 230.
7 *Pilgrims Through Space and Time*, chapter 4.
8 Bernard Bergonzi, *The Early H. G. Wells*, chapter IV.
9 *The War of the Worlds*, book two, chapter 2.

Chapter Three pp 38–63

1 A few of the many examples of such utopias which include immortality, or at least longevity, are Thomasso Campanella's *The City of the Sun* (1623), Francis Bacon's *New Atlantis* (1627), W. H. Hudson's *A Crystal Age* (1887) and William Morris's *News from Nowhere* (1890).
2 *Man and His Future* edited by Gordon Wolstenholme.
3 DNA is deoxyribonucleic acid, large, highly complex molecules of nucleic acids which exist at the centres of cells. DNA is divided into genes (carrying blueprint information of the individual) and two strands of DNA combine to form chromosomes.
4 Information from a BBC TV *Tomorrow's World* programme, 16 November 1978.
5 See *New Scientist* 9 March 1978, p659.
6 Information from a BBC TV *Horizon* programme, 2 April 1979.
7 Ibid.
8 This constraint may be sidestepped if it becomes possible to make a recording of the total personality and memories of a human brain. Such a recording could either be stored and accessed electronically or it could be inserted, perhaps, into the (empty) brain of a newly created clone.
9 There are many fictional accounts of disembodied brains. Best known are Curt Siodmak's *Donovan's Brain* and Anne McCaffrey's *The Ship Who Sang*.

Chapter Four pp 64–86

1 See *New Scientist* 15 March 1979.
2 There are horrifying accounts of field surgeons, from the time of the Franco–Prussian war of 1870, who, when faced with casualties suffering from grievous head injuries which left the

brain exposed, attempted to discover whether any part of the brain was damaged by the use of a needle or an electric current. Apparently this was applied at random and if no part of the body moved in response that area of brain was regarded as dead and cut away with a scalpel.

3 *The Reach of the Mind.*

4 *ESP—A Scientific Evaluation.*

5 The clairvoyants of Victorian times often made their living by bringing supposed messages from deceased persons to their rich and sorrowful relatives, though the element of precognition was rarely present. Sometimes necromancy is presented as a separate category.

6 There is no room here to describe any particular test in detail or to describe the doubts, but several books including Professor Hansell's *ESP—A Scientific Evaluation* provide careful accounts.

7 It seems that Czech researchers have reportedly broken through the ESP barrier by assuming that there has always been a very high noise level on the telepathic waveband; by using a computer to suppress this they have achieved reliable telepathic communication. It sounds hopeful, but . . .

8 *British Medical Journal* 9 December 1978.

9 'The Brains Behind the Operation' by Ed Harriman, *New Scientist* 21 June 1979.

Chapter Five pp 87–114

1 This section and the two which follow it owe much to *Future Shock* by Alvin Toffler, one of the few books which does consider the human factor in future society. Although it is not primarily predictive (it analyses the current problems of society and suggests solutions but does not attempt to predict how society will look in a century or two) and concentrates on western society, it remains an important work which should be read by all those who hope to survive in tomorrow's world.

2 But many firms do practise under-engineering to the extent that a product will begin to fall apart soon after its guarantee period has expired. Also, cosmetic changes and heavy advertising are used to persuade consumers that this year's model is different from last.

3 *Future Shock*, chapter 15.

4 Figures given by BBC radio news, 14 June 1979.

5 For about twenty years the French-based Club Mediterrané has been offering 'get away from it all' holidays in grass huts

situated on exotic beaches, where there are few modern conveniences and formal dress is a swimming costume. Despite high prices the response has always been good.

6   Alvin Toffler reports that a seventy-seven-year-old man turned up at one of his classes on the Sociology of the Future wanting to know about the future. If all mankind had as much spirit as that there would be less chance of future shock, and the future would be a better place.

7   'The Still Small Voice Inside' in *Pulsar 1* edited by George Hay.

8   Ibid.

9   Ibid.

Chapter Six pp 115–138

1   In fact this event will probably be celebrated a year early by many people. It seems to be a popular misconception that the millennium will have changed as soon as it becomes necessary to put a '2' rather than a 1' at the beginning of the year number —at the beginning of the year 2000 rather than, as correct, at the beginning of 2001.

2   Much more detail on this, together with statistical examples of the chronic 'shortage' of petroleum in the USA, is to be found in *The Next 200 Years*, chapter IV.

3   This is in contrast to *primary* economic activities, which consist of basic food production—agriculture, fishing, trapping, etc—*secondary*, which are industrial pursuits, and *tertiary*, which are the service industry support for secondary activities. At present the industrialised nations have just shifted from a majority of secondary activities to a majority of tertiary ones. In the LDCs a very high proportion of the populations are still concerned with primary activities.

4   But this is, of course, just another extrapolation of a trend. One can obtain amazingly ridiculous results that way. For example, a three per cent per annum growth in the world's energy consumption would, at the end of 350 years, mean enough heat being liberated to make the oceans boil. This is quoted in chapter VII of *The Next 200 Years* by Kahn, Brown and Martel. The most absurd extrapolation of all, calculated by Fred Hoyle and quoted by Walter Sullivan in *We Are Not Alone*, is that if the present rate of increase in the human population continues the total mass of humanity will, within 5,000 years, exceed the mass of all planets, stars and galaxies visible through Mount Palomar's 200 inch telescope.

5   Certainly there is something of a world petrol shortage at

the time of writing—June 1979—which has been the result of power supply levels from Iran since the overthrow of the Shah's regime and the higher prices charged by some other producers. There is not a true lack of supplies.

6   There is a masterly fictional treatment of a Malthusian near future, John Brunner's *The Sheep Look Up*, a sufficiently convincing novel to make frightening reading.

7   While solar, wind and wave power can easily be converted to electrical energy, this is not very suitable for cars and, in particular aircraft. Liquid hydrogen (LH_2) is being developed as the new petrol substitute for all motorised transport. The big advantage is that hydrogen can be obtained from seawater. Prototype road vehicles are already in operation. Supersonic aircraft could be using it as a fuel by 1986.

8   And just to prove the point, Herman Kahn has thought about it sufficiently to produce three books dealing with it: *On Thermonuclear Warfare*, *Thinking About the Unthinkable* and *On Escalation*.

9   Mordecai Roshwald's novel, *A Small Armageddon*, explores this possibility to its logical conclusions.

10   BBC TV programme *Wildlife on One*, 21 June 1979.

Chapter Seven pp 139–164

1   The amount of *insolation*, that is, of Sun power falling on the Satellite's receptors, will be six times as great as could be achieved anywhere on Earth. On the other hand, ideal low-cost solar receptors have yet to be designed.

2   It is often mentioned that a low-gravity environment such as a space colony, would be an ideal place for the elderly or infirm to live, especially those suffering from a weak heart. So it would be, except that the multi-g forces inherent in escaping from Earth's grip would probably kill anyone with a weak heart. Also the cost would be too high. No, the only infirm people whom low-g will help are those who leave Earth while they are still young and healthy.

3   This account of space colonies is necessarily non-technical. For more details see Gerard K. O'Neill's *The High Frontier* and T. A. Heppenheimer's *Colonies in Space*.

4   A mass accelerator will probably be used for this, rather than a powered shuttle. It was first suggested by Arthur C. Clarke as early as 1950 and will take the form of a straight stretch of railway track, several miles in length, carrying electrically powered trucks which are accelerated enormously quickly. See Clarke's *The Promise of Space*, chapter 19.

5 Venus's land area is 186 million square miles, more than three times that of the Earth, which is only fifty-seven million square miles.

6 In fact Venus's period of axial rotation is 243 Earth days, slightly longer than its orbital period of 225 Earth days, but its axial rotation is retrograde, giving rather less than two nights and two days per year.

7 A light year, the distance light can travel in one Earth year, is almost six million million miles. The speed of light is usually given as 186,283 miles per second.

8 Adrian Berry, in *The Iron Sun*, has suggested that man might be able to cross the galaxy quickly by using black holes, which would instantaneously transport matter across thousands or millions of light years, spewing it out through a white hole. There are problems involved (apart from not having the faintest idea of where one might be transported to). Black holes are thought to rotate extremely fast, and one which was big enough to drive a spaceship through would need to have a mass at least ten times as great as the Sun and would thus rotate a thousand times a second. The spaceship would need to match this speed (which is about sixty per cent of the speed of light) and pass through the black hole at just the right angle to avoid being torn apart by its singularity (see *The Iron Sun* for an explanation of all this). Another snag is that the nearest black hole known to exist is 6,000 light years away from us; so Adrian Berry suggests that man should build one just outside the Solar System by sweeping up enough interstellar dust with magnets.

9 See, for example, Brian Aldiss's *Non-Stop* and Robert A. Heinlein's *Orphans of the Sky*.

10 It should not be forgotten that UFO stands for Unidentified Flying Object and *must not* automatically be equated with 'alien spaceship'. The vast majority of unidentified flying objects reported have, after investigation, been identified (as aircraft, flocks of birds, clouds, mirages, fireballs, and so on). Where they have not been so identified it is due to lack of reliable evidence. No UFO has ever been positively identified as an alien spacecraft. Nor is there any good reason for believing that alien spacecraft have visited Earth in the past, though this cannot be ruled out entirely; such craft may even have left evidence of their visit, though this has still to be found.

11 Adapted from Walter Sullivan's *We Are Not Alone*. It was originated by Dr Frank Drake of Green Bank Observatory.

12 This has been pointed out to the author by Dr Jack Cohen of Birmingham University.

13 Science fiction contains many bizarre forms of alien intelligence, far too diverse and interesting for any meaningful examples to be given here. But see the present author's chapter 'Alien Encounter' in *Encyclopaedia of Science Fiction* edited by Robert Holdstock.

14 'Extraterrestrial Linguistics', *Astronautics* May 1961. Reprinted in *The Coming of the Space Age* edited by Arthur C. Clarke.

Chapter Eight pp 165–192

1 Hermann J. Muller in *Man and His Future* edited by Gordon Wolstenholme.

2 The actual figures are that to give a tenfold increase in size each dimension will have increased by an amount equal to the cube root of ten, in other words by a factor of 2·1543 ('slightly more than double') and a cross-sectional area will have increased by $2 \cdot 1543^2$ which is equal to 4·6410 ('about four and a half times').

3 This optimum size presupposes life under normal Earth gravity. Life away from Earth is dealt with in chapter seven and such future inventions as the null-grav field, beloved of many science fiction authors, can be ignored here even though it may well be a reality within a few centuries.

4 A BBC TV *Horizon* programme shown on 2 April 1979 showed a man living in Texas who has not eaten or drunk for over two years. Most of his digestive system was removed due to cancer and he receives a continuous drip-feed but is able to walk around and live an almost normal life.

5 'The Chronic Argonauts' is reprinted (as far as it ever went) in Bernard Bergonzi's *The Early H. G. Wells.*

6 In *Extraterrestrial Encounter* Chris Boyce suggests that (page 78) 'man will be made biologically incapable of killing his fellow man in almost every situation. This limiter may be written into the DNA itself, if possible.'

7 From late Victorian times until fairly recent years it was widely accepted that there would occur a melting pot effect among genetic types as among cultures, the end result being a world full of people with light brown skin. An example is John Langdon-Davies in *A Short History of the Future*, Routledge 1936, who prophesies that 'by AD 4000 race problems will all be solved. There will be one race in the world, with a pale coffee-coloured skin, mongoloid eyes, rather shorter than the average Englishman today.' But, of course, advances in genetic engineering will enable future men to assume the colour of their choice—and pass it on to their offspring.

8 This observation is borrowed from Dr Jack Cohen of Birmingham University, who likes to puzzle his genetics students by assuring them that 'ninety per cent of all I'm teaching you is wrong. Unfortunately we don't know which ninety per cent'.

9 There is a short story by Frederic Brown entitled 'Preposterous' in which a father castigates his son for reading a science fiction magazine which includes 'sheer balderdash' such as 'travel to other galaxies by means of space warps, whatever they are. Time machines, teleportation and telekinesis', but they live in a future which already possesses antigravity, space travel, telepathy and immortality.

10 *The Daily Telegraph Magazine* 20 December 1974. His prophecy assumes massive urban growth (into a sprawling global conurbation, Ecumenopolis), floating nuclear power stations all round the coasts, and most of the world's land area devoted to farming.

11 'Ethical Considerations' in *Man and His Future* edited by Gordon Wolstenholme.

12 This reduction of the degree of alienness is deliberate by most authors; they need to trade off true alienness against readability. Most readers will not put up with a very alien future for more than a few pages, so the best 'alien future man' stories are short ones like Frederik Pohl's 'Day Million'.

13 As already mentioned in chapter two, Lytton's *The Coming Race* (1871) shows a race of subterranean supermen, but no hint of their origin is given and they are shown as living in the present (ie 1871). To all intents and purposes, though, they are future men. The author will only commit himself as far as saying that they will eventually come to save man from his own shortcomings.

14 Richard Gerber in *Utopian Fantasy: a Study of English Utopian Fiction Since the End of the Nineteenth Century.*

15 *More Issues at Hand* by William Atheling jr (James Blish), Advent (Chicago) 1967.

16 H. G. Wells' article 'The Man of the Year Million' in the *Pall Mall Gazette*, 1893. Reprinted in Stover and Harrison's *Apeman, Spaceman.*

17 *The Educated Imagination*, quoted in an article by Susan Glicksohn in *SF: the Other Side of Realism* edited by Thomas D. Clareson.

Bibliography

Listed below are the editions used by the author, which are not necessarily first editions. All were published in London unless otherwise mentioned. Science fiction titles are not included.

Aldiss, Brian W. *Billion Year Spree* Weidenfeld & Nicolson 1973
Allanby, Michael *Inventing Tomorrow* Abacus 1977
Armytage, W. H. G. *Yesterday's Tomorrows* Routledge & Kegan Paul 1968
Baier, Kurt and Rescher,, Nicholas (eds) *Values and the Future* Macmillan (New York) 1969
Bailey, J. O. *Pilgrims Through Space and Time* Argus (New York) 1947
Berry, Adrian *The Next Ten Thousand Years* Coronet 1976
Berry, Adrian *The Iron Sun* Coronet 1979
Bergonzi, Bernard *The Early H. G. Wells* Manchester University Press (Manchester) 1961
Boyce, Chris *Extraterrestrial Encounter* David & Charles (Newton Abbot) 1979
Brown, Harrison, Bonner, James and Weir, John *The Next Hundred Years* Weidenfeld & Nicolson 1958
Churchill, R. C. *A Short History of the Future* Werner Laurie 1955
Clareson, Thomas D. (ed) *SF: the Other Side of Realism* Bowling Green University (Ohio) 1971
Clarke, Arthur C. *The Promise of Space* Penguin 1970
Clarke, Arthur C. (ed) *The Coming of the Space Age* Panther 1970
Clarke, I. F. *The Tale of the Future* The Library Association 1972 (2nd edition)
Clarke, I. F. *The Pattern of Expectation* Cape 1979
Cook, Peter *Architecture: Action and Plan* Studio Vista 1967
Cotgrove, Stephen *The Science of Society* Allen & Unwin 1968
d'Albe, E. E. Fournier *Quo Vadimus?* Kegan Paul 1927
Dawkins, Richard *The Selfish Gene* Granada 1978
George, Frank *Science Fact* Angus & Robertson 1977
Haldane, J. B. S. *Possible Worlds* Heinemann 1940
Hansell, C. E. M. *ESP: a Scientific Evaluation* MacGibbon & Kee 1966
Hay, George (ed) *Pulsar 1* Penguin 1978

Heppenheimer, T. A. *Colonies in Space* Warner Books (New York) 1978

Holdstock, Robert (ed) *Encyclopaedia of Science Fiction* Octopus 1978

Huxley, Julian *Essays of a Humanist* Penguin 1966

Jennings, H. S. *Prometheus or Biology and the Advancement of Man* Kegan Paul (no date)

Joad, C. E. M. *Diogenes or the Future of Leisure* Kegan Paul (no date)

Kahn, Herman *On Thermonuclear War* Princeton University Press (New Jersey) 1960

Kahn, Herman *On Escalation* Princeton University Press (New Jersey) 1965

Kahn, Harman and Wiener, Anthony J. *The Year 2000* Macmillan 1967

Kahn, Herman, Brown William and Martel, Leon *The Next 200 Years* Associated Business Programmes 1977

Karlins, Marvin and Andrews, Lewis M. *Biofeedback* Abacus 1975

Kurten, Bjorn *Not From the Apes* Gollancz 1972

Langford, David *War in 2080* David & Charles (Newton Abbot) 1979

Macfie, R. C. *Metanthropos or the Body of the Future* Kegan Paul 1928

Meadows, Donella H., et al *The Limits to Growth* Pan 1974

Moore, Patrick *Concise Atlas of the Universe* Mitchell Beazley 1974

Nicholls, Peter (ed) *Explorations of the Marvellous* (*Science Fiction at Large*) Fontana 1978

Nicolson, Iain *The Road to the Stars* David & Charles (Newton Abbot) 1978

O'Neill, Gerard *The High Frontier* Morrow (New York) 1976

Pedler, Kit *The Quest for Gaia* Souvenir Press 1979

Pierce, Henry W. *Science Looks at ESP* Signet (New York) 1970

Rhine, J. B. *The Reach of the Mind* Penguin 1954

Roberts, M. B. V. *Biology: a Functional Approach* Nelson 1976

Rook, Arthur (ed) *The Origins and Growth of Biology* Penguin 1964

Rorvik, David *As Man Becomes Machine* Abacus 1975

Rorvik, David *In His Image: the Cloning of a Man* Lippincott (New York) 1978

Rosen, Stephen *Future Facts* Heinemann 1976

Sagan, Carl *Other Worlds* Bantam (New York) 1975

Shaw, George Bernard *Prefaces* Odhams Press 1938

Stover, Leon E. and Harrison, Harry (eds) *Apeman, Spacemen* Penguin 1972

Stubbs, Peter (ed) *New Science in the Solar System* IPC 1975

Sullivan, Walter *We Are Not Alone* Penguin 1970

Taylor, John *The Shape of Minds to Come* Panther 1974

Teilhard de Chardin, Pierre *The Phenomenon of Man* Collins 1959

Thompson, Alan E. *Understanding Futurology* David & Charles (Newton Abbot) 1979

Thomson, Sir George *The Forseeable Future* Cambridge University Press 1955

Toffler, Alvin *Future Shock* Pan 1971

Vassiliev, M. and Gouschev, S. *Life in the Twenty-First Century* Penguin 1961

Walter, W. Grey *The Living Brain* Penguin 1961

Wells, H. G. *Anticipations* Chapman & Hall 1901

Wolstenholme, Gordon (ed) *Man and His Future* J. & A. Churchill 1963

Wood B. A. *Human Evolution* Chapman & Hall 1978

Young, Michael *The Rise of the Meritocracy* Penguin 1961

Index

Ad-hocracy, 93, 121
Aldiss, Brian W., *Billion Year Spree,*
    195; *Hothouse,* 190-91; *Non-Stop,*
    199
Alien contact, 158-64, 200
Alien planets, survival on, 62, 152-57
Alternative technology, 124-5
Anderson, Paul, 'The Pugilist', 48;
    Twilight World, 138
Androids, 52-53, 62
Apollo space programme, 140, 149,
    183
Archetypes (of future man), 166-73
Artificial body parts, *see* Cyborgis-
    ation
Artificial mind, 86
Artificial organic man, *see* Androids
Atrophy, 165, 168, 170
Australopithecus, 17-22, 166
Automation, 91, 120, 122, 130, 145,
    155

Bacteria, 13, 49, 153-54
Beresford, J.D., *The Hampdenshire
    Wonder,* 37, 59
Berg, Professor Paul, 48
Bergonzi, Bernard, *The Early H.G.
    Wells,* 195, 200
Berry, Adrian, *The Iron Sun,* 199; *The
    Next Ten Thousand Years,* 138
Bester, Alfred, *The Demolished Man,*
    78-79
Biocomp, 110-11
Bio-feedback training (BFT), 72, 80,
    84, 114
Bionic-implant computer terminal, *see*
    Biocomp
Birth control, 73, 131, 144, 166, 182
Blish, James; as William Atheling Jr
    201; *Pantropy,* 155-56; *The Seedling
    Stars,* 155
Boyce, Chris, *Extraterrestrial Encoun-
    ter,* 158, 161, 200
Brain, 64, 69; disembodied, 56, 195;
    electrodes implanted in, 83-84;
    stimulation of, 85; transplants, 63
Brunner, John, *The Sheep Look Up,*
    198
Bulwer-Lytton, E.G., *The Coming Race,*
    34, 201
Butler, Samuel, *Erewhon,* 34, 186

Caidin, Martin, *Cyborg,* 56
Capital, 8, 9, 127, 135

Change, 116, 130, 140, 164, 184;
    acceleration of, 90-91, 97; climatic,
    18; cultural, 164; evolutionary, 168;
    in laws, 93; management of, 104-5;
    mental, 113, 140, 166; of
    occupation, 91-92; political, 7;
    social, 177; transcendental, 113-14
Children of the atom, 57-60
Clairvoyance, 74, 75, 196; *see also*
    ESP
Clarke, Arthur C., *Childhood's End,*
    59; *The City and the Stars,* 196; *The
    Coming of the Space Age,* 200; *The
    Promise of Space,* 198
Clarke, Professor I.F., *The Tale of the
    Future,* 195
Cloning, 50-52, 150, 195; of humans,
    38, 62; *in situ,* 47; *see also* Genetic
    engineering
Cohen, Dr Jack, 199, 201
Colonies, interstellar, 152-56
Colonies, orbital, 140-45, 157, 163,
    181
Comfort, Dr Alex, 41
Communications, extrasensory, *see*
    ESP
Control, behavioural, 85; by biofeed-
    back training, 72-73; environmental,
    65; hypnotic, 80; of mind, 65,
    79-83; of mood, 72, 81; of pain, 84;
    of pollution, 132; of population,
    123, 125, 131
Cosmetic transplants, 48
Cranial capacity, early man, 19-21, 24-
    25, 169; future man, 167-169;
    modern man, 24, 169
Creation, 12-14, 31, 193; spontaneous,
    13, 29
Crystal Age, A, W.H. Hudson, 35,
    172, 184-86, 195
Cult of the Millennium, the, 115-16
Cybernetics, *see* Cyborgisation
Cyborgisation, 38, 53-57, 62, 83, 147

Darwin, Charles, 27, 29-33, 184, 194
Darwin, Erasmus, 30
Darwinism, 30, 33-37, 170, 186
Death, criteria for, 46; definitions of,
    45
Delany, Samuel R., *Babel,* 17, 48
DNA, 48-49, 60, 171, 195, 200; repairs
    to, 42
Dream studies, 69-72, 84
Dropping out, 100, 135

Drosophila melanogaster (fruit fly), 33, 49
Dyson sphere, 148, 157, 181-83

Early hominids, 17-19
Earth, creation of, 31; formation of, 12
Ecology, 9, 154; balance of, 124; damage to, 135
Economic growth, 88, 119, 125, 132-34
Educational systems, 94, 108-9
Electrode implantation, in brain, 83-86
Electroencephalogram (EEG), 69-70
Energy, crises, 127; shortages, 197; solar, 139, 183, 198; sources, 124, 129, 183, 198; *see also* Fuel reserves
Enkephalin, 64, 71-72
Environment, 175, 179-84; closed, 143; new, 140, 144, 168
ESP, 51, 73-79, 114, 196
Eugenics, 43, 66, 185-86
Evolution, 10, 156, 160, 165; before Darwin, 29-30; common ancestor, 27; Darwinism, 30-31; evidence for, 26-28; Lamarckism, 30; regression, 42, 181; spiritual, 33
Exploring the mind, 69-70
Extrapolation, 115, 122, 129, 133, 138, 167, 177, 197
Extrasensory perception, *see* ESP
Extraterrestrial sources (of materials), 118, 181
Extraterrestrials, 113, 158-64

Faster-than-light travel (FTL), 155, 178, 183
Fossil fuels, 127, 130, 134, 193; *see also* Energy
Fossils, 13-14, 17-21, 25-26
Frankenstein's monster, 52, 102
Freezing (of humans), 43-45
Fremlin, Professor John, 181
Fuel reserves, 8; *see also* Energy
Future shock, 98-99, 101-102, 106, 109, 116, 135, 197

Geller, Uri, 77-78; *see also* ESP
Genes, 41, 49, 51, 66, 82, 166, 195; defective, 166; recessive, 59
Genetic engineering, 11, 33, 38, 48-50, 66, 82, 135, 156, 171, 200; *see also* Cloning
Genetic mutation, spontaneous, 37, 59, 60, 156
Genetics, research in, 32-33
Genus *'Homo'*, 19-26
Gigantopithecus, 17
Gravity, 141, 145, 147, 198; Earth, 140, 157, 200; zero, 140, 157
Growth, economic, 119, 125, 132, 133, 134

Haemophilia, 60, 166
Haldane, Professor J.B.S., 138, 166
Hansell, Professor C.E.M., 74, 195
Hay, George, *Pulsar 1,* 197
Heinlein, Robert A., *Farnham's Freehold,* 176; *Orphans of the Sky,* 199; *Time Enough for Love,* 43
Heppenheimer, T.A., 145; *Colonies in Space,* 198
Heredity, 32, 66; *see also* Genetic mutation, spontaneous; Genetics
Hive society, 172-73
Hominids, cranial capacity, 19; early, 17-19
Homo erectus, 20-22, 24
Homo (genus), 17, 19-26
Homo habilis, 20-22
Homo megacephalus, 167, 168, 172
Homo sapiens, 20, 41, 58, 59, 165, 174, 176, 184, 186, 189
Homo sapiens neanderthalis, 22-24
Homo sapiens sapiens, 10, 25-26, 156, 184
Homogenisation of lifestyles, 89, 129, 135
Hothouse, Brian W. Aldiss, 190-91
Hoyle, Professor Fred, 14, 197
Hudson, W.H., *A Crystal Age,* 35, 172, 184-86, 195
Huxley, Aldous, *After Many a Summer,* 42; *Brave New World,* 50, 62, 68, 178
Huxley, T.H., 13, 32, 35
Hypnosis, 79-80, 84, 85

Immortality drug, 42; *see also* Longevity
Increased life expectancy, 41; *see also* Longevity
Industrialisation, 88, 106, 119, 124, 126, 130, 133, 178
Innovation, technological, 7, 90-91, 97, 109, 111-13, 118, 130-131, 133
Intelligence, 64-69, 113; alien, 158-64, 200
Interbreeding for longevity, 43; *see also* Longevity
Intermediate scenarios, 130-35
International co-operation, 131-33, 179-80
Interstellar travel, 130, 148-52, 154, 158

Jupiter, 147, 182

Kahn, Herman, 107, 117, 120, 130, 135ff, 167, 179, 193, 197, 198
Kurten, Dr Bjorn, *Not From the Apes,* 18, 24, 194

Lamarckism, 30

Langford, David, 110, 137
Last and First Men, Olaf Stapledon, 156, 186-90
Less developed countries (LDCs), 90-91, 101-2, 106-7, 112, 118-19, 123, 125, 126, 128, 130-132, 134, 180, 197
Life before man, 14-17
Life expectancy, cyborg, 56; increased by restricted diet, 41; natural, 39, 41; *see also* Longevity
Limbs, artificial, 53-54; cloned, 47; transplanted, 47
Limited predictions, 174-79
Longevity, freezing for, 43; increased, 37, 39-45, 62, 121, 180; side-effects of, 42

Macrofutures, 87, 115
Malthus, Thomas, 123, 134
Malthusianism, 123-30, 134, 198
Mars, 35-36, 146-47, 159
Matter transmitter, 122, 178, 183
Meadows, Donella H., *The Limits to Growth,* 124, 128
Meditation, 72
Memory, enhancement, 67; long- and short-term, 103; recording of, 150, 195
Mental disorders, treatment of, 71, 81-82, 121
Mental maturity, 43, 113-14
Microfutures, 87
Millennium, 197; cults of, 115-16
Mind, artificial, 86
Mind control, 79-83
Mind over matter, 72-73
Mineral resources and reserves, 8, 120
Mood control, 72, 81
Moon, 118, 122, 140-42, 145-46, 188, 190
Morgan, Chris, 'Alien Encounter', 200
Morris, William, *News From Nowhere,* 35, 195
Multi-generation starships, 149-50
Mutation, 31, 37, 38, 57-60, 156

Neanderthal man, 20, 22-26
Nuclear war and weapons, 57, 135-83

O'Neill, Dr Gerard K., 140, 182-83, 198
Optimism, technological, 116-23, 128, 130
Orbital colonies, 140-45
Organ banks, 46
Organ transplants, 11, 45-48
Organs, artificial, 55
Origin of Species, Charles Darwin, 29-32
Orwell, George, *1984,* 83, 111

Overpopulation, 179

Pacemakers, electronic, 54; *see also* Cyborgisation
Pain, suppression of, 73, 80, 84
Pantropy, 147, 156-58
Pessimism, economic, 123-30; *see also* Malthusianism
Planets (other than Earth), 118, 145, 152-54, 158, 182, 193
Pleasure-centre stimulation, 85, 111
Pohl, Frederik, 147, 201
Pollution, 10, 119, 123-26, 128, 132, 134, 179
Population, ageing, 43; controls of, 123, 125, 131; increase in, 43, 118, 124-25, 131, 133, 179, 182, 197; predicted totals, 118, 127, 180; stable, 131, 133
Post-catastrophe future, 35, 57-59, 138
Precognition, 74, 75; tests for, 76; *see also* ESP
Prediction, 7-11, 106, 109, 115, 122, 158, 161, 174-79
Project Ozma, 159
Prosthetics, 11, 53-57; *see also* Cyborgisation
Psi, *see* ESP
Psychokinesis (PK), 74, 75, 78; tests for, 76; *see also* ESP

Radiation, 57-58, 128, 137-38
Ramapithecus, 17-19, 166, 168
Random eye movements (REMs), 70
Raw materials, 9, 134, 139
Regression, evolutionary, 42, 166, 181; technological, 155-56
Religion, 95, 113
Reserves, fuel and mineral, 8-9, 117, 126
'Resonant' orbit, 142
Resources, 117, 123, 124, 129, 130-34
Rhine, Dr J.B., 73-74, 76-77
Robots, 62, 122, 153
Rorvik, David, *In His Image,* 51-52
Roshwald, Mordecai, *Level 7,* 138; *Small Armageddon, A,* 198

Satellites, orbital colonies in, 140-45
Satellites, solar-power, 118, 129, 134, 139-40
Scrap recovery, 9, 118
Search for Extra-Terrestrial Intelligence (SETI), 159
Sensory deprivation, 56, 71, 83
Shaw, George Bernard, 132; *Back to Methuselah,* 37, 42, 172
Silverberg, Robert, *Tower of Glass,* 52; *Up the Line,* 50; *World Inside, The,* 180
Situational grouping, 104

Sleep, 70, 84; *see also* Dream studies
Social problems, 60-63
Solar-power satellites, 118, 129, 134, 139-140
Space colonies, orbiting, 89, 129-30, 135, 140, 157, 171
Space colonisation, 121, 145-48
Space programme, 119, 126
Spaceship Earth, 125
Stability zones, 103-4, 107
Stanford torus, 141, 144, 149, 151
Stapledon, Olaf, 191; *Last and First Men,* 156, 186-90; *Odd John,* 59; *Sirius,* 186
Starships, 148-52, 154, 157, 160
Sterilisation, 128, 144; *see also* Population control
Stress, 98-100
Sullivan, Walter, *We Are Not Alone,* 197, 199
Sun, creation of the, 12; future life of, 26

Technological interface, 109-13
Technological regression, 155, 156
Telekinesis (psychokinesis), 114; *see also* ESP
Telepathic abilities, 58-59; *see also* ESP
Telepathic societies, 114, 138, 173; *see also* ESP
Telepathy, 74-75, 114, 170, 189; tests for, 75-76; *see also* ESP
Teleportation (levitation), 74, 114; *see also* ESP
Tenn, William, 'Null-P', 176-77
Terra nova, 152-56
Terraforming, 146, 153-55, 157, 188
Time travel, 11, 105, 106, 178
Toffler, Alvin, *Future Shock,* 26, 93, 98, 103, 193-94, 196-97
Transcendental change, 113-14
Transcendental meditation (TM), 72, 80, 95, 103, 114
Transcience, 96-98

Transplant donors, animal, 46-47; foetal, 47
Transplant surgery, 38, 44, 45-48
Trauma, avoidance of, 102-9; causes of, 90-98; manifestations of, 98-102
Tucker, Wilson, *Wild Talent,* 78

UFOs, 158, 199
Undersea cities, 171, 180-81
USSR, ESP research in, 78
Utopia, 36, 39, 115, 119, 131

Varley, John, 'Gotta Sing, Gotta Dance', 158; *The Ophiuchi Hotline,* 51
Venus, 146, 153, 157, 188-89, 199
Verne, Jules, *Journey to the Centre of the Earth,* 33
Vestigial organs, 38
Victorian England, 35, 170

War, nuclear, 57, 135-38
Wells, H.G., 32, 191; 'Fiction of the Future', 7; 'The Man of the Year Million', 37, 201; 'A Story of the Stone Age', 34; *The Time Machine,* 35, 190; various works, 36-37; *The War of the Worlds,* 36, 161
Wilhelm, Kate, *Where Late the Sweet Birds Sang,* 52
Wolfe, Bernard, *Limbo 90,* 56
Wood, B.A., *Human Evolution,* 21, 194
World government, 121
Wyndham, John, *The Chrysalids,* 58; triffids, 49

Xenophobia, 162

Young, Michael, *The Rise of the Meritocracy,* 68-69

Zener symbols, 75; *see also* ESP
Zero-gravity, 140, 157
Zero population growth, 131, 133